700 TRADITIONAL PATCHWORK PATTERNS

CD-ROM AND BOOK

Susan Winter Mills

DOVER PUBLICATIONS, INC.
MINEOLA, NEW YORK

The CD-ROM on the inside back cover contains all of the images shown in the book. There is no installation necessary. Just insert the CD into your computer and call the images into your favorite software (refer to the documentation with your software for further instructions). Each image has been scanned at 600 dpi and saved in six different formats—BMP, EPS, PICT, TIFF, and Internet-ready GIF and JPEG.

The "Images" folder on the CD contains six different folders. All of the TIFF images have been placed in one folder, as have all of the PICT, all of the EPS, etc. The images in each of these folders are identical except for file format. Every image has a unique file name in the following format: xxx.xxx. The first 3 characters of the file name, before the period, correspond to the number printed with the image in the book. The last 3 characters of the file name, after the period, refer to the file format. So, 001.TIF would be the first file in the TIFF folder.

An index to the patterns is included on the CD-ROM as well as in the book. Also included on the CD-ROM is Dover Design Manager, a simple graphics editing program for Windows, that will allow you to view, print, crop, and rotate the images.

For technical support, contact:
Telephone: 1 (617) 249-0245
Fax: 1 (617) 249-0245
Email: dover@artimaging.com
Internet: **http://www.dovertechsupport.com**

The fastest way to receive technical support is via email or the Internet.

Bibliographical Note

700 Traditional Patchwork Patterns CD-ROM and Book, first published in 2004, includes all of the designs featured in the *Illustrated Index to Traditional American Quilt Patterns,* first published by Arco Publishing, Inc., New York, in 1980.

International Standard Book Number: 0-486-99626-3

Manufactured in the United States of America
Dover Publications, Inc., 31 East 2nd Street, Mineola, N.Y. 11501

Stars

Alice's Favorite
002

Arkansas Traveller 005
Travel Star

All Hallows 003

Aunt Eliza's Star
006

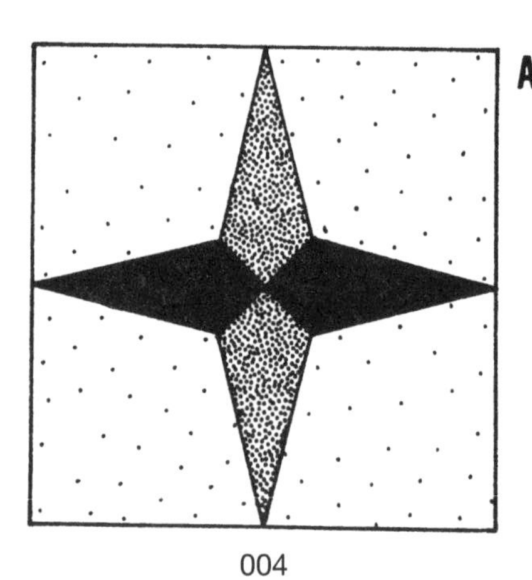

Arkansas Snowflake
Four-Point
Job's Troubles, Var. 2
Kite
Snowball, Var. 3

004

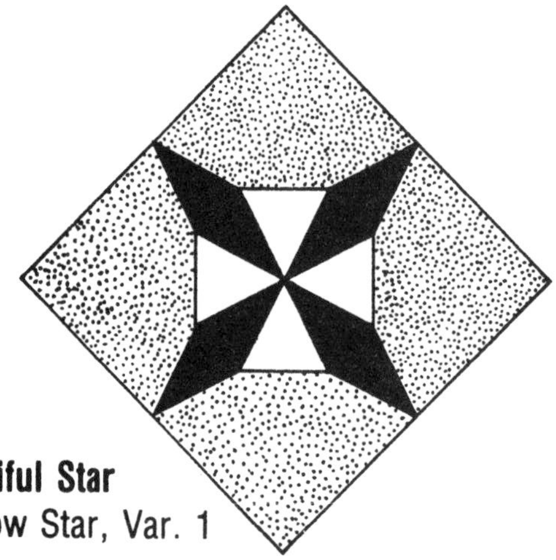

Beautiful Star
Arrow Star, Var. 1

007

Blazing Star Variation 1 008

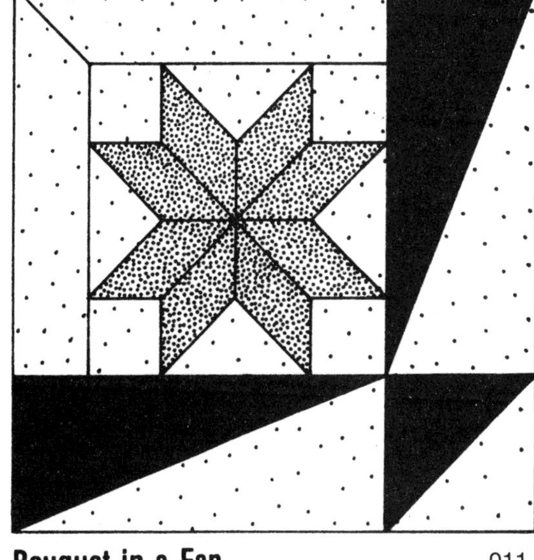

Bouquet in a Fan 011

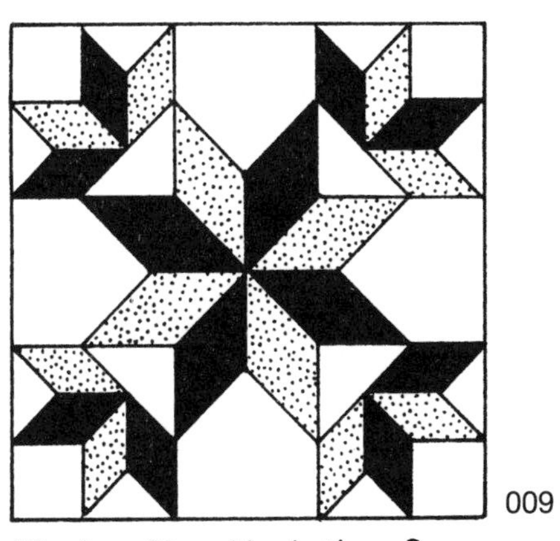

009

Blazing Star Variation 2
Lemon Star, Var. 3

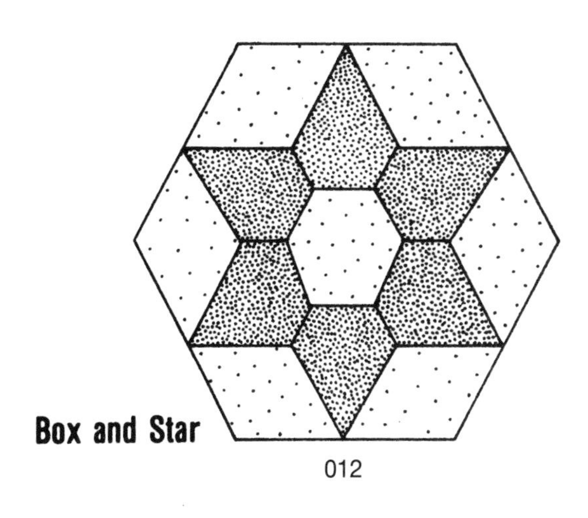

Box and Star
012

Blazing Sun

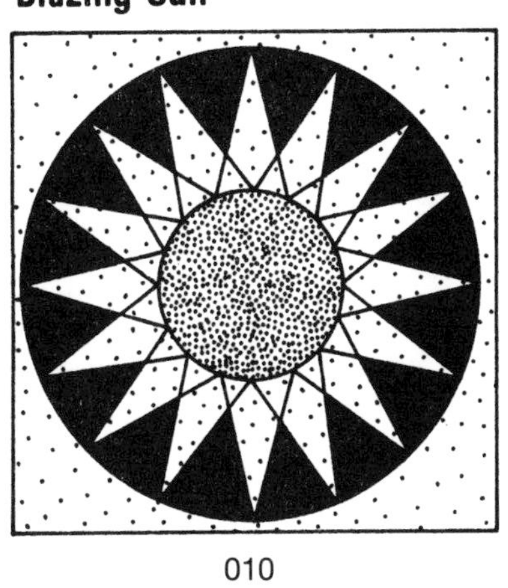

010

Caesar's Crown

013

California Star Variation 1

014

Carpenter's Wheel Variation 2

016

California Star Variation 2

015

017

Chained Star
Brunswick Star, Var. 1
Rolling Star, Var. 3

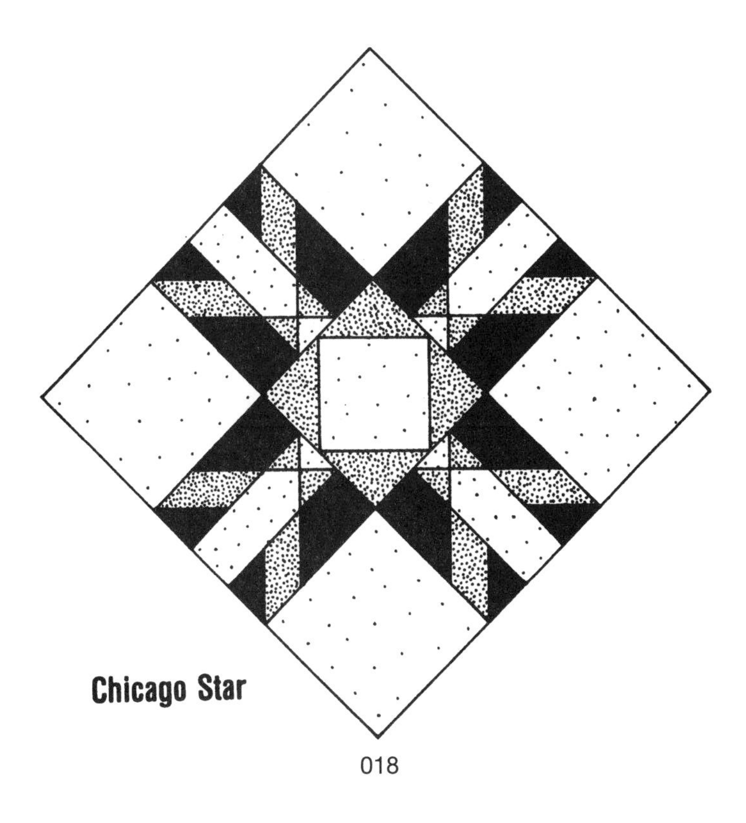

Chicago Star

018

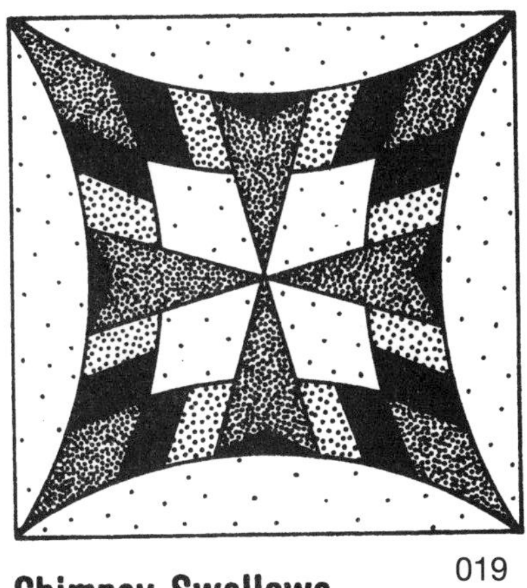

Chimney Swallows 019

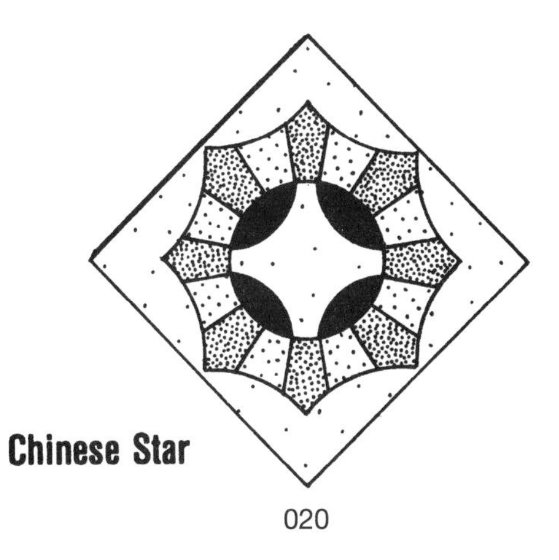

Chinese Star

020

Chips and Whetstones 021
Variation 1

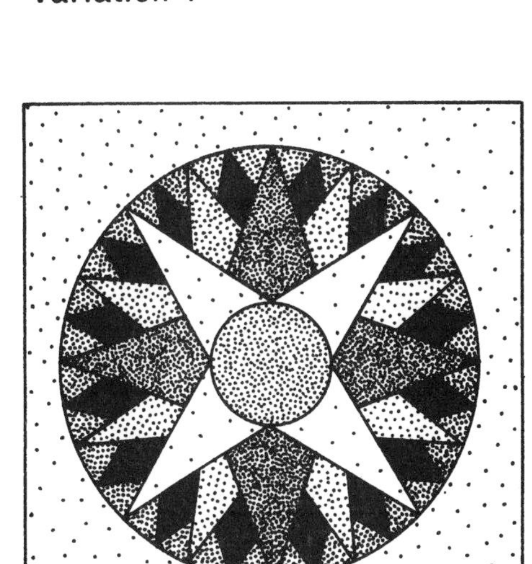

Chips and Whetstones 022
Variation 2

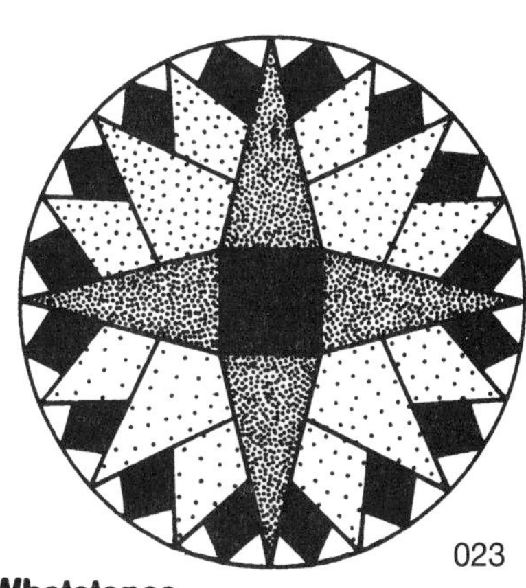

023
Chips and Whetstones
Variation 3

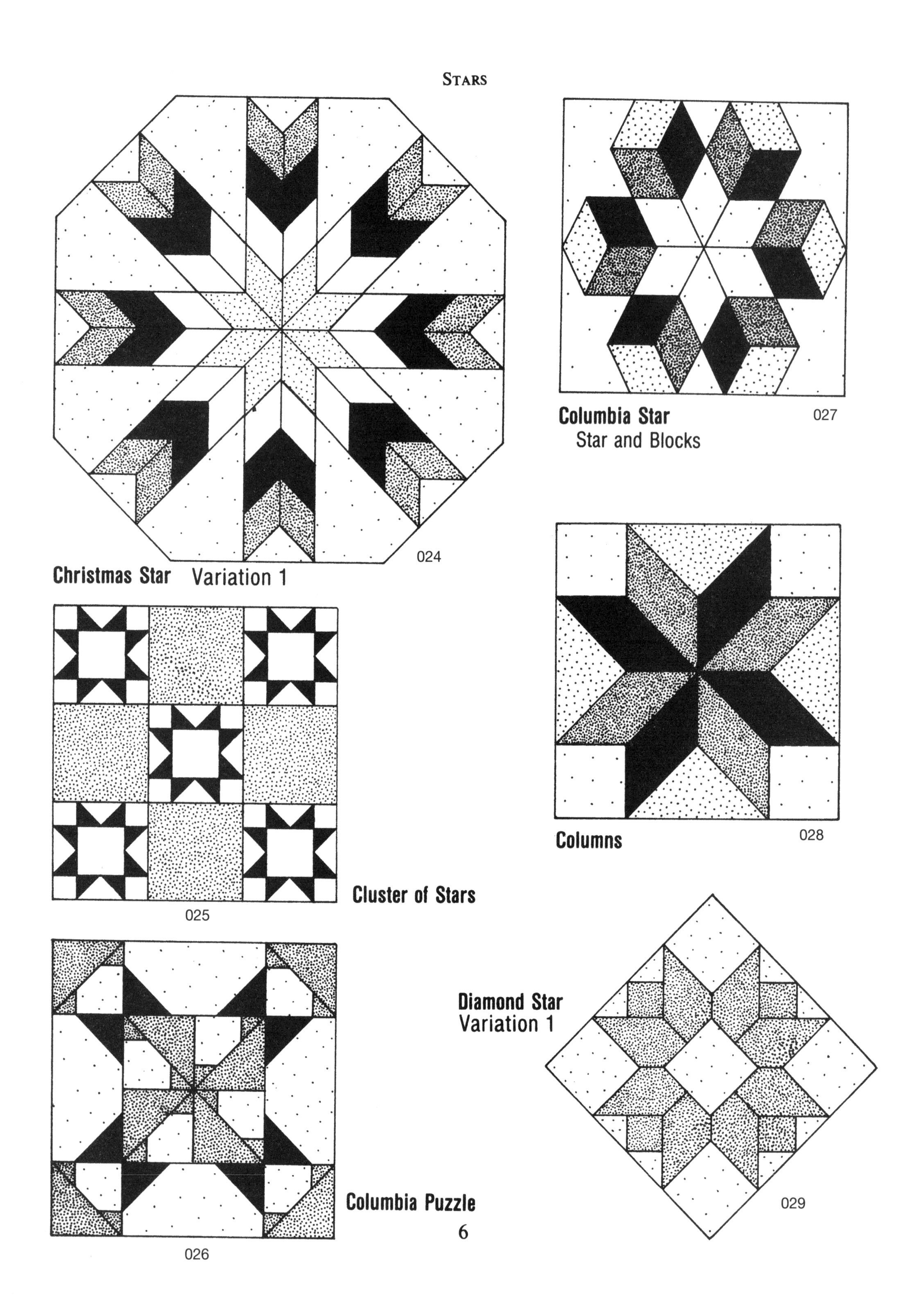

Christmas Star Variation 1

Columbia Star
Star and Blocks

Cluster of Stars

Columns

Columbia Puzzle

Diamond Star
Variation 1

030

Diamond Star Variation 2

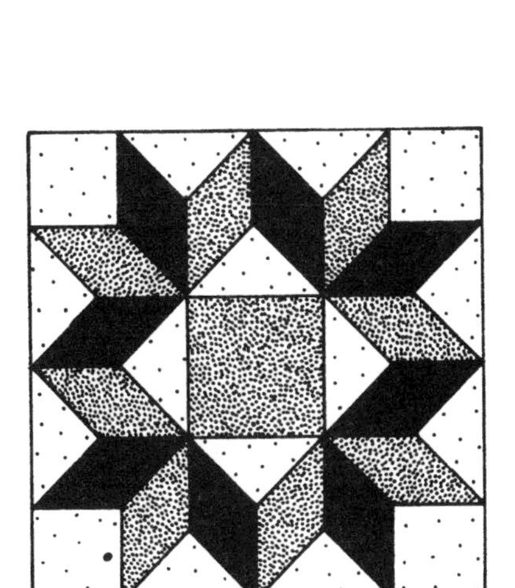

031

Dove at the Window

032

Dutch Rose
Octagonal Star, Var. 1

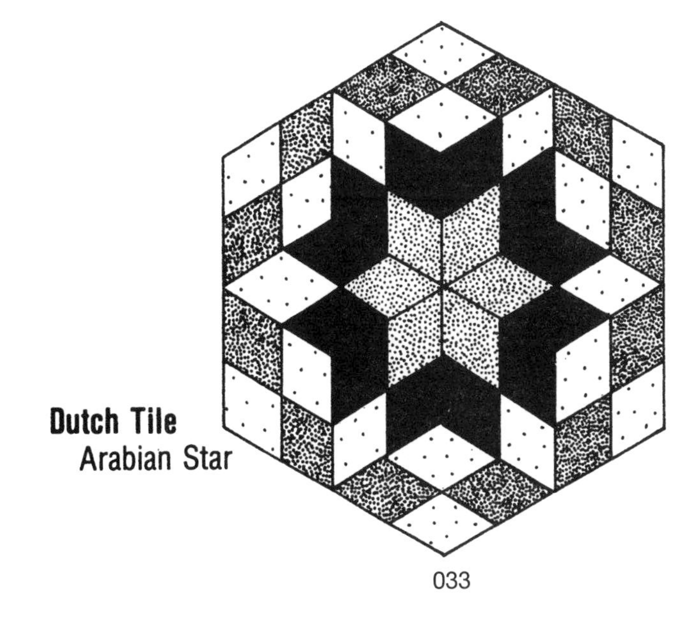

033

Dutch Tile
Arabian Star

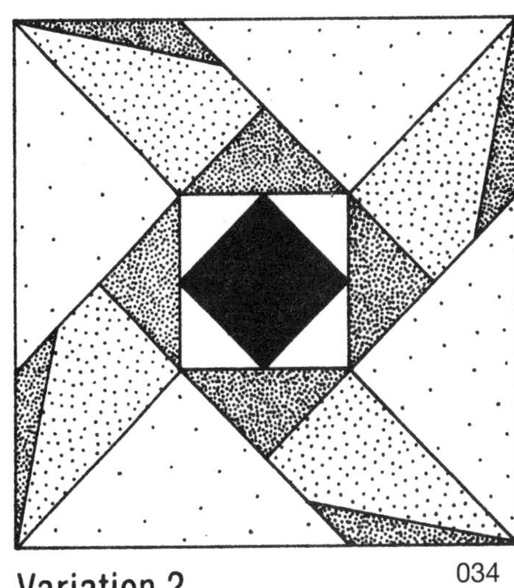

034

Eccentric Star Variation 2

035

Eight-Pointed Star Variation 2

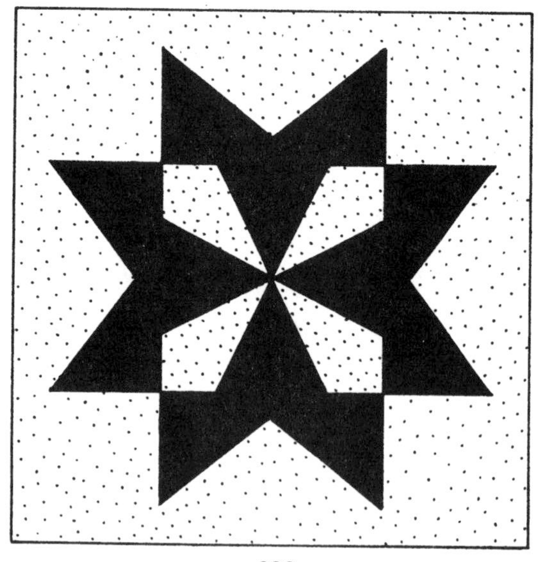

Enigma Star

036

039

Evening Star Variation 3

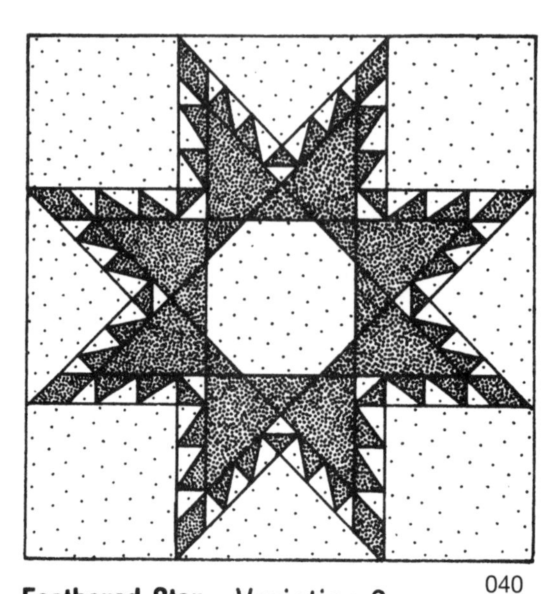

Feathered Star Variation 2

040

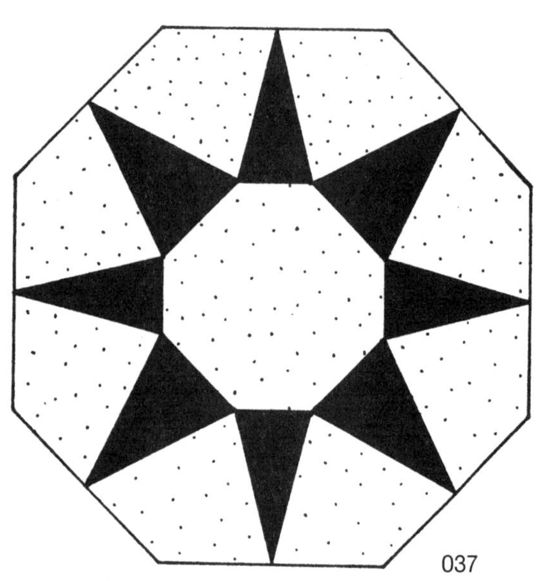

037

Evening Star Variation 1

Feather Star
Feathered Star, Var. 1
Sawtooth, Var. 1
Star of Bethlehem
Twinkling Star, Var. 1

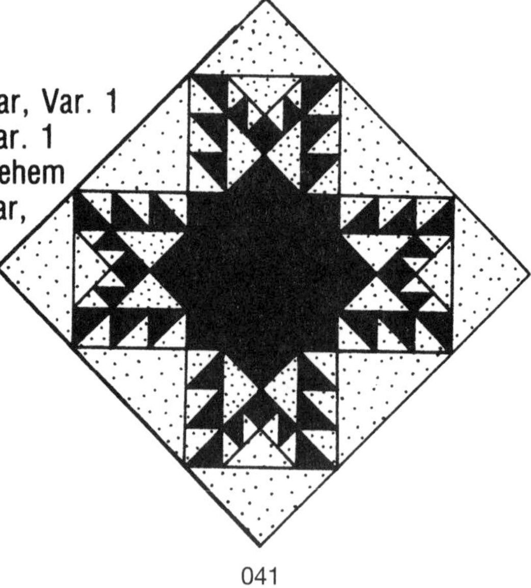

041

Evening Star Variation 2
Sawtooth, Var. 5

038

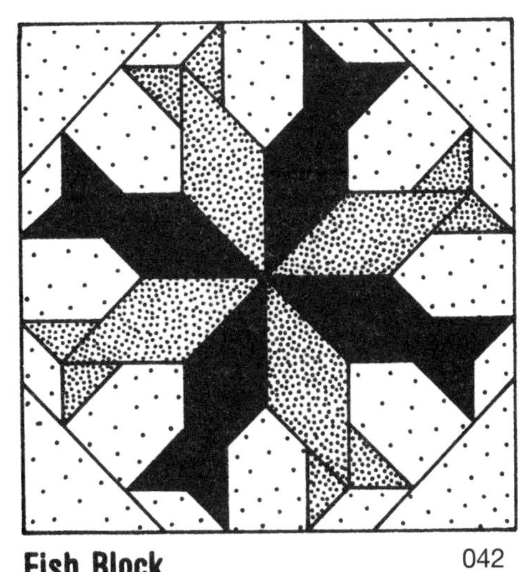

Fish Block 042
Goldfish

Flying Bat
Polaris Star

045

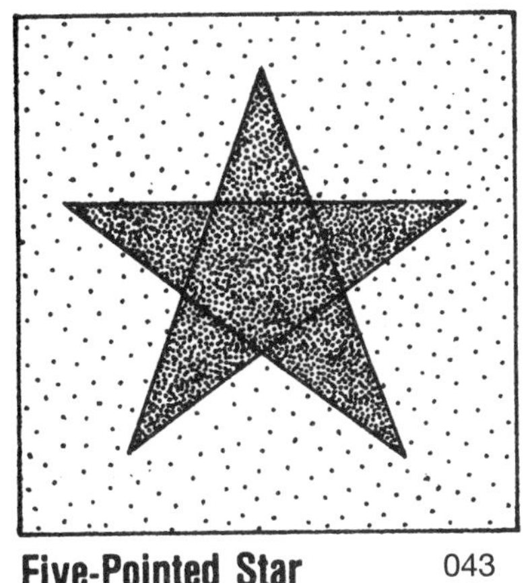

Five-Pointed Star 043

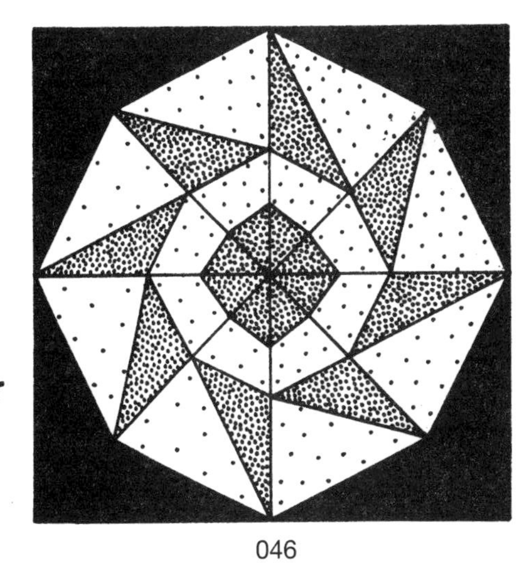

Flying Saucer

046

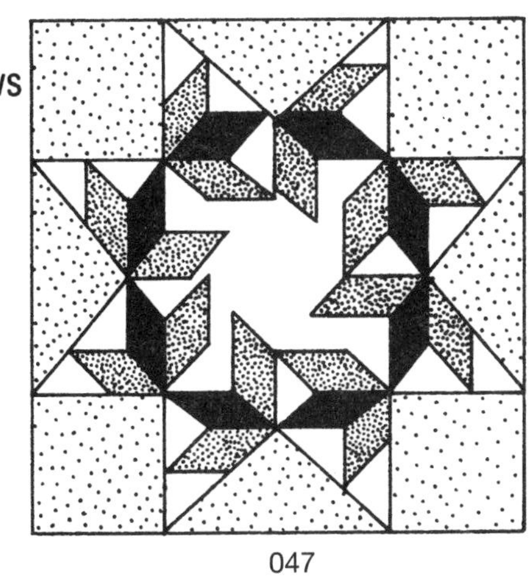

Flying Swallow
Circling Swallows
Falling Star
Flying Star

047

Flower Star Variation 1 044

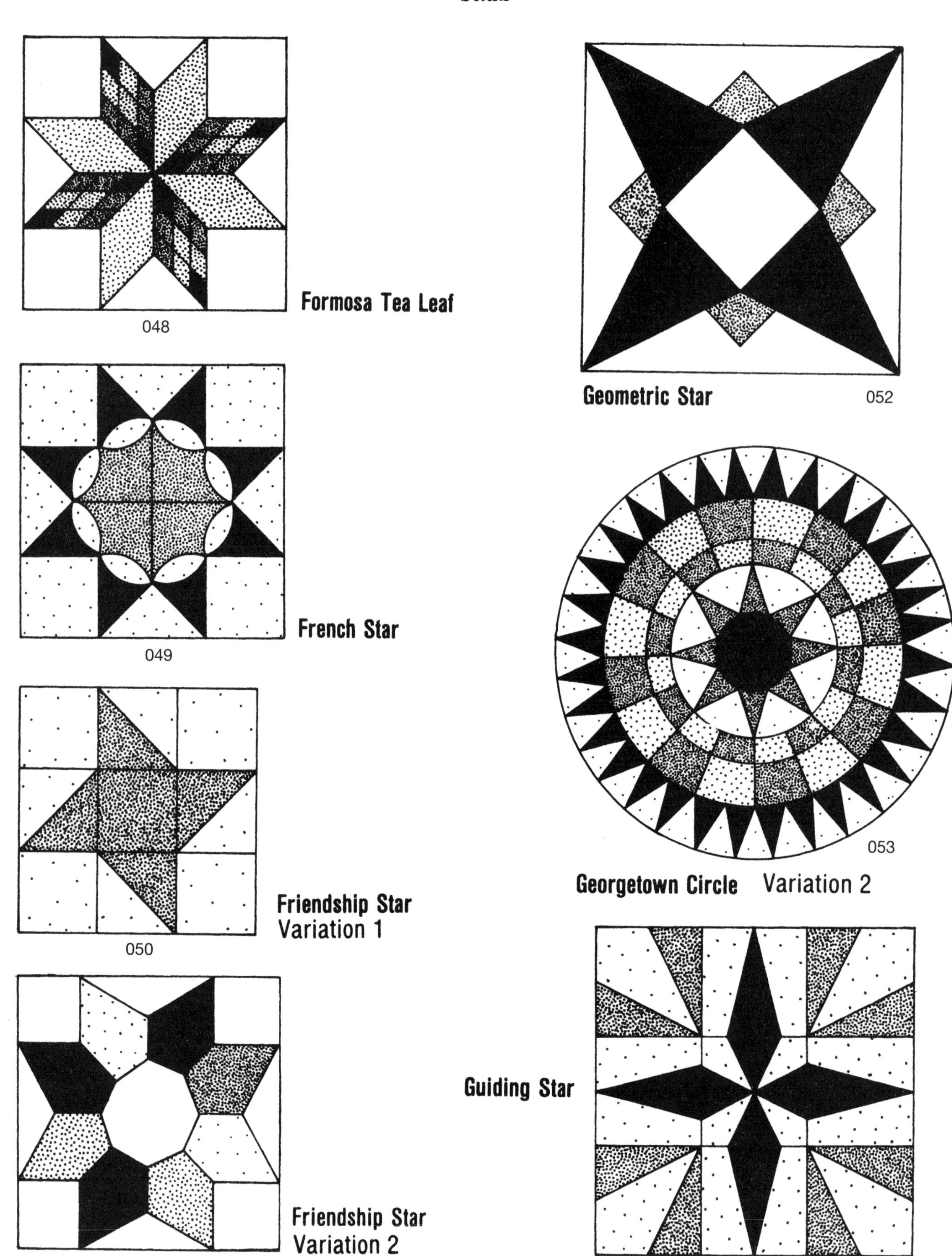
Formosa Tea Leaf
048
French Star
049
Friendship Star
Variation 1
050
Friendship Star
Variation 2
051
Geometric Star
052
053
Georgetown Circle Variation 2
Guiding Star
054

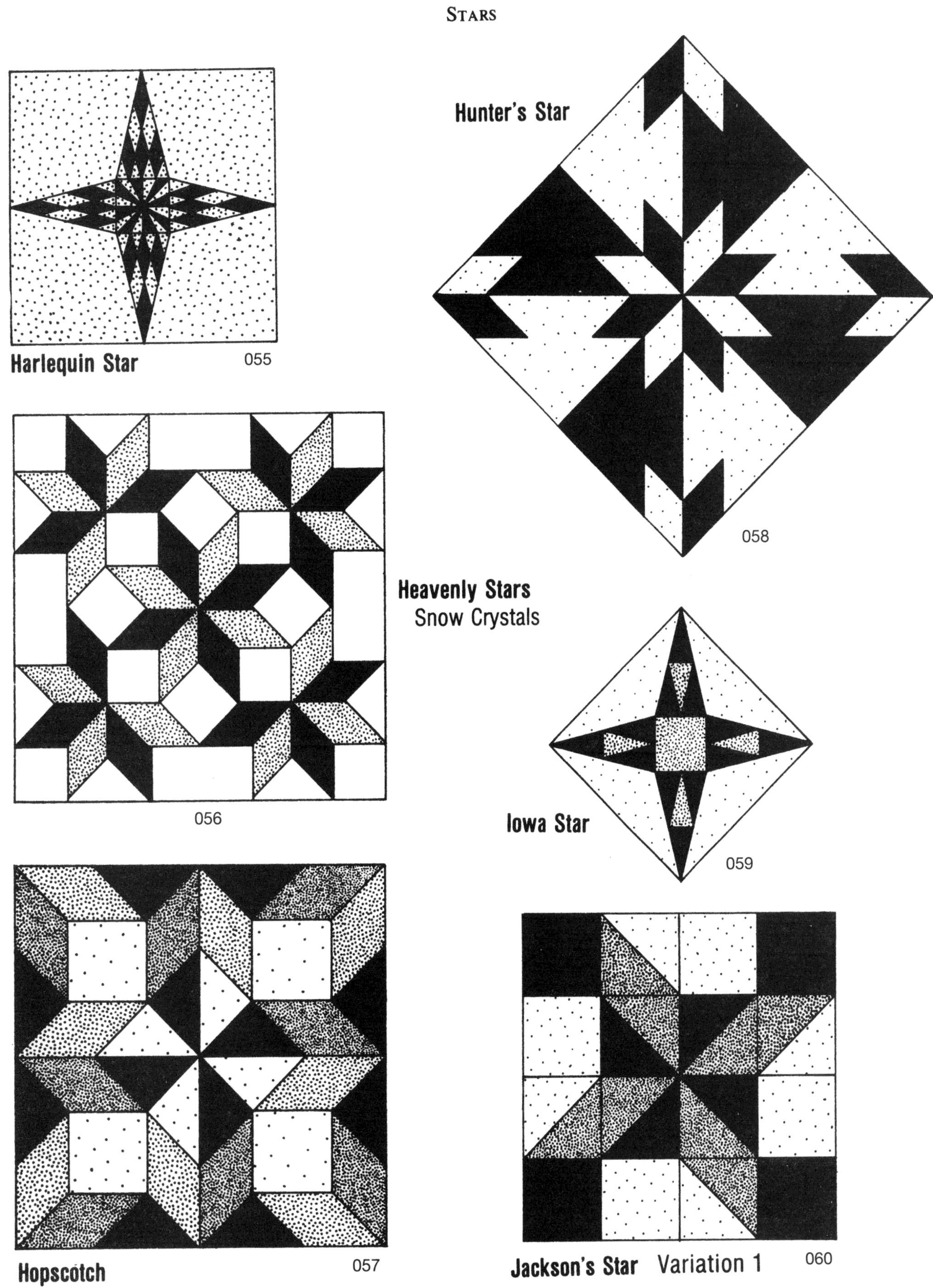
Harlequin Star
055
Hunter's Star
058
056
Heavenly Stars
Snow Crystals
Iowa Star
059
057
Hopscotch
Jackson's Star Variation 1
060

Jackson Star
Four Stars

061

Key West Star 064

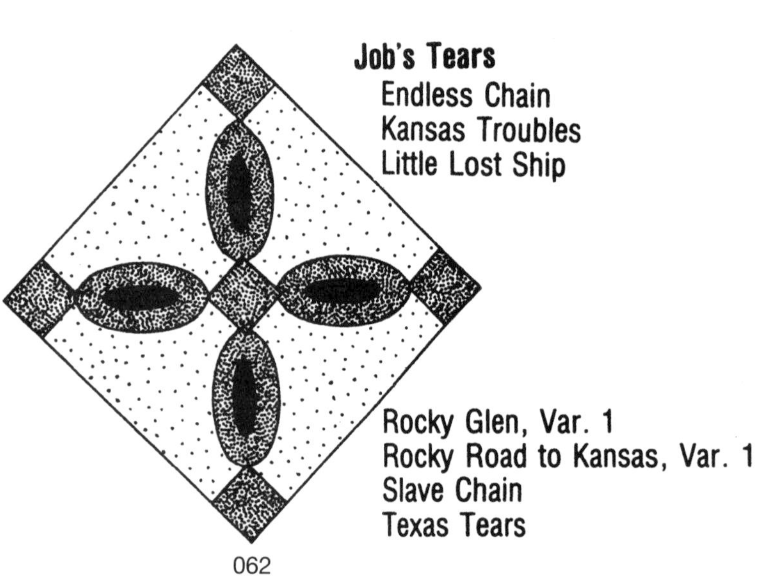

Job's Tears
Endless Chain
Kansas Troubles
Little Lost Ship
Rocky Glen, Var. 1
Rocky Road to Kansas, Var. 1
Slave Chain
Texas Tears

062

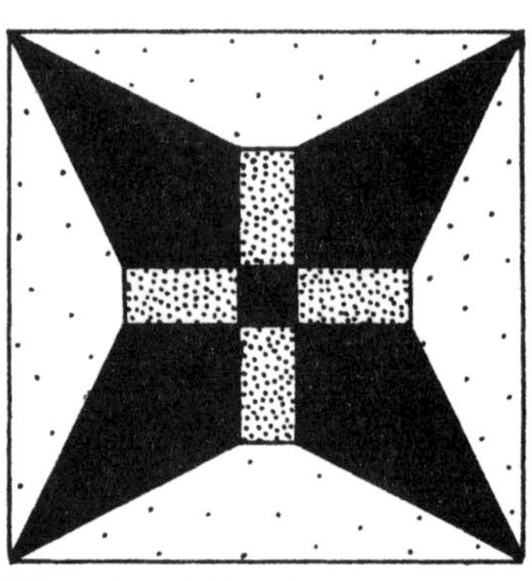

King David's Crown 065
Variation 1

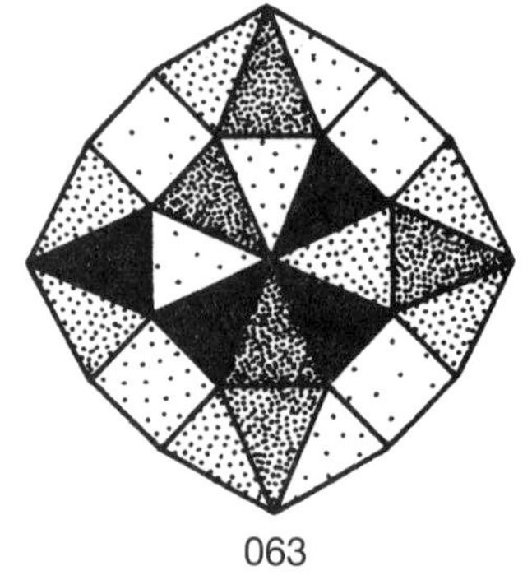

063

Kaleidoscope Variation 1

066

King's Star Variation 1

Lazy Daisy Variation 2 067

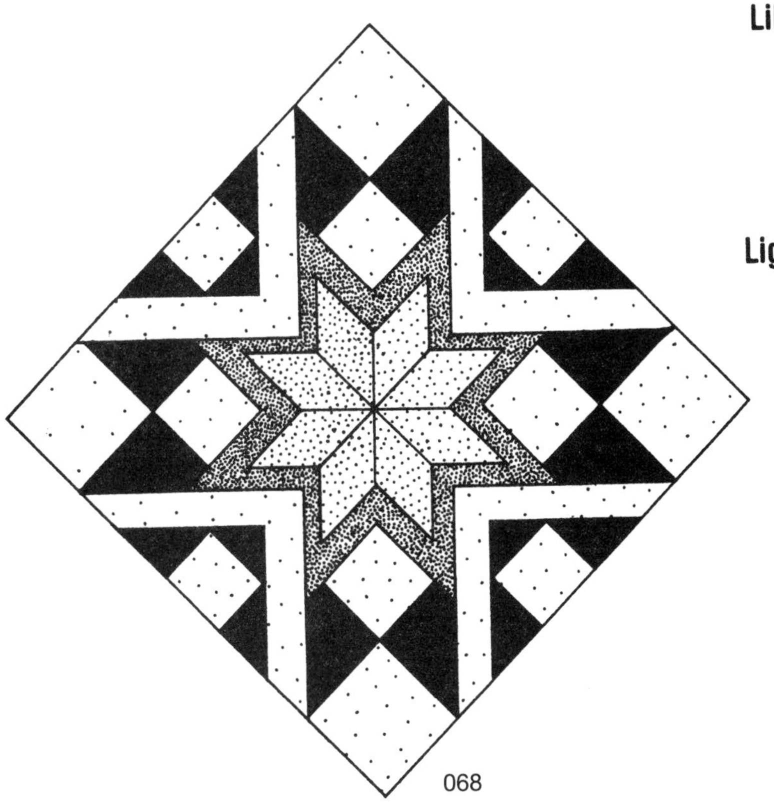

068

Leavenworth Star

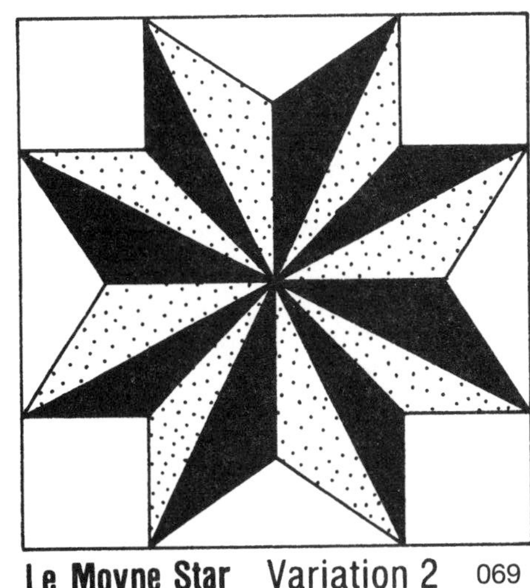

Le Moyne Star Variation 2 069

Divided Star
Lemon Star, Var. 2
Star of LeMoine, Var. 2
Star of LeMoyne, Var. 2

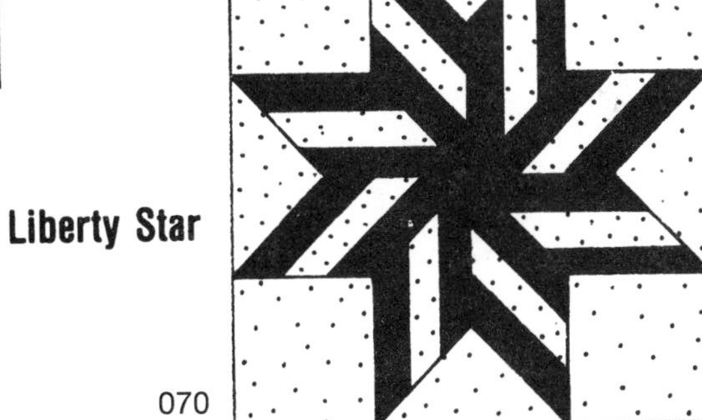

Liberty Star

070

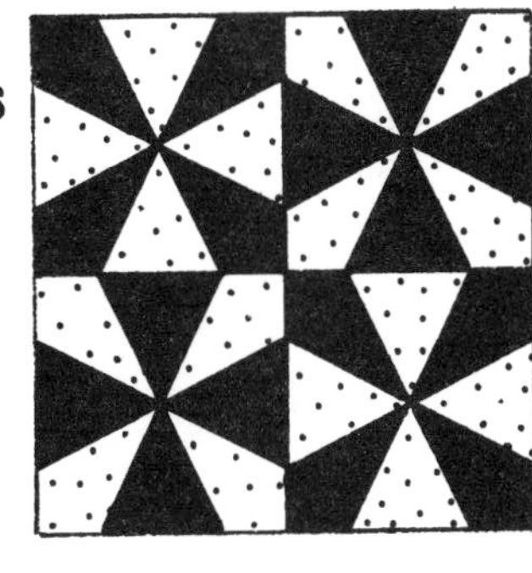

Light and Shadows

071

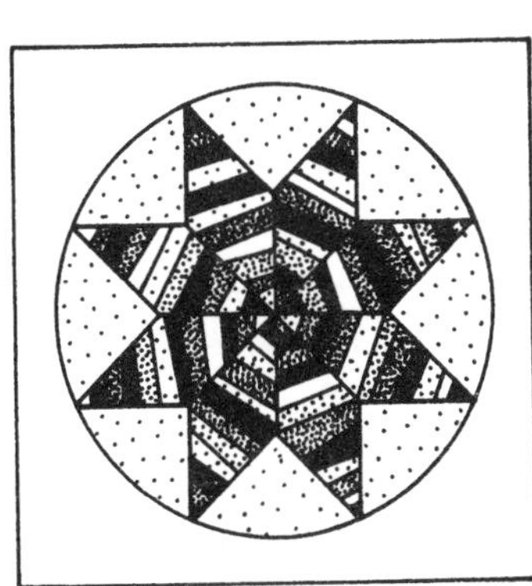

Log Cabin Star

072

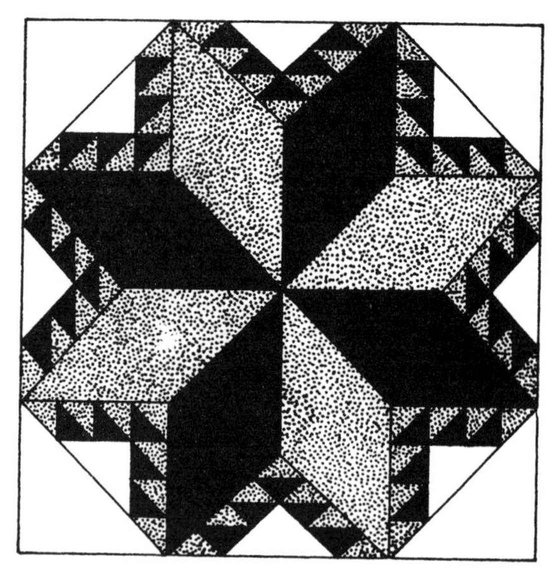

Lucinda's Star 073

Martha Washington Star
076

Many-pointed Star 074

Mexican Rose 077
Mexican Star, Var. 1

075 **Mariner's Compass**
Rising Sun, Var. 1

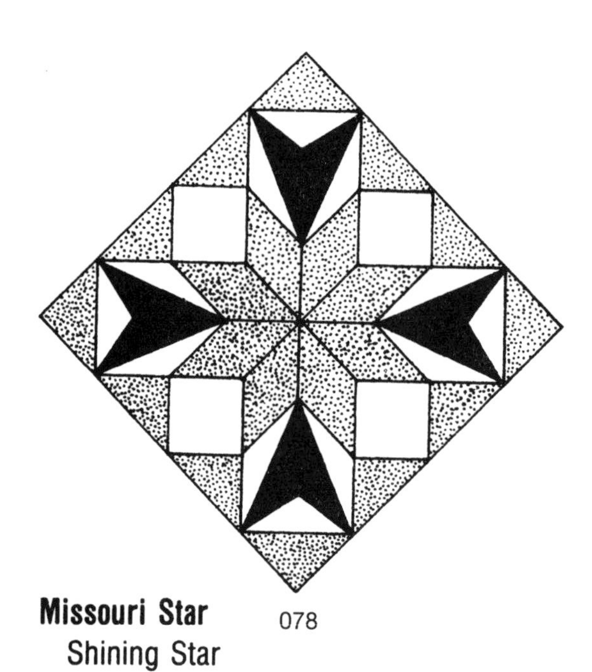

Missouri Star 078
Shining Star

Modern Star 079

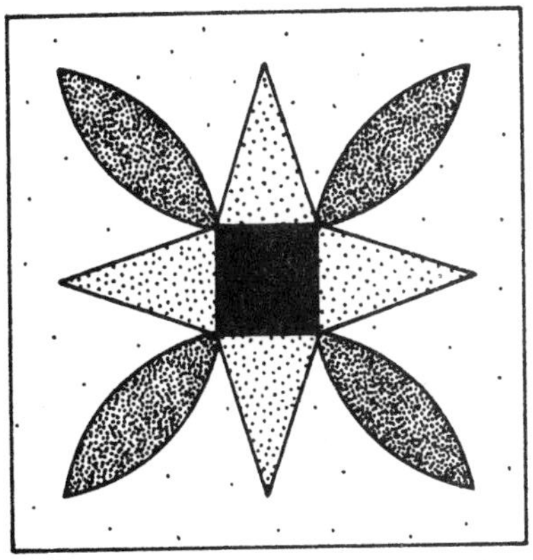

082

Morning Star Variation 3

Northern Lights
Blazing Star, Var. 3
Four-Pointed Star
Star, Var. 2

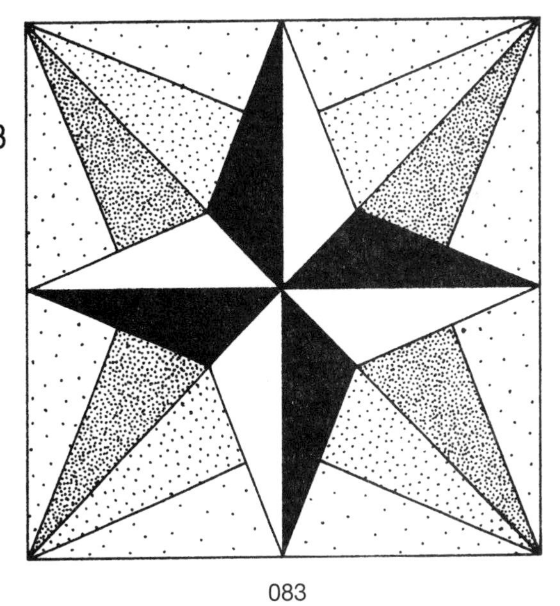

083

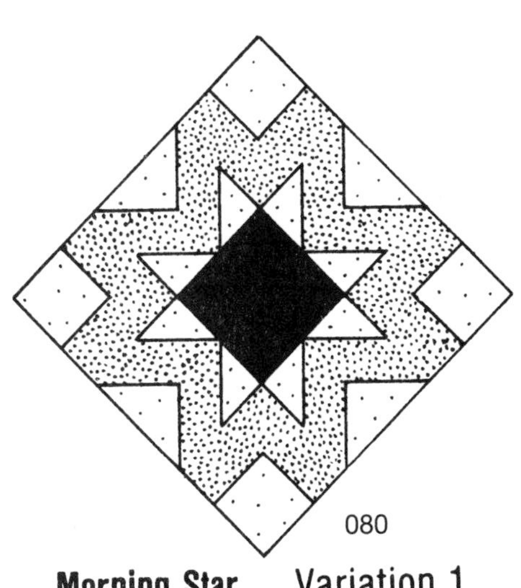

080

Morning Star Variation 1

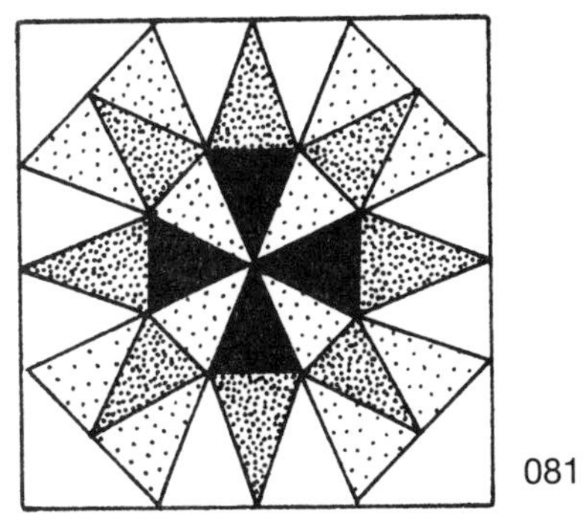

081

Morning Star Variation 2

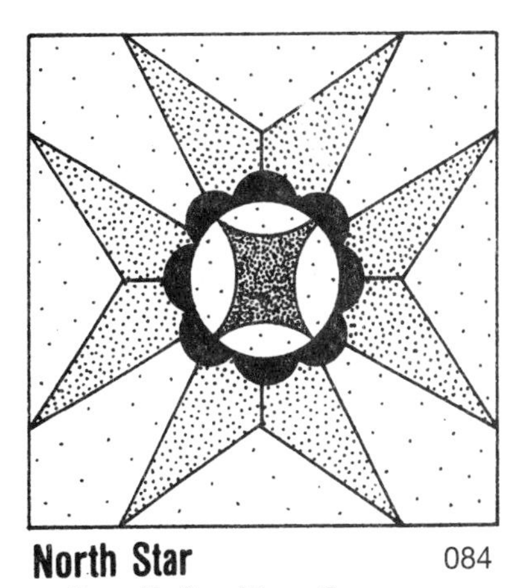

North Star 084
Star Tulip, Var. 2

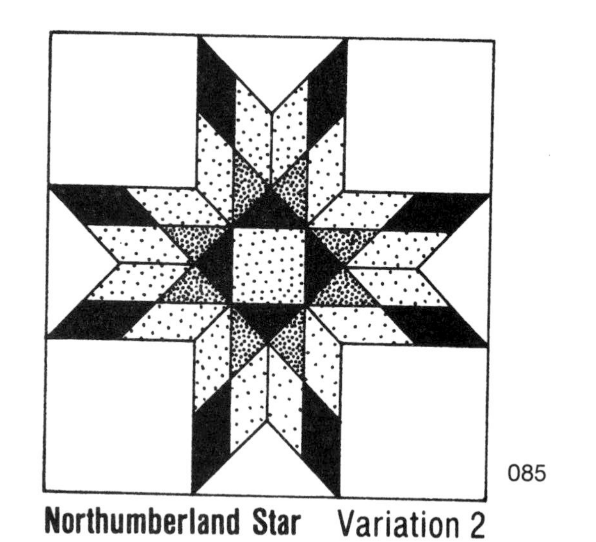

085

Northumberland Star Variation 2

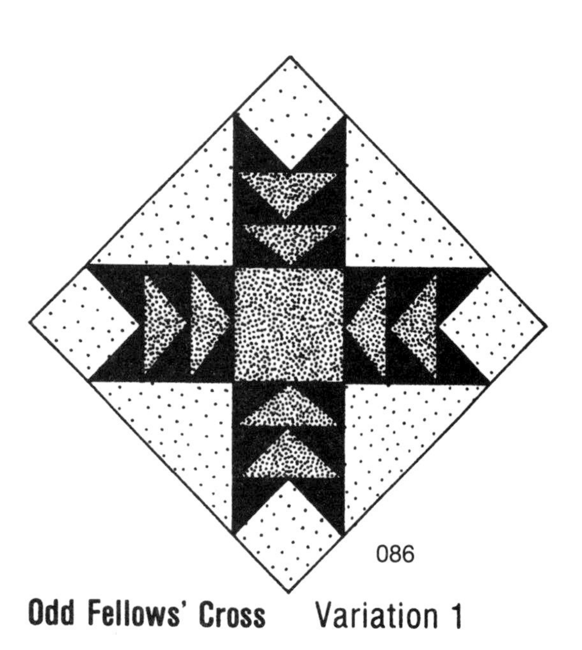

086

Odd Fellows' Cross Variation 1

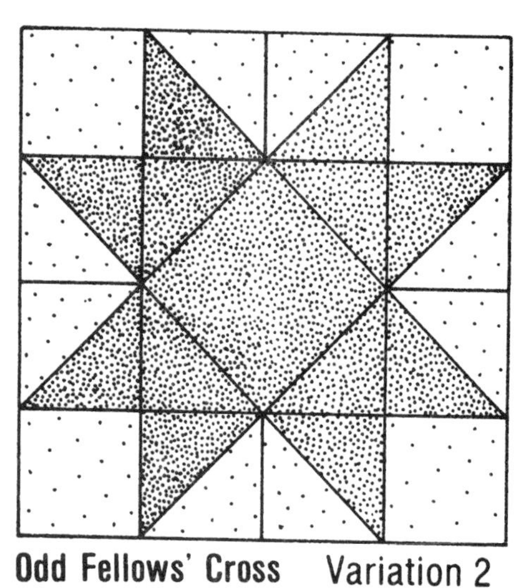

Odd Fellows' Cross Variation 2

087

Odd Star

088

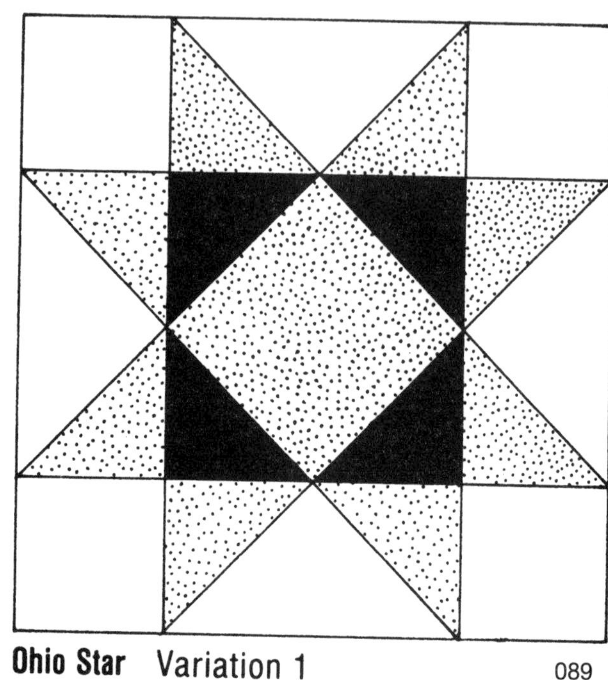

Ohio Star Variation 1

089

Lone Star, Var. 1
Old Tippecanoe and Tyler Too
Variable Star

Ohio Star Variation 2

Eastern Star, Var. 1
Eight-Point Star
Lone Star, Var. 2
Lucky Star
Shoofly, Var. 2
Texas
Tippecanoe and Tyler Too

090

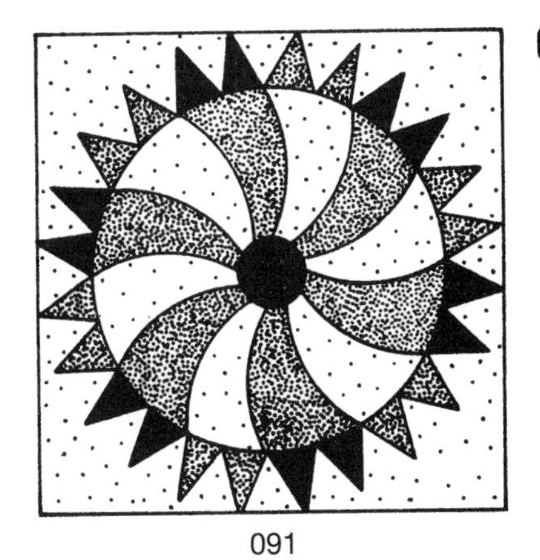

Oklahoma Star
Rising Sun, Var. 2

091

Ozark Star
Ozark Diamond

094

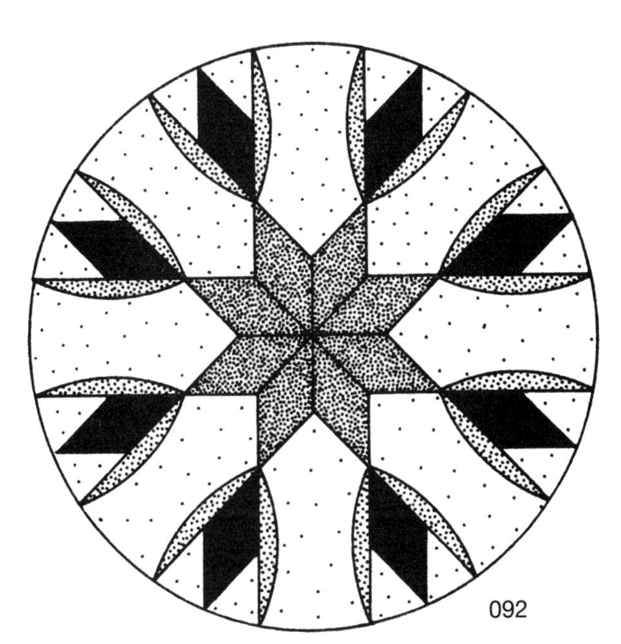

092

Olive's Yellow Tulip

Patty's Star

095

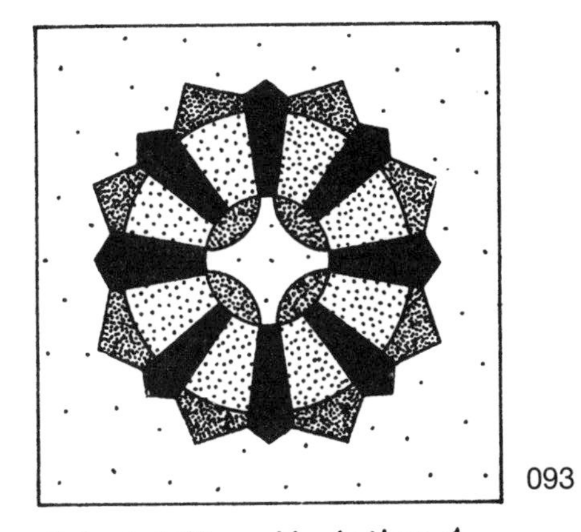

093

Oriental Star Variation 1

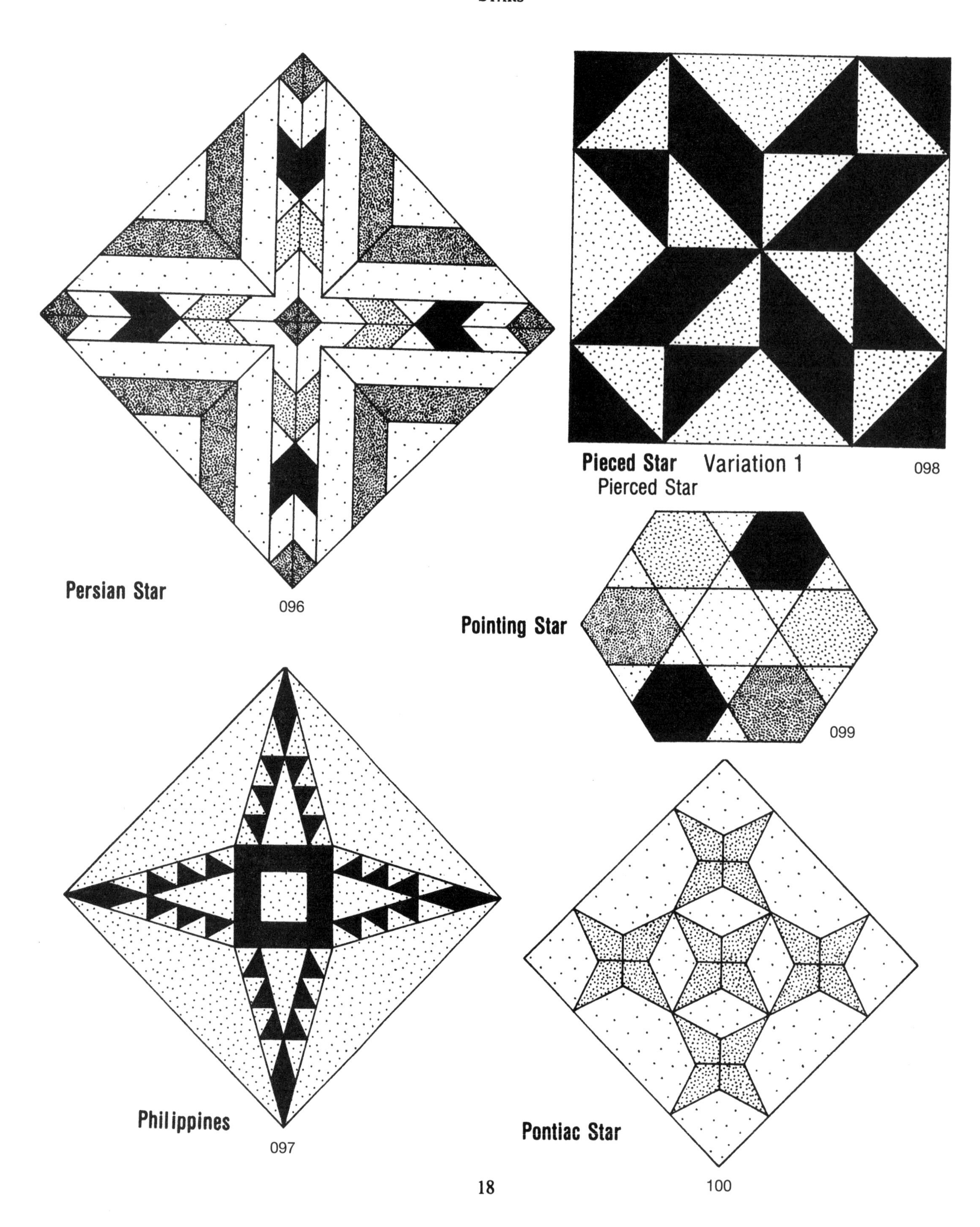
Persian Star
096
Pieced Star Variation 1
Pierced Star
098
Pointing Star
099
Philippines
097
Pontiac Star
100

Prairie Queen
Variation 2
101
Purple Cross
103
Prairie Star
Harvest Star
Harvest Sun
Ship's Wheel
102
Queen of the May
104
Ring Around the Star
Rolling Star, Var. 2
Star and Chains
105

Rising Star Variation 1 106
Stars and Squares

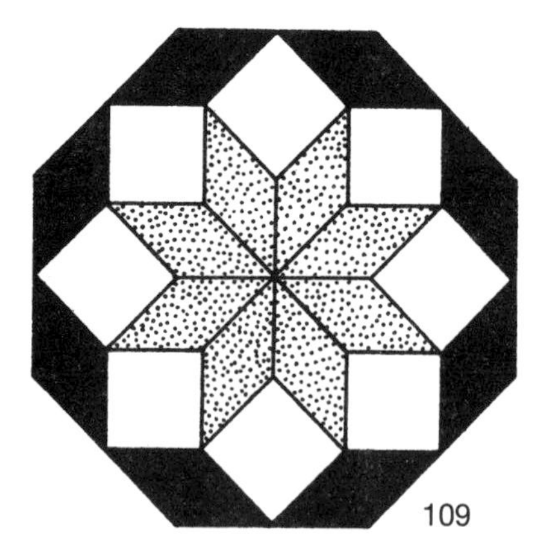

109

Rolling Star Variation 1
Virginia Reel

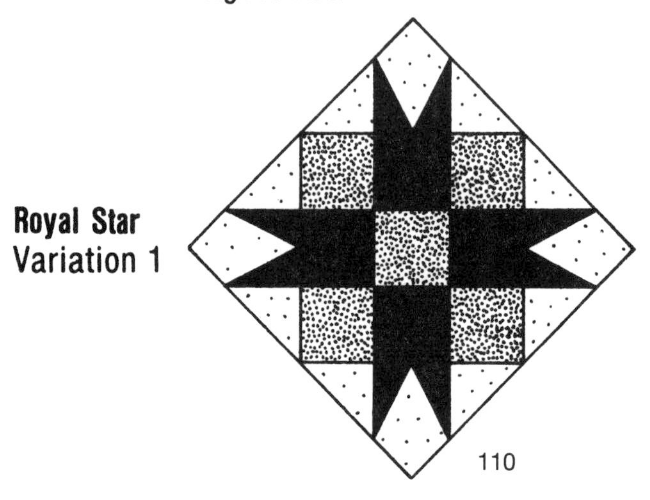

Royal Star
Variation 1

110

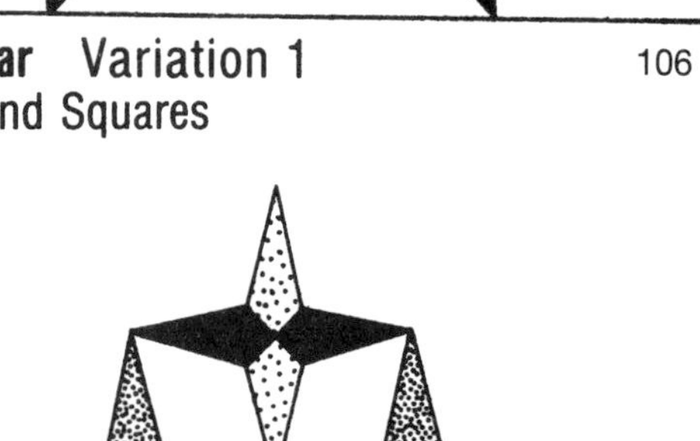

107

Rock Garden

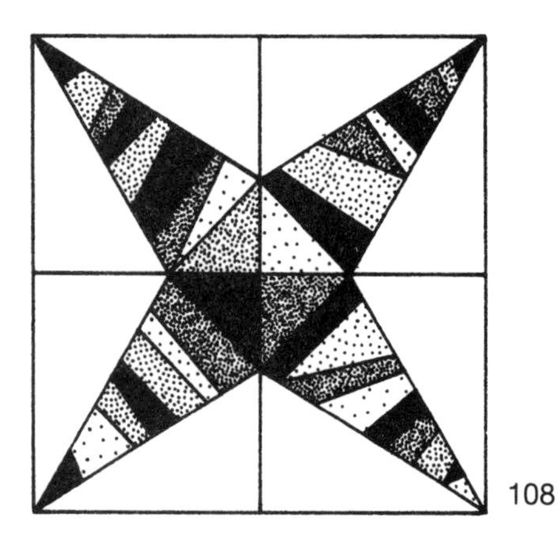

108

Rocky Road to Kansas Variation 2

Royal Star Variation 2

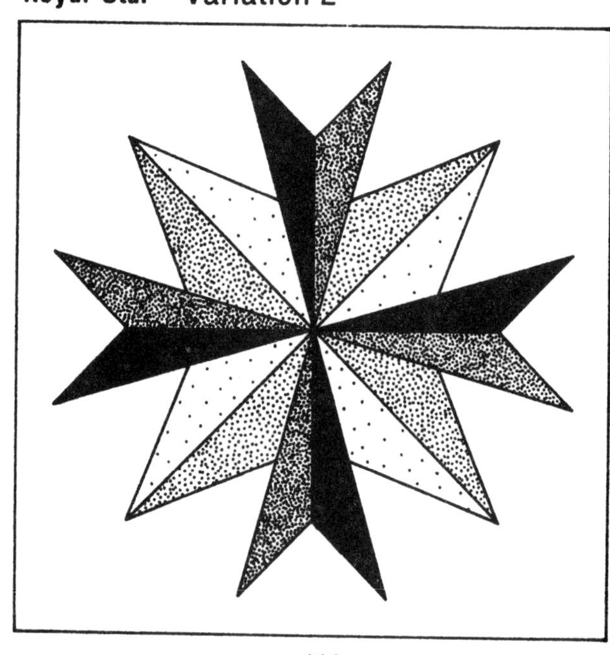

111

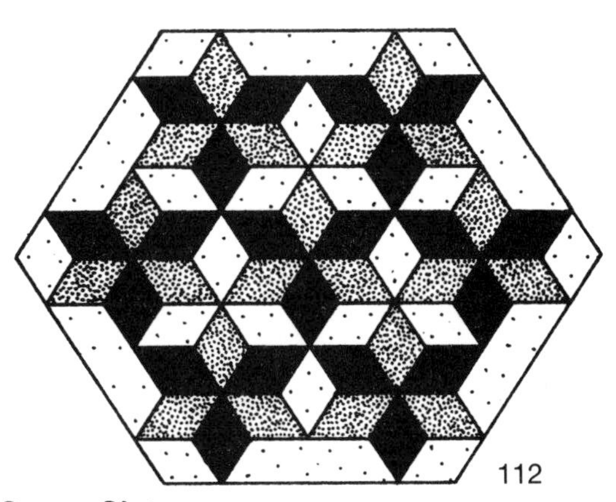

112

Seven Sisters
Evening Star, Var. 4

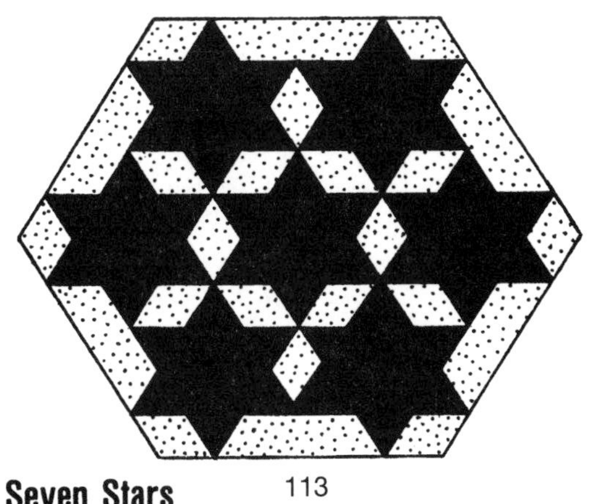

Seven Stars 113
Boutonniere

Sky Rocket

114

Slashed Star 115
Sunflower

Small Business

116

Spiderweb
Variation 2

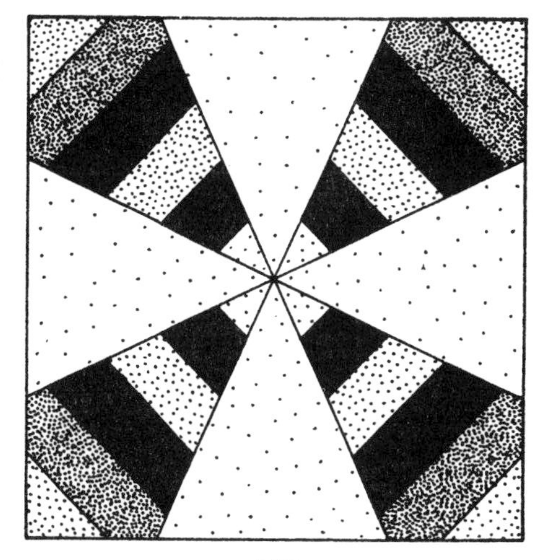

117

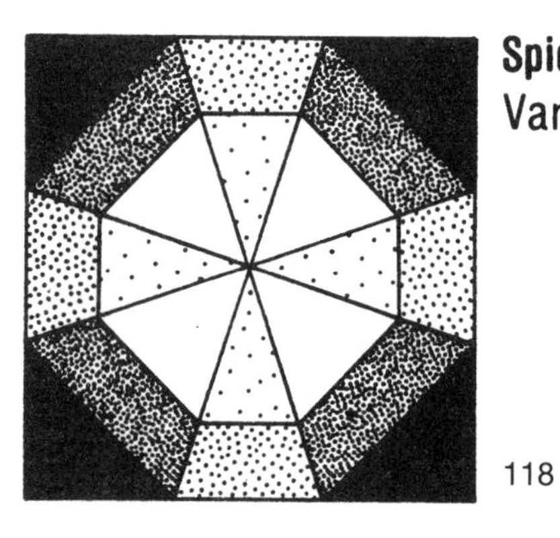

Spiderweb
Variation 3

118

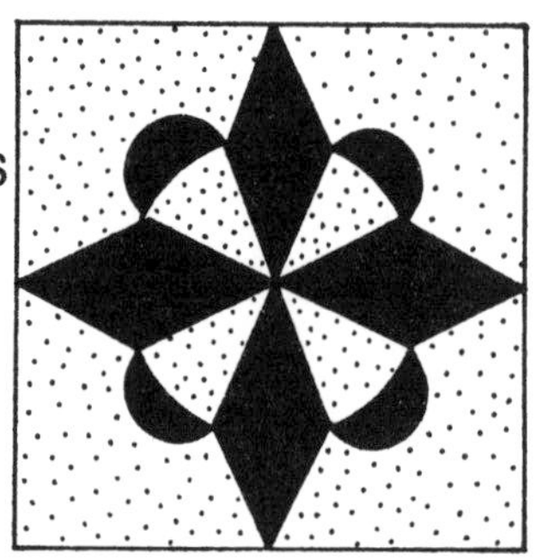

Star and Crescent
Variation 2
Star of the Four Winds

122

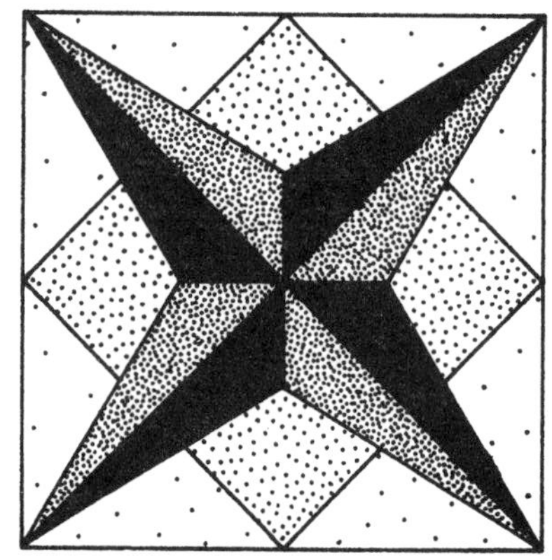

Star Variation 1

119

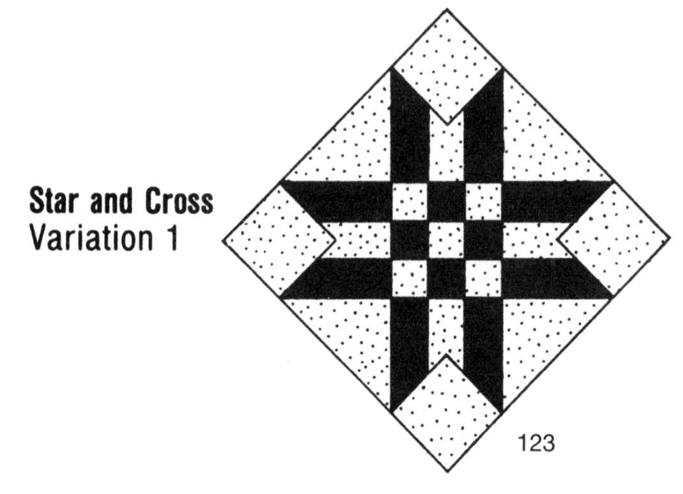

Star and Cross
Variation 1

123

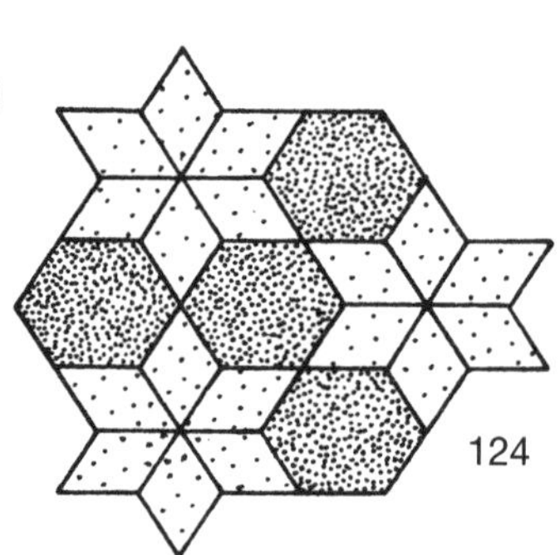

Star and Cone

120

Star and Hexagon
Tiny Star

124

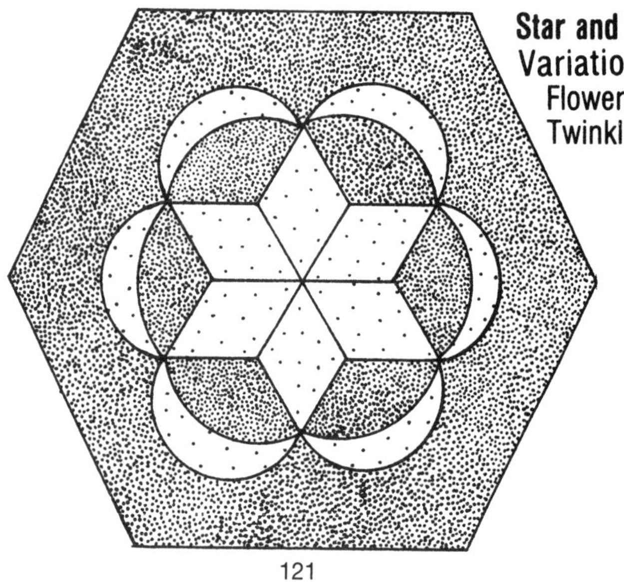

Star and Crescent
Variation 1
Flower Star, Var. 2
Twinkling Star, Var. 2

121

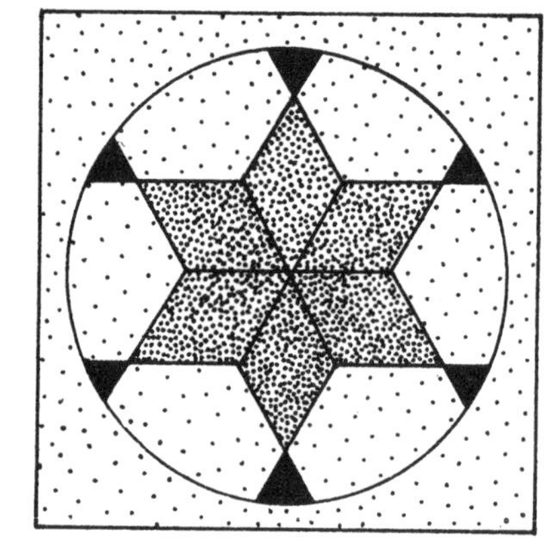

Star and Planets

125

Star Flower Variation 2

126

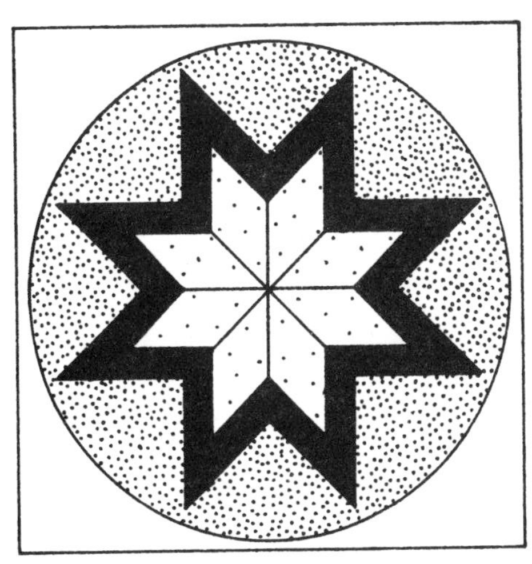

Star of Hope Variation 2

129

Starlight Variation 1

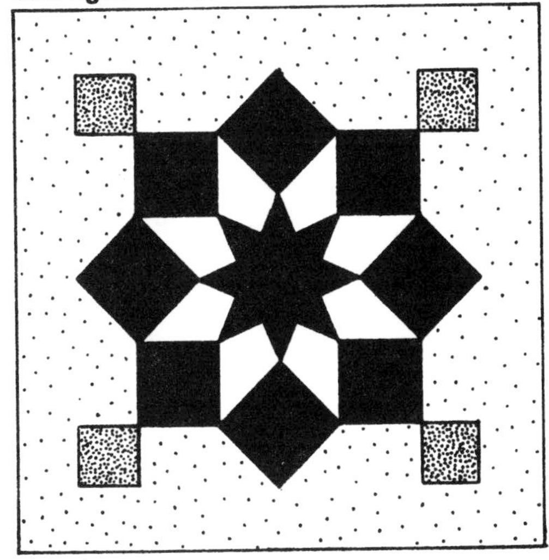

127

Star of Le Moyne Variation 1
Brunswick Star, Var. 2
Eight-Pointed Star, Var. 1
Lemon Star, Var. 1
LeMoyne Star, Var. 1
Star of the East, Var. 1
Star of LeMoine, Var. 1

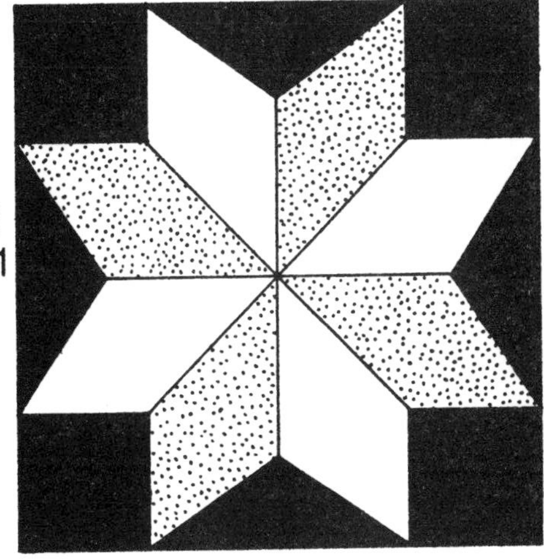

130

Starlight Variation 2

128

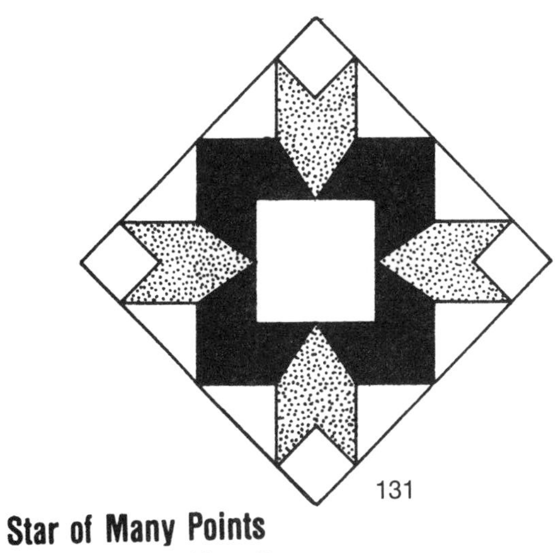

131

Star of Many Points
Arrow Star, Var. 2

Star of North Carolina 132
North Carolina Star

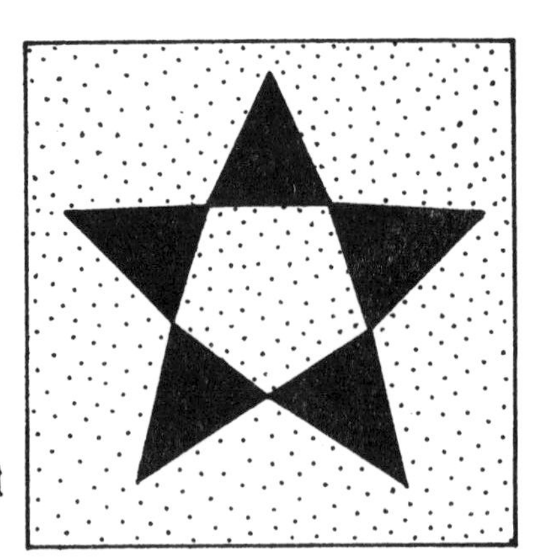

Star of the West
Variation 2
135

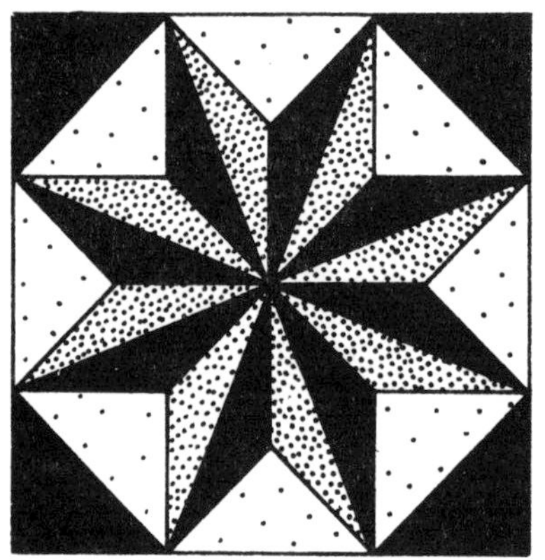

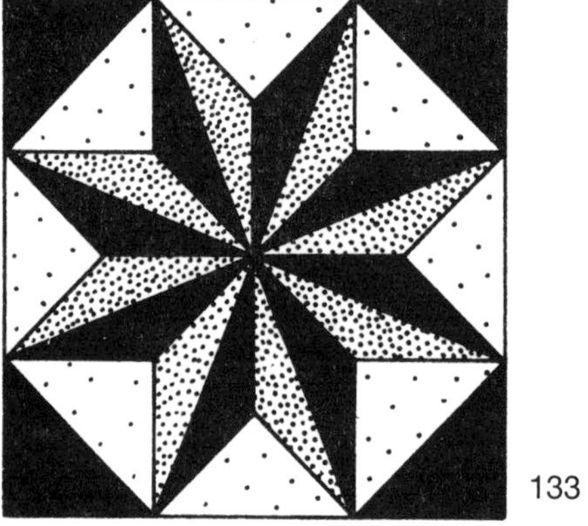

133

Star of the East Variation 3
Silver and Gold

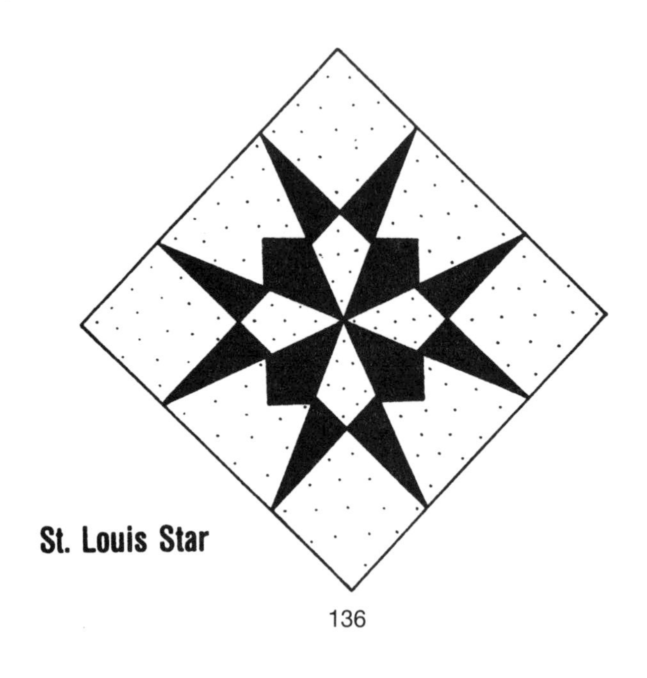

St. Louis Star
136

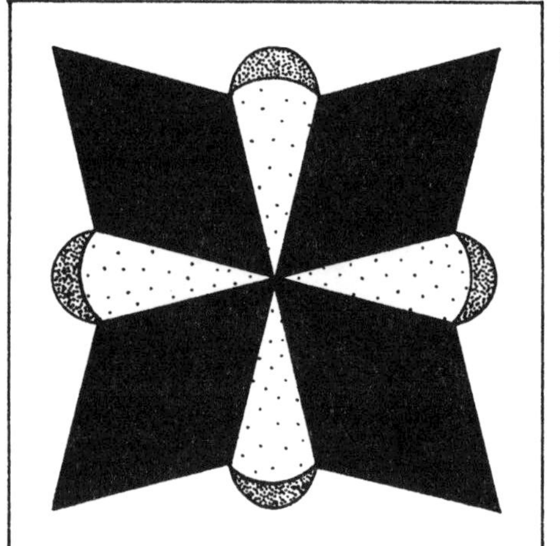

134

Star of the West
Variation 1
Compass, Var. 1
Four Birds
Four Winds
King's Star, Var. 2

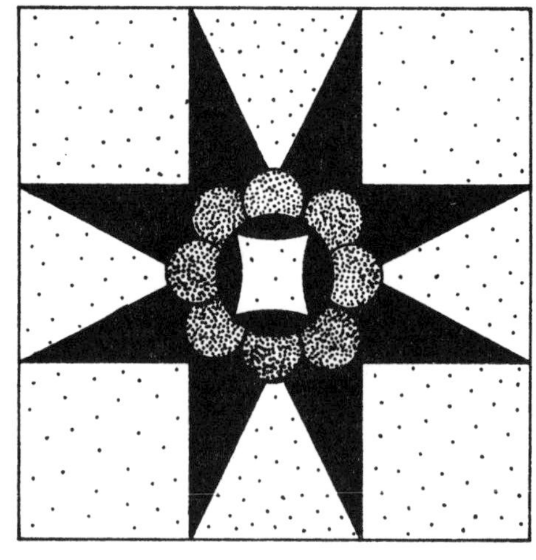

Star Tulip
Variation 1
137

Sunburst
Variation 1
141
Star Within a Star
Carpenter's Wheel, Var. 1
Double Star
Star of the East, Var. 2
138
142
String Quilt
Sunburst Variation 2
139
Sunbeam
Sunburst Variation 3
140
143

Sunburst Variation 4 144

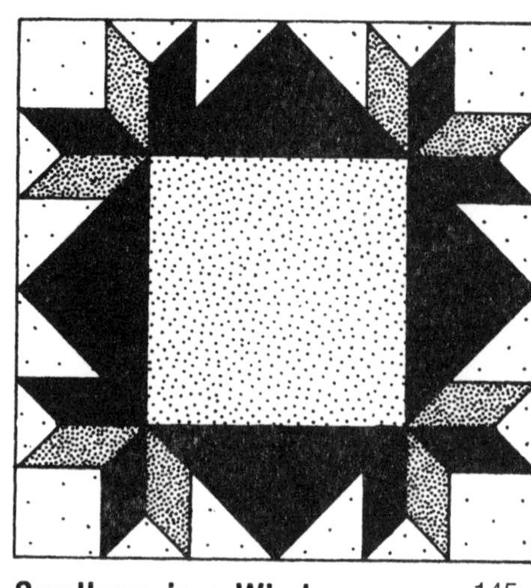

Swallows in a Window 145

Tennessee Star 147

Tangled Cobwebs 146

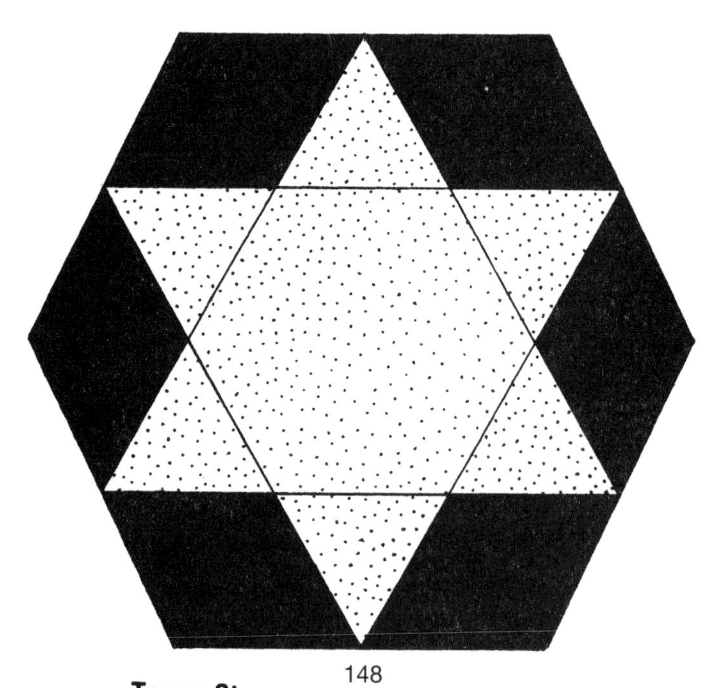

148 Texas Star

Union Star 149

Yankee Pride
Maple Leaf, Var. 3

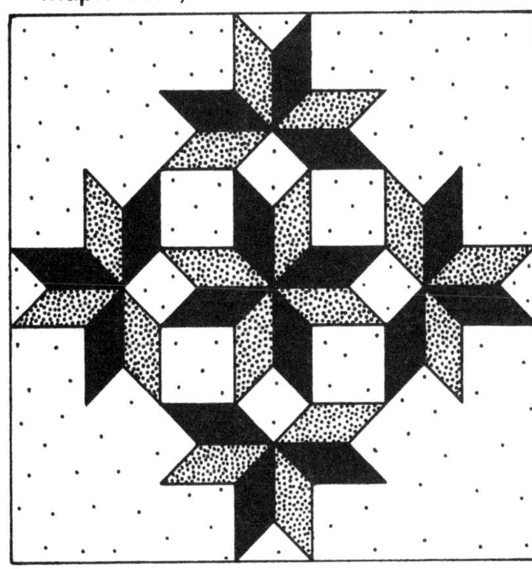

152

Virginia Star
Eastern Star, Var. 2
Star upon Stars
Virginia's Star

150

World Without End
Amethyst
Golden Wedding Ring
Windmill Star

151

SUPPLEMENT

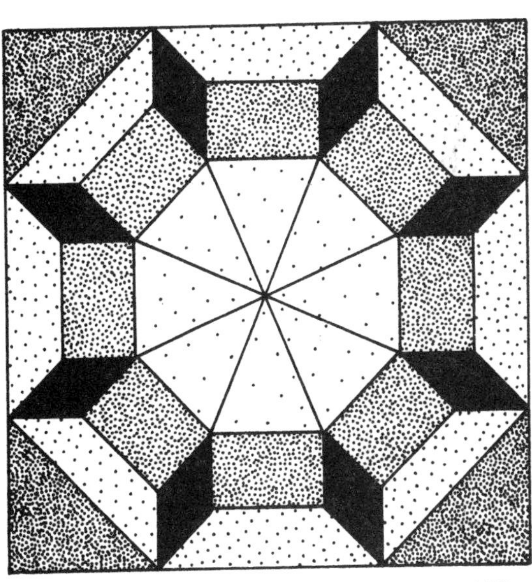

Castle Wall 153

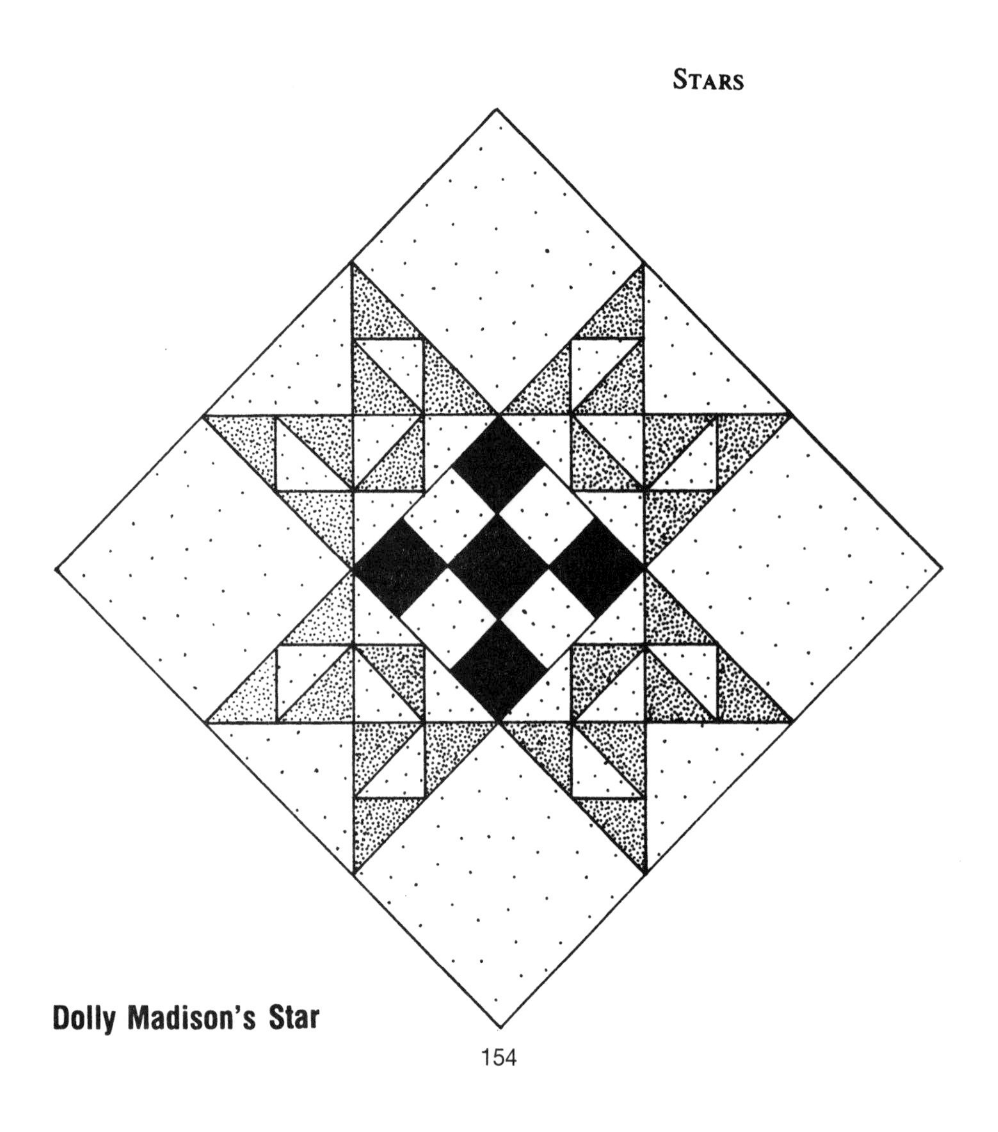

Dolly Madison's Star

154

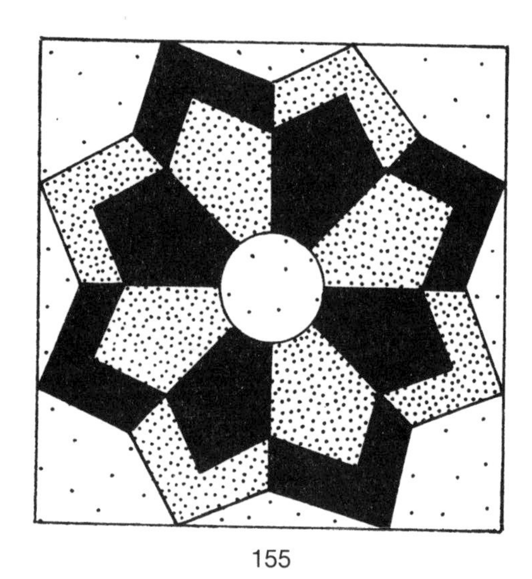

155

Eight-Pointed Star Variation 3

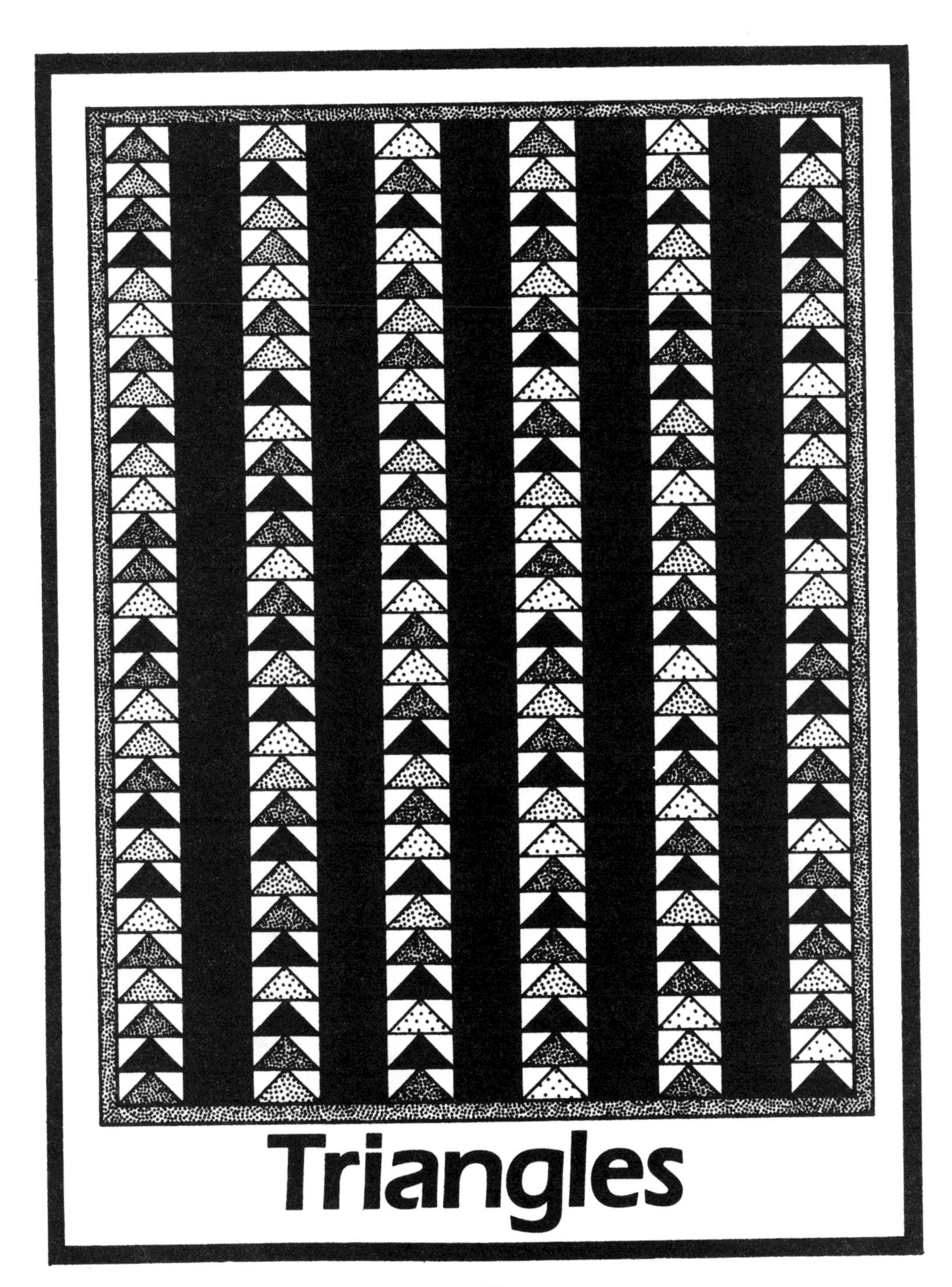

Triangles

Aircraft
157

Album
Variation 4
158

Album
Variation 5
159

Anvil
160

Barbara Frietchie Star
Star Puzzle
161

Barn Raising
162

Barrister's Block
Lawyer's Puzzle
163

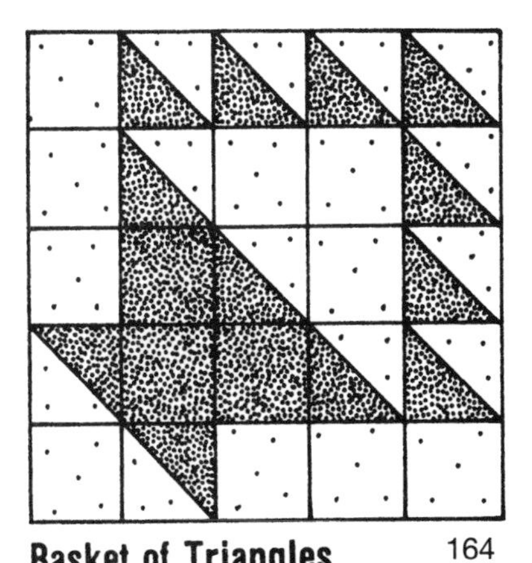

Basket of Triangles 164
Fruit Basket, Var. 2

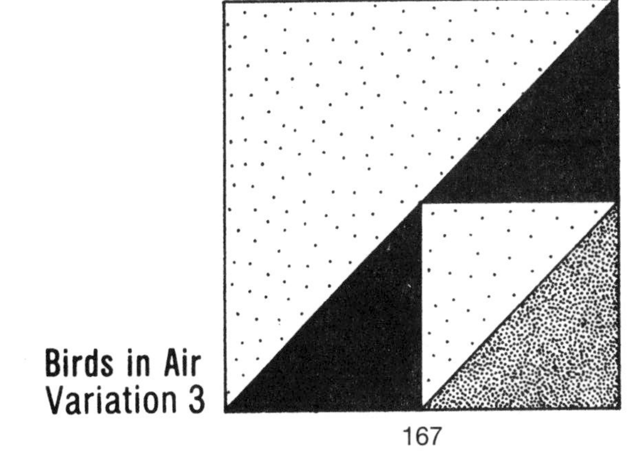

Birds in Air
Variation 3
167

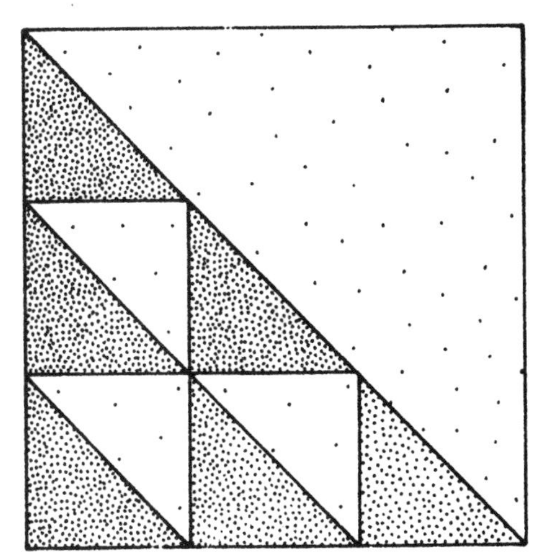

Birds in Air Variation 1 165
Flying Birds
Flying Geese, Var. 1
Flock of Geese

Blindman's Fancy 168

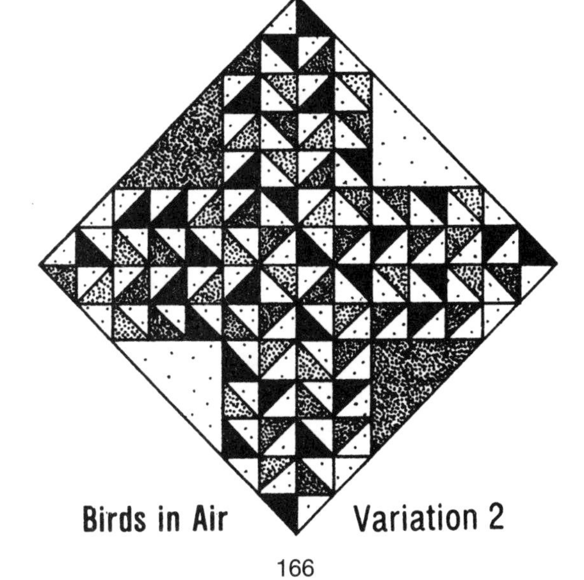

Birds in Air Variation 2
166

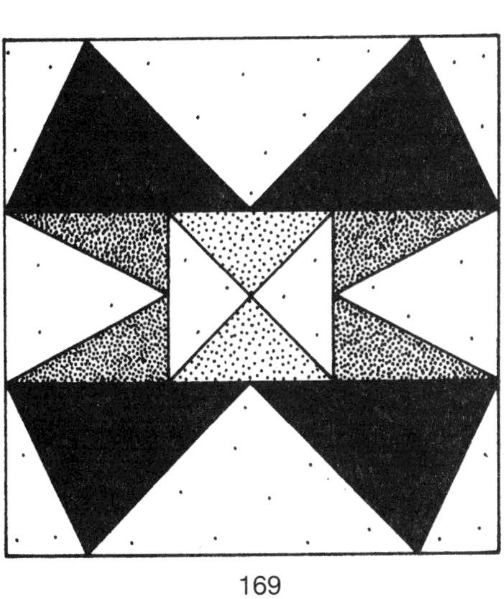

Bow
169

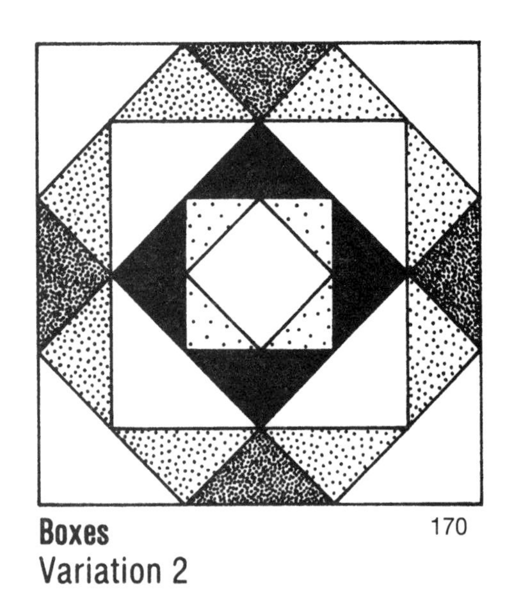

Boxes 170
Variation 2

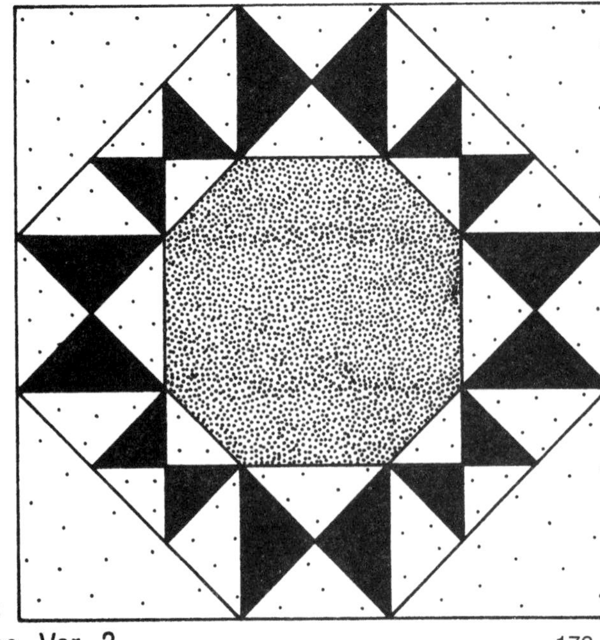

Buttons and Bows 173
Wheel of Fortune, Var. 3

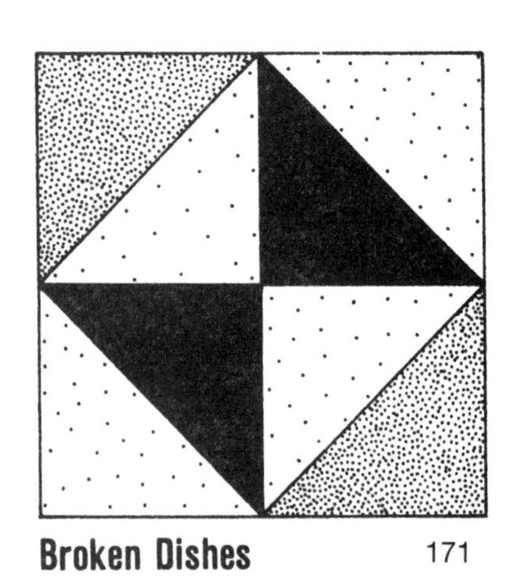

Broken Dishes 171

Cactus Flower 174

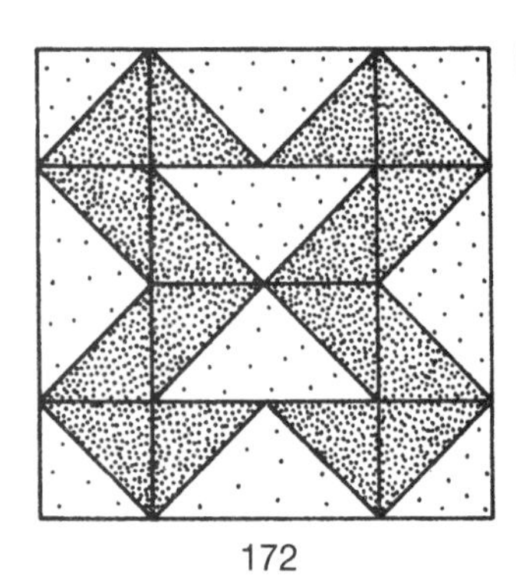

172

Brown Goose
Brown
Devil's Claws, Var. 1
Double Z
Grey Goose

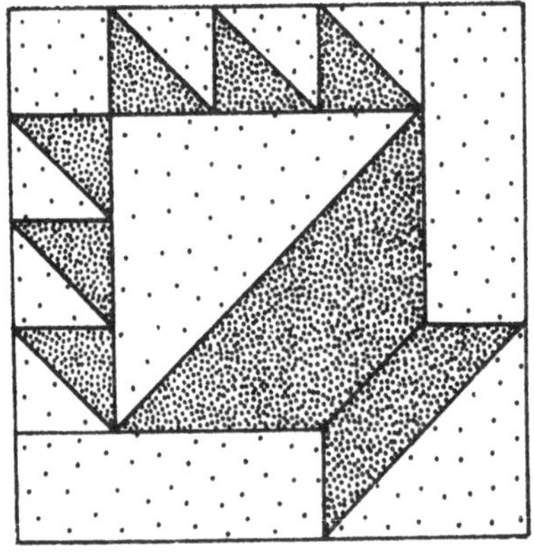

Cakestand 175

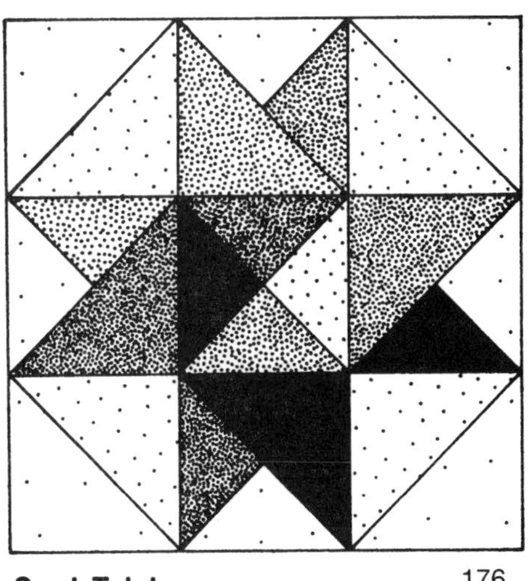
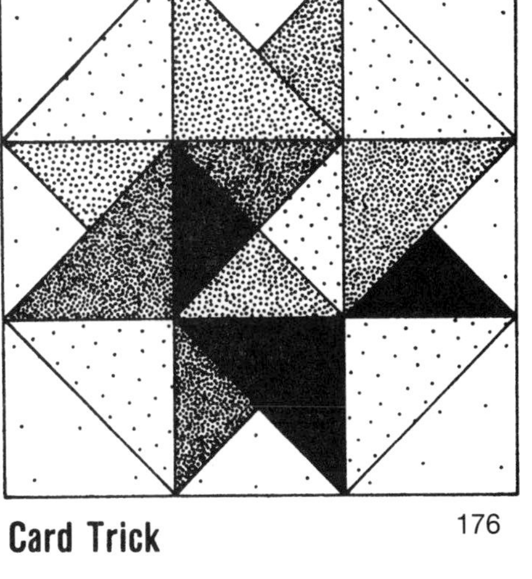

Card Trick 176

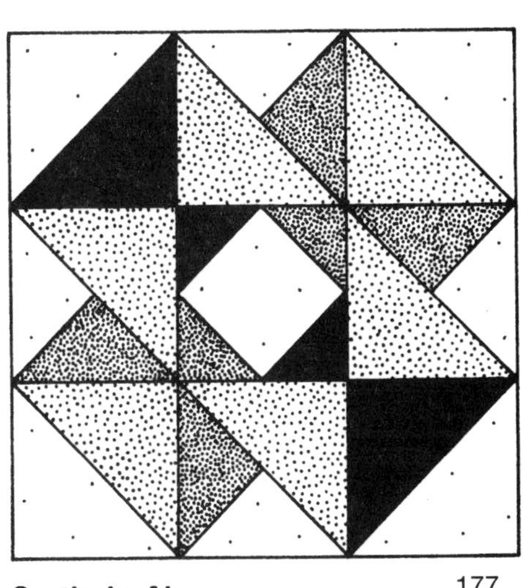

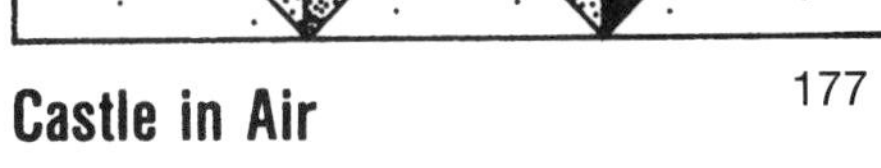

Castle in Air 177

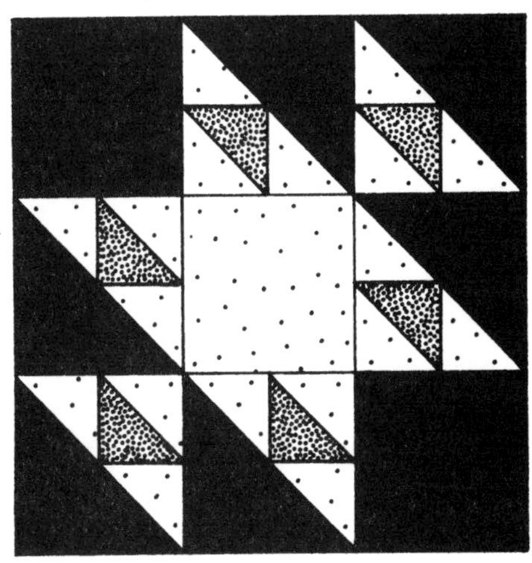

Cat's Cradle 178

Century
Variation 2

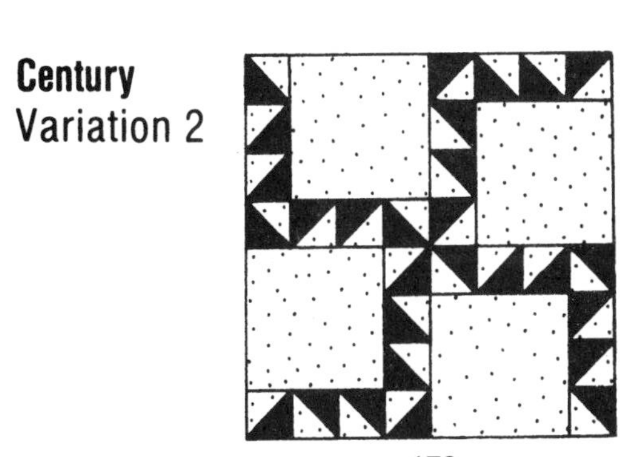

179

Cherry Basket Variation 1
Flower Basket

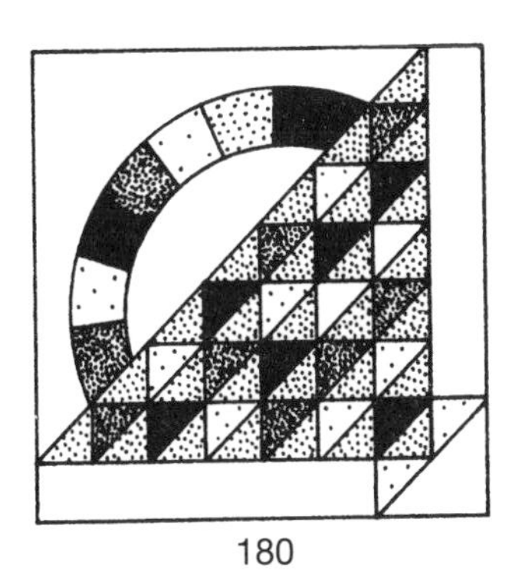

180

Cherry Basket
Variation 2

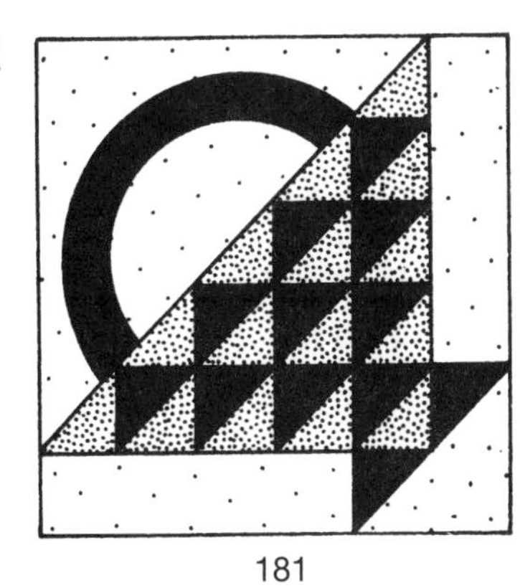

181

Christmas Tree
Tree of Life, Var. 3

182

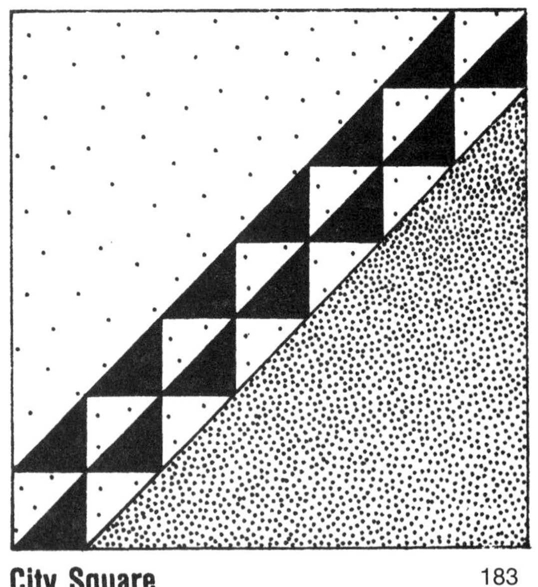

City Square 183
London Square

Crazy Ann Variation 1
Follow the Leader
Twist and Turn

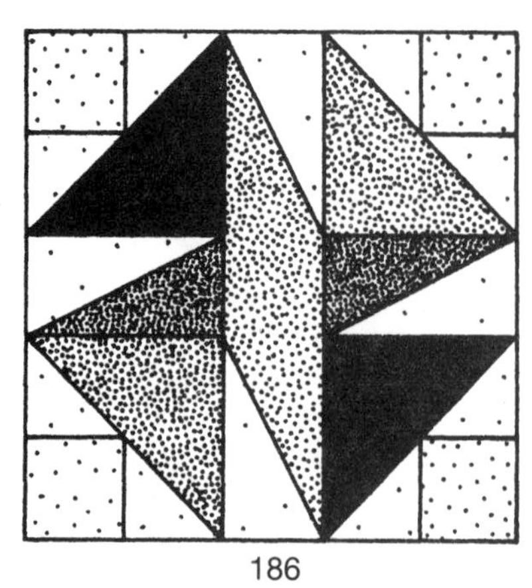

186

Cross
Variation 1

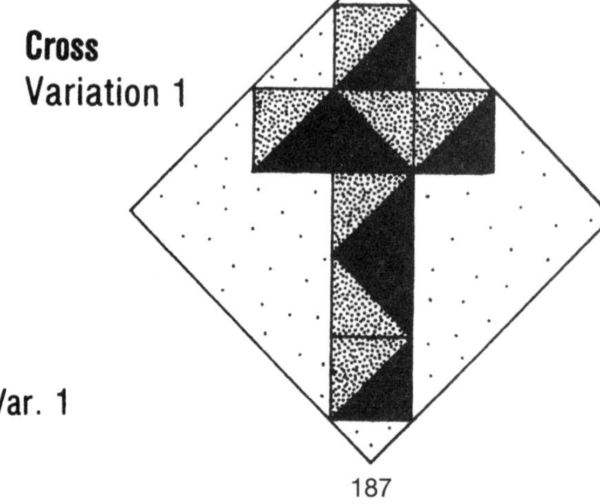

187

Corn and Beans
Variation 2
Duck and Duckling
Handy Andy, Var. 4
Hen and Chickens, Var. 1
Shoofly, Var. 4

184

Crossed Canoes
Tippecanoe

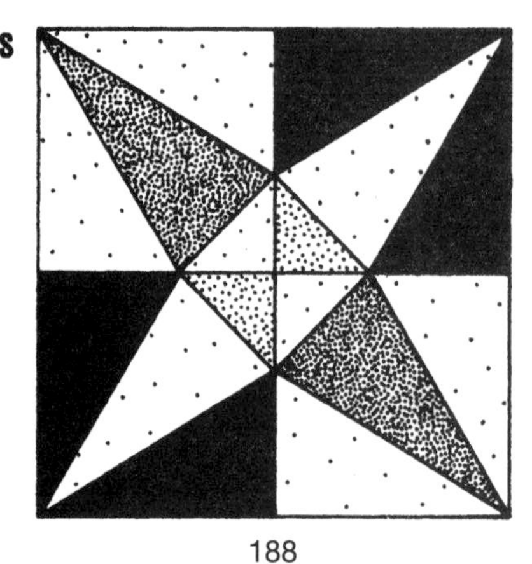

188

Cotton Reel 185

Crosses and Losses
Double X, Var. 2
Fox and Geese
Old Maid's Puzzle
X

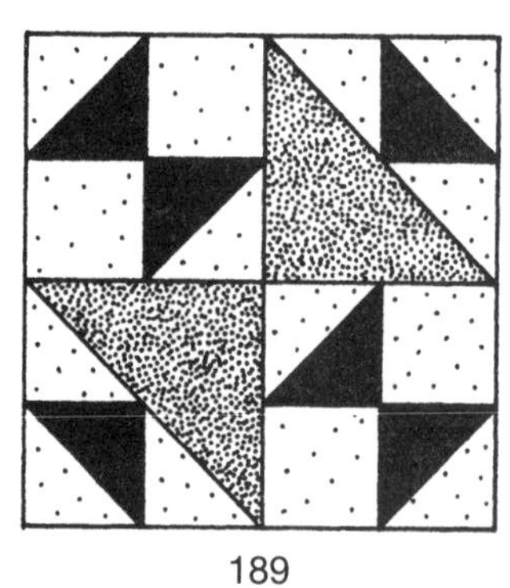

189

Double Pyramid 190

Double Sawtooth 191

Double T Variation 1 192

Dove in the Window Variation 1 193

Duck and Ducklings
Corn and Beans, Var. 1
Handy Andy, Var. 5
Hens and Chickens, Var. 1
Shoofly, Var. 3
Wild Goose Chase, Var. 2

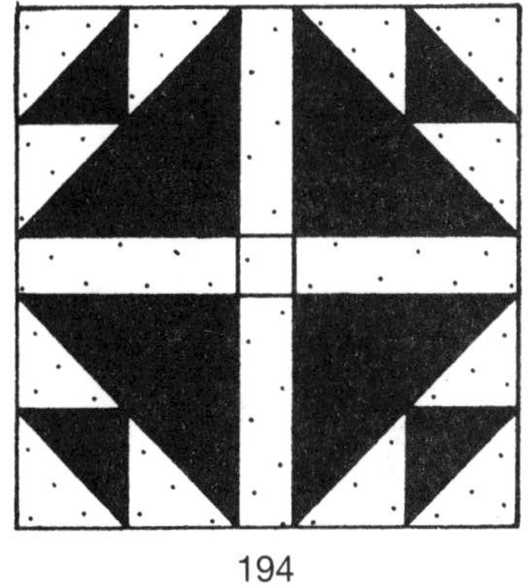

194

Dutchman's Puzzle
Dutch Windmill

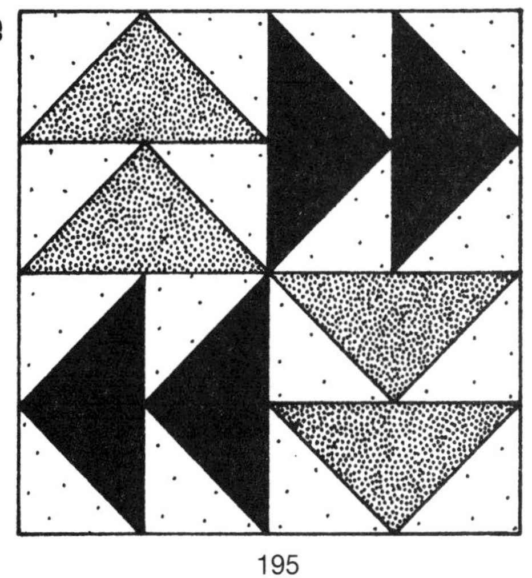

195

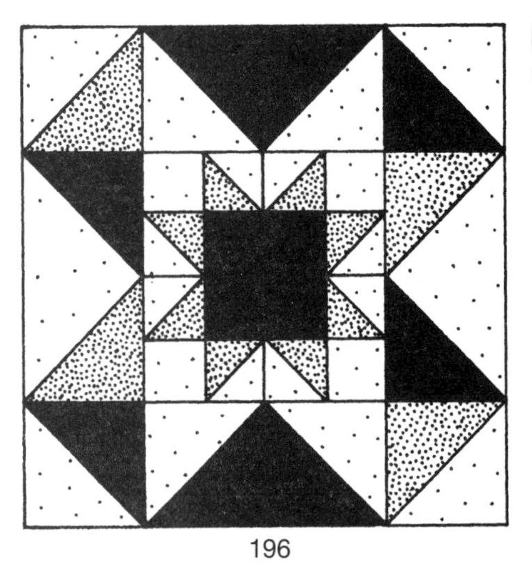

Eight Hands Round
Variation 1

196

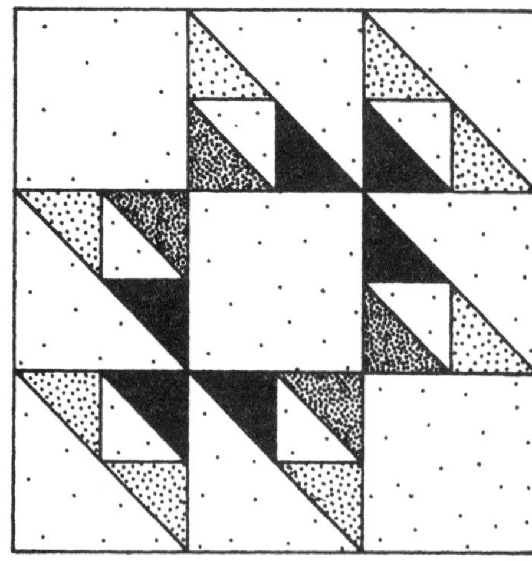

Flying Bird 200

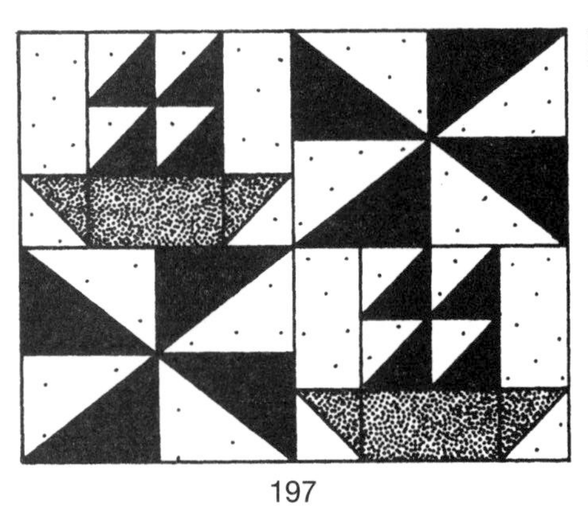

Flags and Ships

197

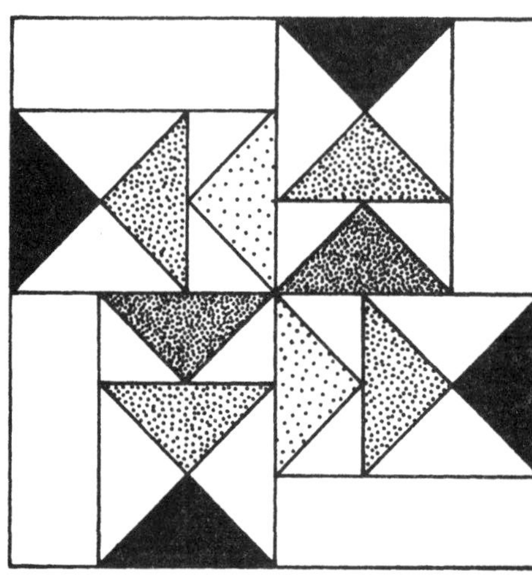

Flying Dutchman Variation 3 201

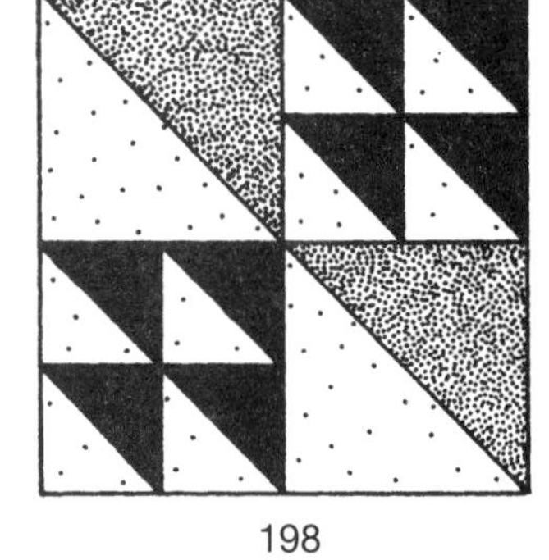

Flock

198

Forbidden Fruit
Forbidden Fruit Tree

202

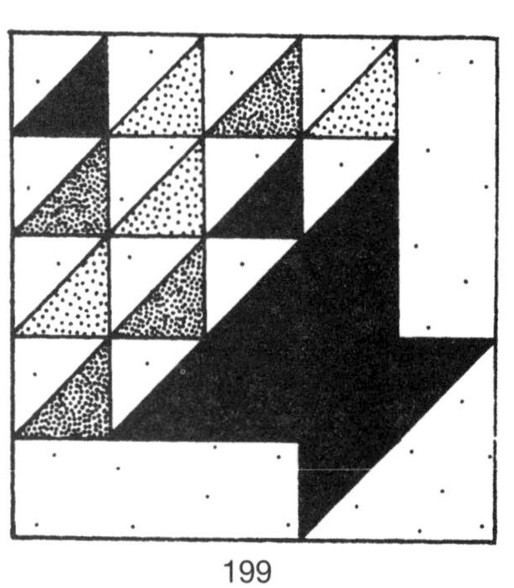

Flower Pot
Variation 3

199

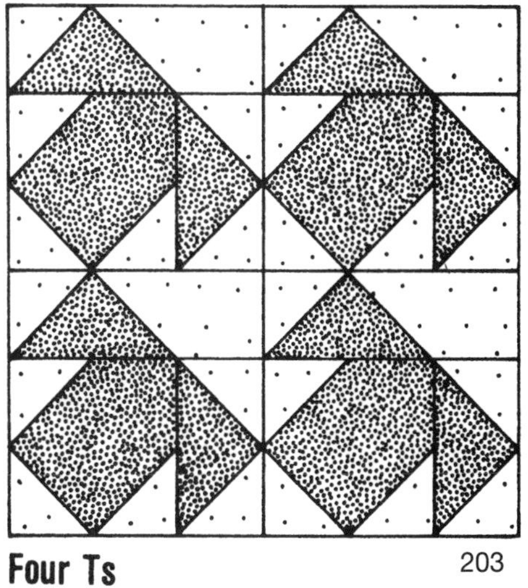

203

Four Ts
Mixed T

Geese in Flight
Battlegrounds
Indian Trails, Var. 2
Rambling Road, Var. 2
Soldiers March
Storm at Sea, Var. 3

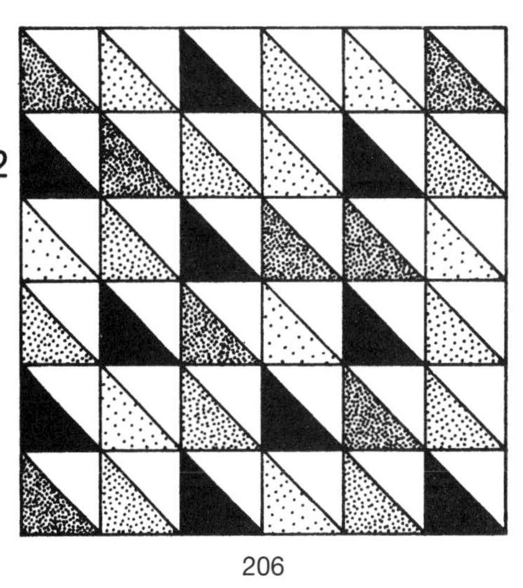

206

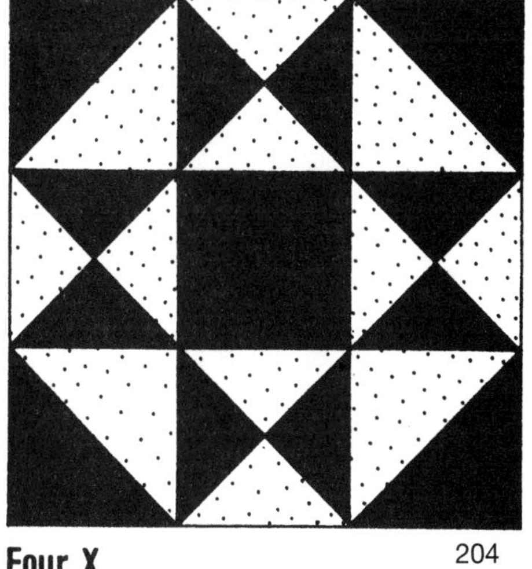

Four X

204

Georgetown Circles

207

Fruit Basket Variation 1

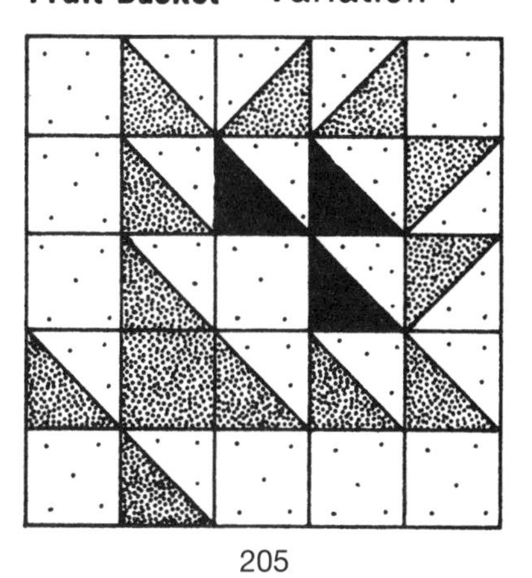

205

Golden Stairs

208

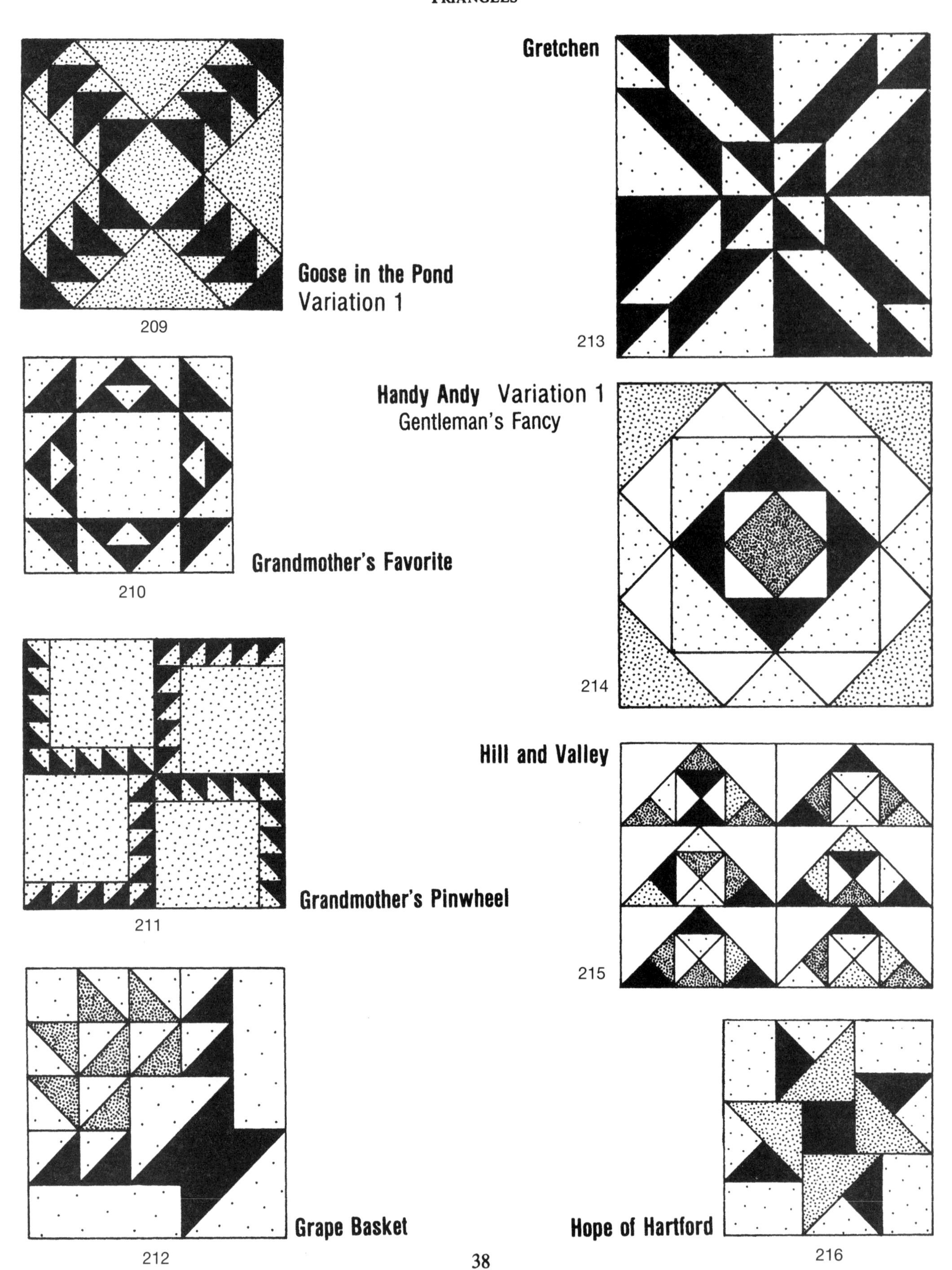
Goose in the Pond
Variation 1
209
Gretchen
213
Handy Andy Variation 1
Gentleman's Fancy
214
Grandmother's Favorite
210
Grandmother's Pinwheel
211
Hill and Valley
215
Grape Basket
212
Hope of Hartford
216

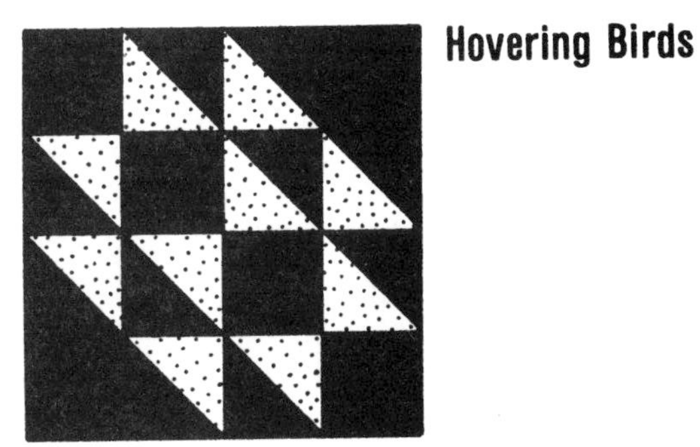

Hovering Birds

217

Ice Cream Bowl

218

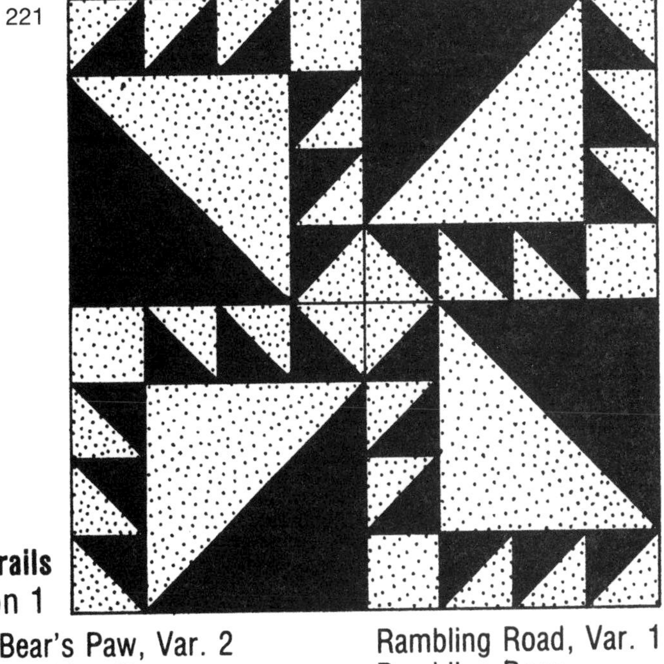

221

Indian Trails
Variation 1

Bear's Paw, Var. 2
Climbing Rose
Flying Dutchman, Var. 2
Forest Path
Irish Puzzle
Kansas Trouble, Var. 1
North Wind, Var. 1
Old Maid's Ramble, Var. 1
Prickly Pear, Var. 2
Rambling Road, Var. 1
Rambling Rose
Storm at Sea, Var. 1
Tangled Tares
Weather Vane, Var. 1
Winding Walk

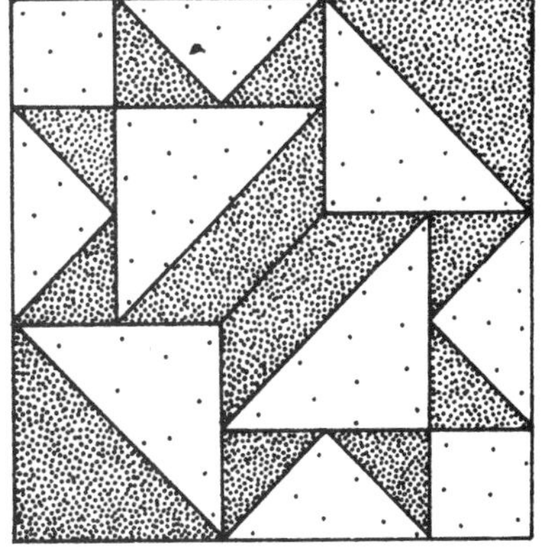

Indian Meadows
Variation 2
Queen Charlotte's Crown, Var. 2

219

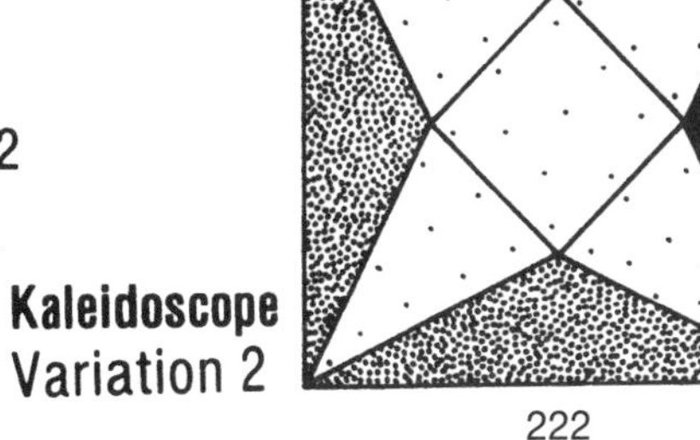

Kaleidoscope
Variation 2

222

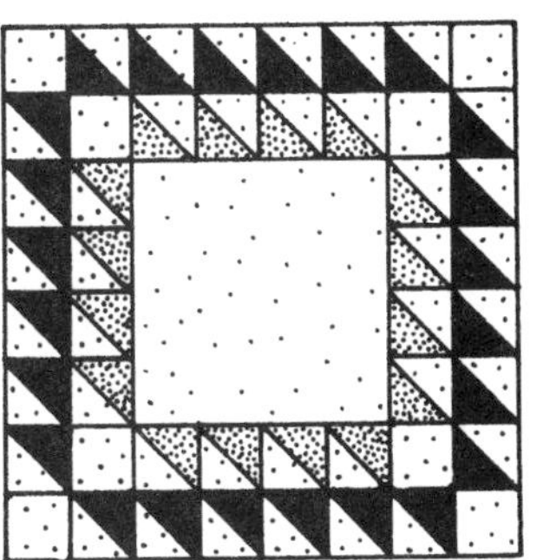

Indian Plumes

220

Kaleidoscope
Variation 3

223

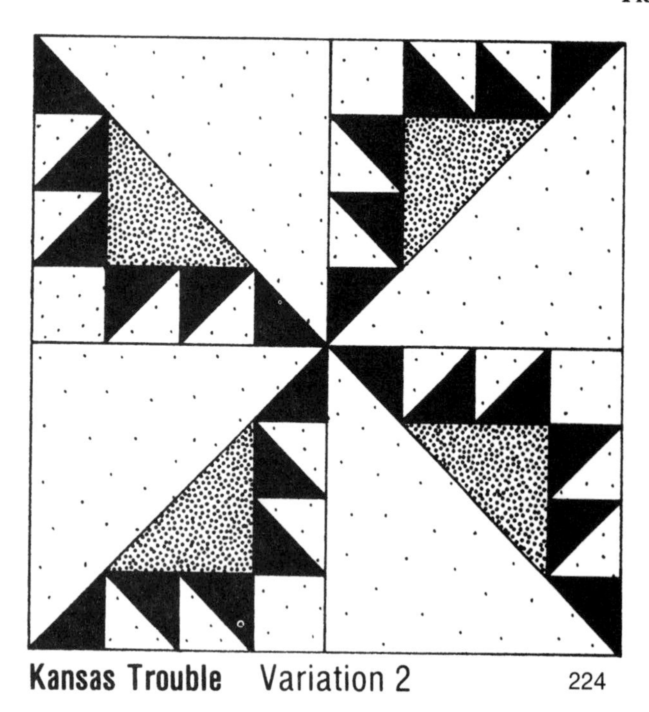

Kansas Trouble Variation 2 224

Lost Ships Variation 1 227
Lady of the Lake, Var. 2
Rockly Glen, Var. 2

Letter X
Clown's Choice
Flying X

225

Maltese Cross
Variation 1

228

Lightning Strips
Chevron
Rail Fence
Snake Fence, Var. 1
Streak of Lightning
Zigzag, Var. 1
1,000 Pyramids

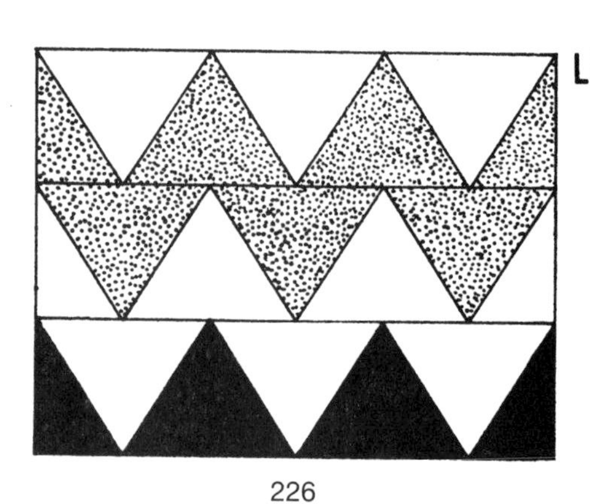

226

Maryland Beauty

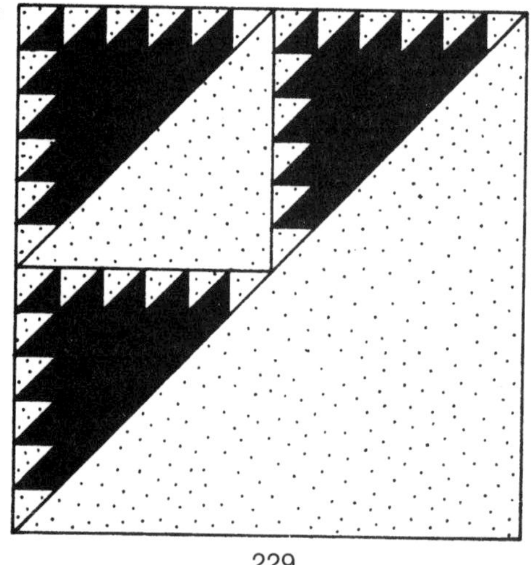

229

Merry Go Round

230

New York Beauty Variation 2 233
Rocky Mountain Road

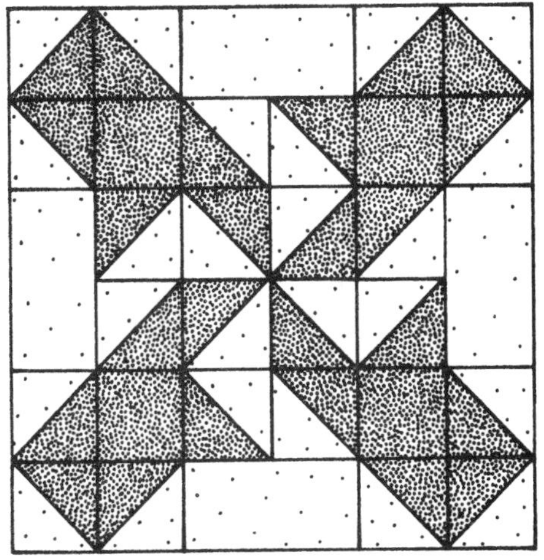

Mrs. Morgan's Choice 231

Next-door Neighbor

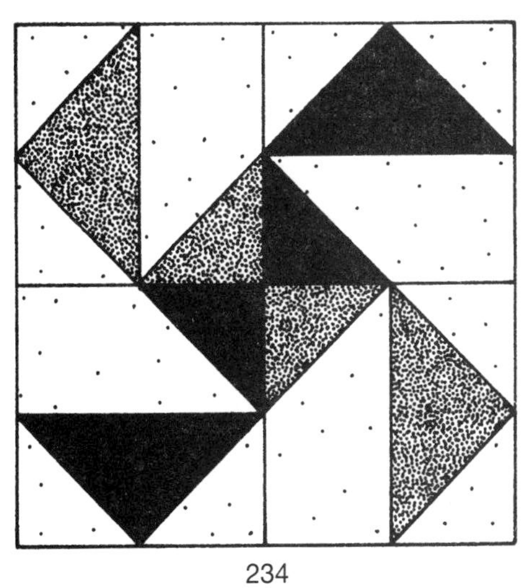

234

232

Night and Day

235

New York Beauty
Variation 1

North Wind
Variation 2

236

Odd Fellows' Chain

240

Ocean Waves
Variation 1

237

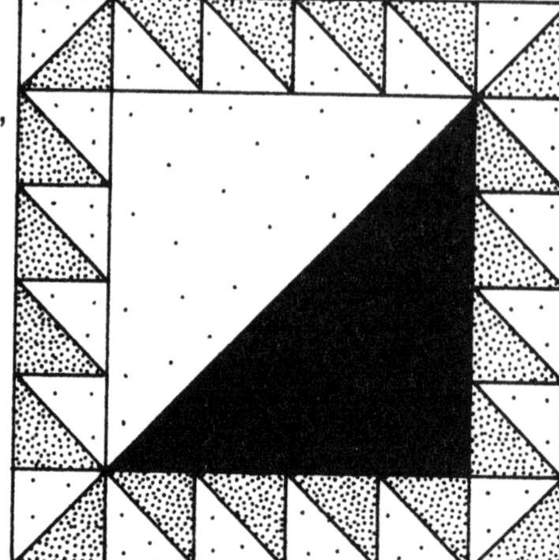

Old Maid's Ramble
Variation 2
Lady of the Lake, Var. 1

241

Ocean Waves
Variation 2

238

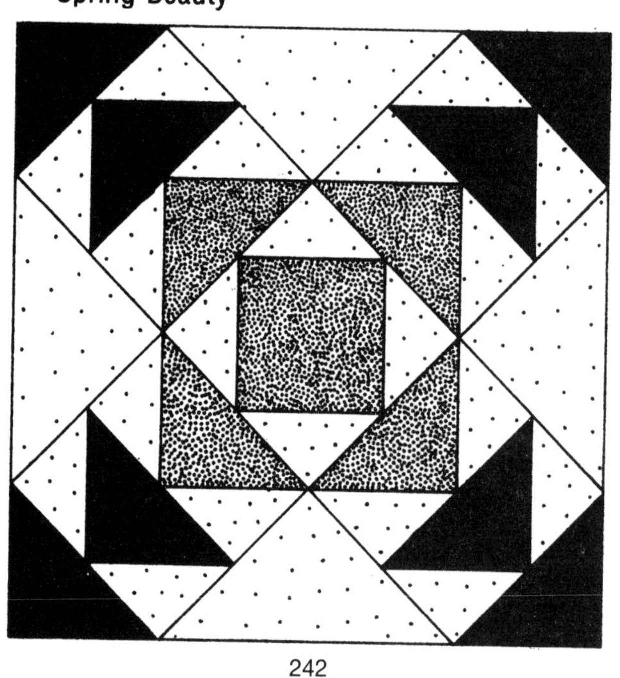

Old Maid's Ramble Variation 3
Crimson Rambler
Rambler
Spring Beauty

242

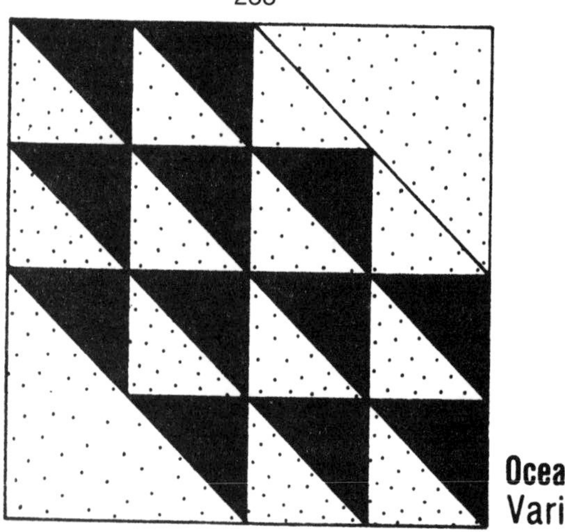

Ocean Waves
Variation 3

239

243

Old Maid's Ramble
Variation 4
Lady of the Lake, Var. 3

Path Through the Woods 246

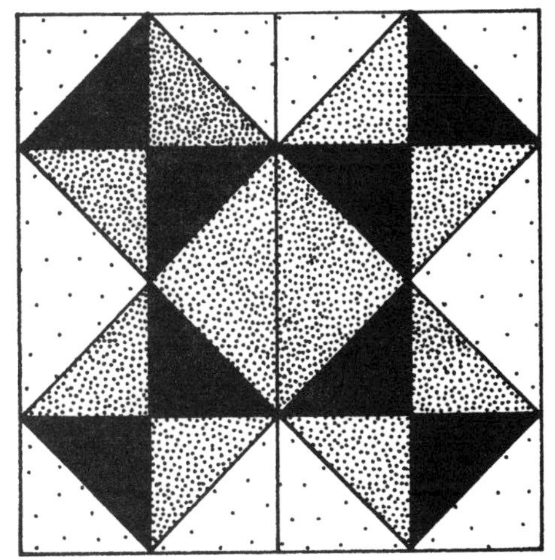

Old Tippecanoe 244

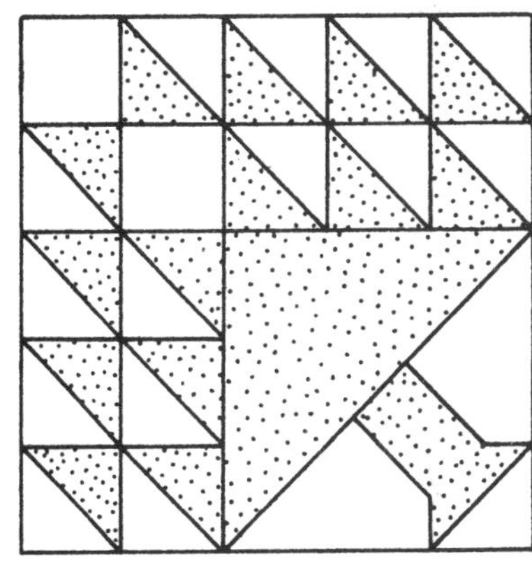

Pine Tree
Variation 2

247

245

Palm Leaves Hosannah!
Hosanna
Palm
Palm Leaf, Var. 1

Pine Tree Variation 3
Temperance Tree

248

Pine Tree
Variation 4

249

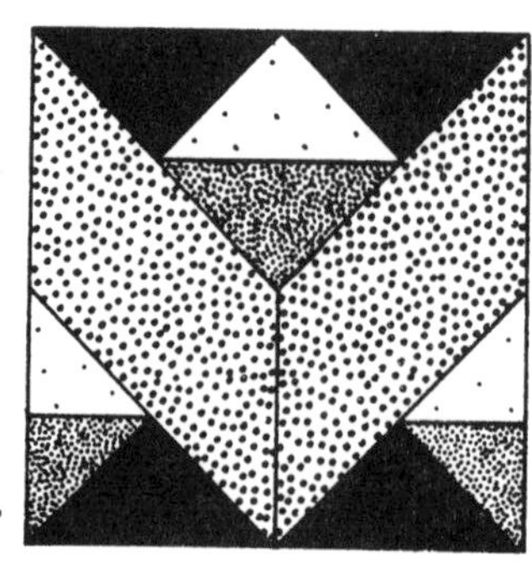

Ribbon Border

252

Pinwheel Star

250

Ribbons

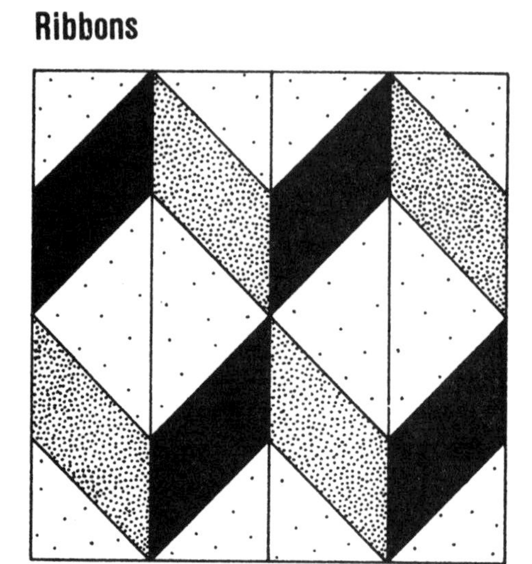

253

Railroad Crossing
Variation 1

251

Rolling Pinwheel
Variation 1

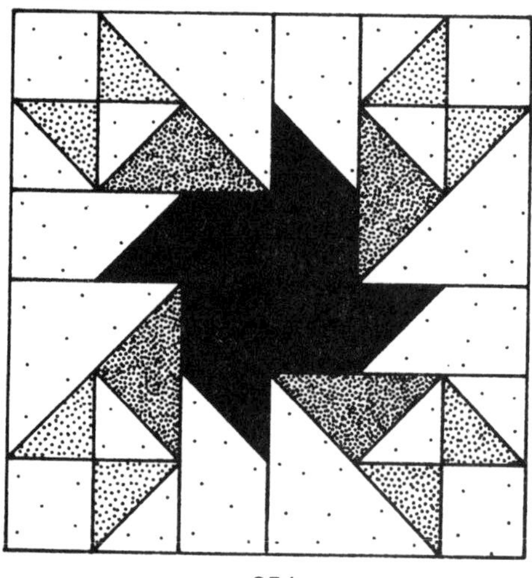

254

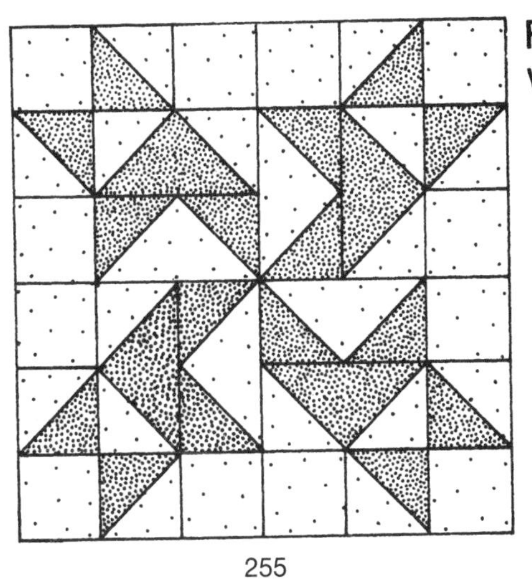

Rolling Pinwheel Variation 2

255

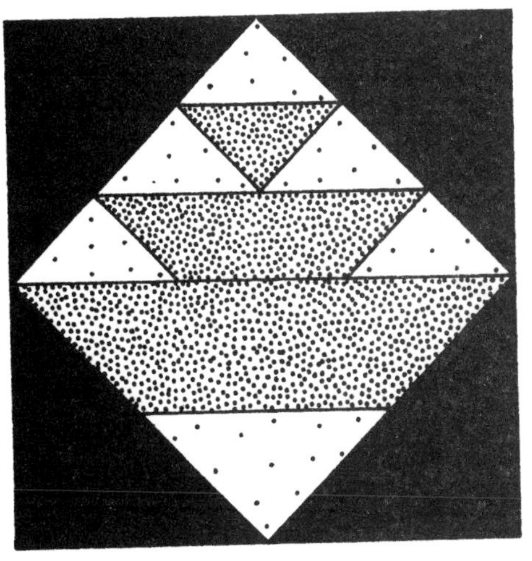

Sailboats

258

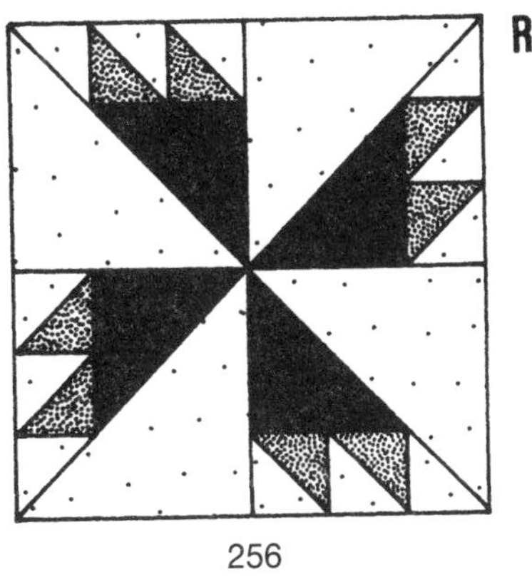

Rose Bud

256

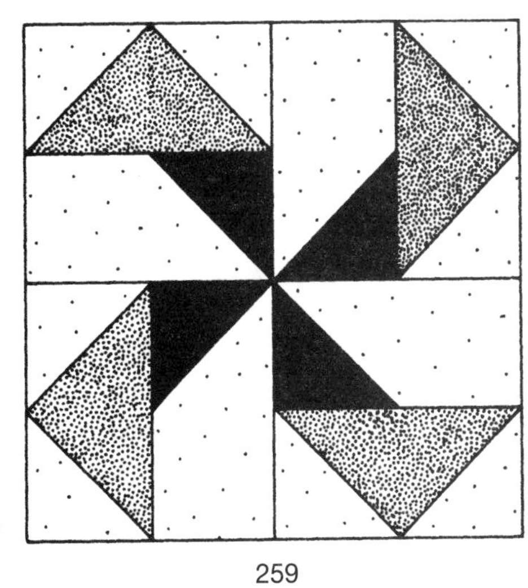

Seesaw

259

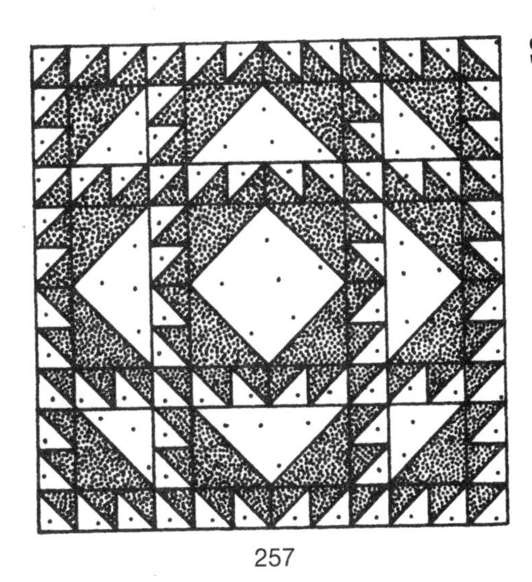

Sailboat

257

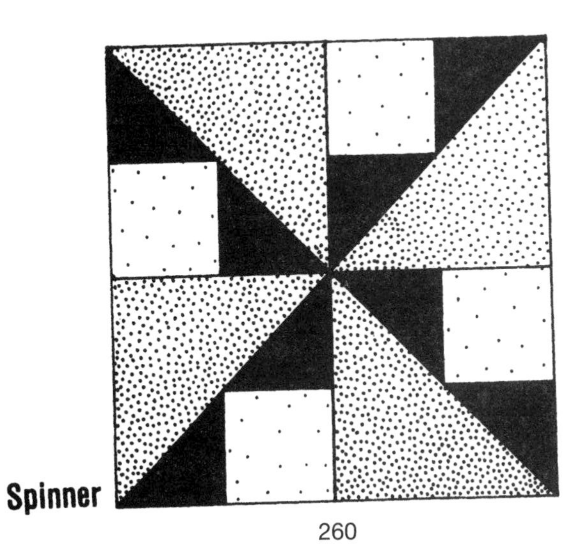

Spinner

260

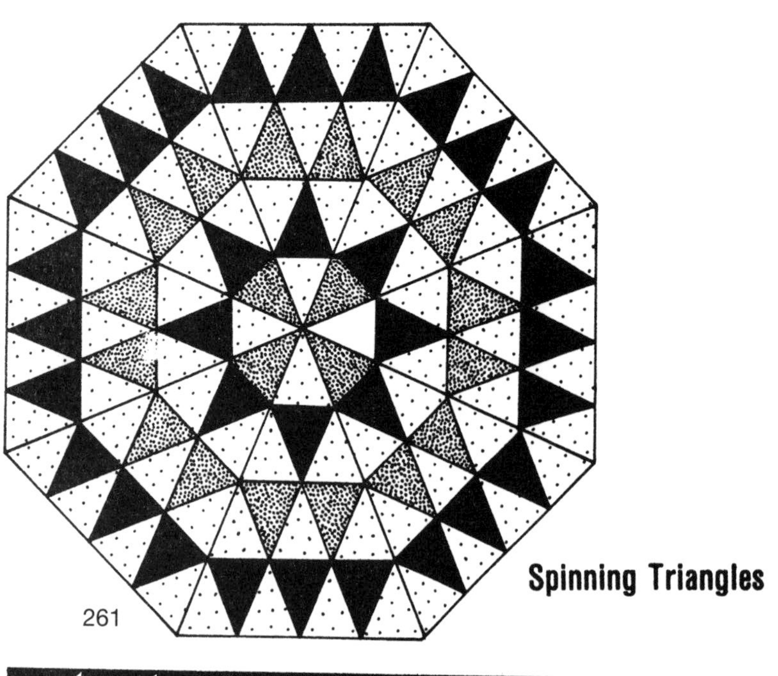

Spinning Triangles

261

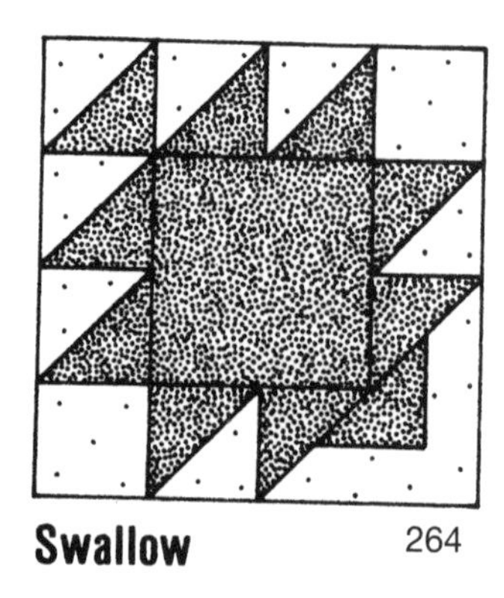

Swallow 264

Square Deal

262

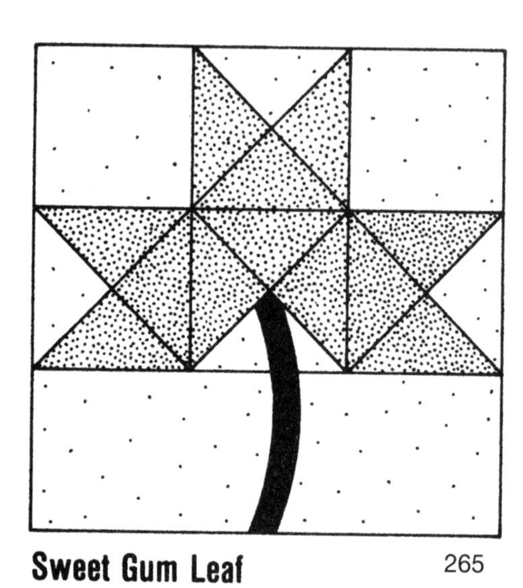

Sweet Gum Leaf 265

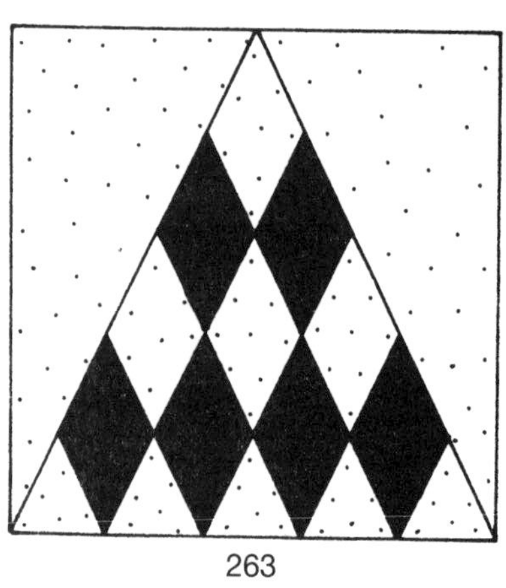

Sugar Loaf

263

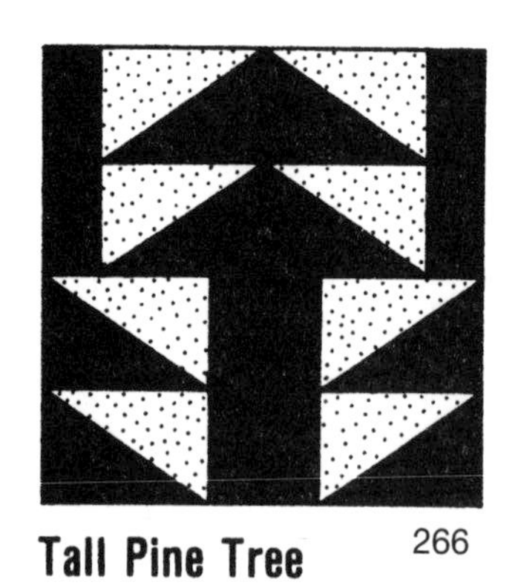

Tall Pine Tree 266

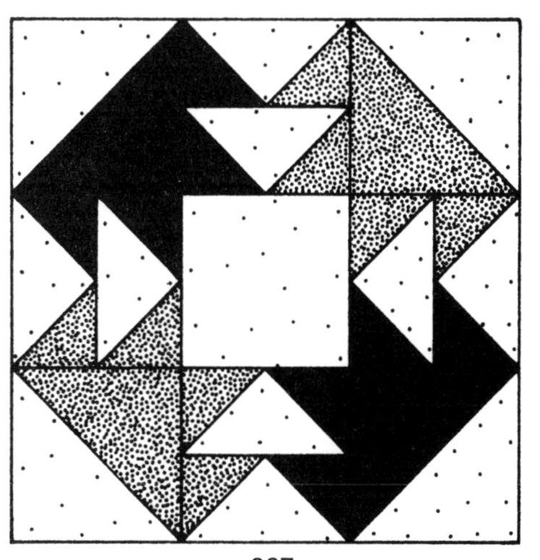

T-Blocks
Variation 1
Capital T
Double-T, Var. 2

267

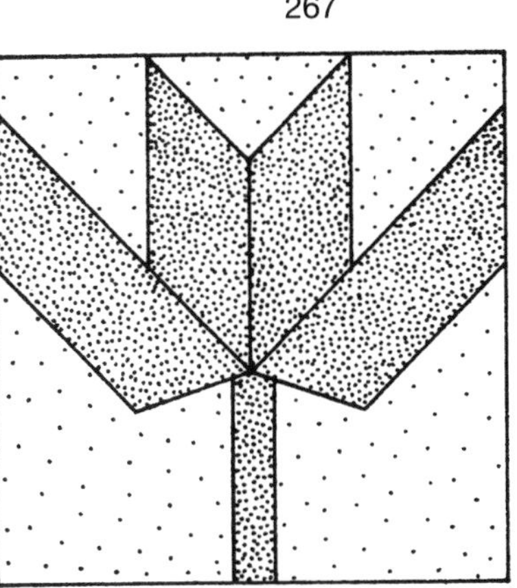

Tea Leaf
Variation 1

268

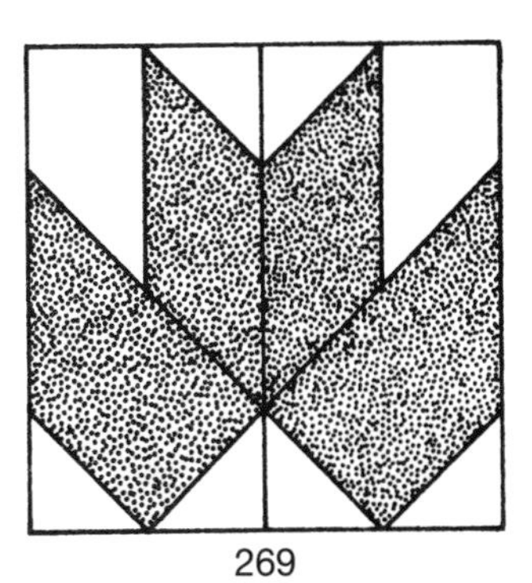

Tea Leaf
Variation 2

269

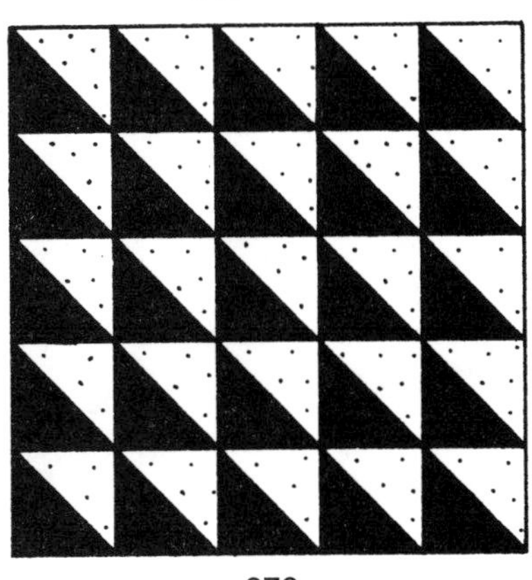

Tents of Armageddon

270

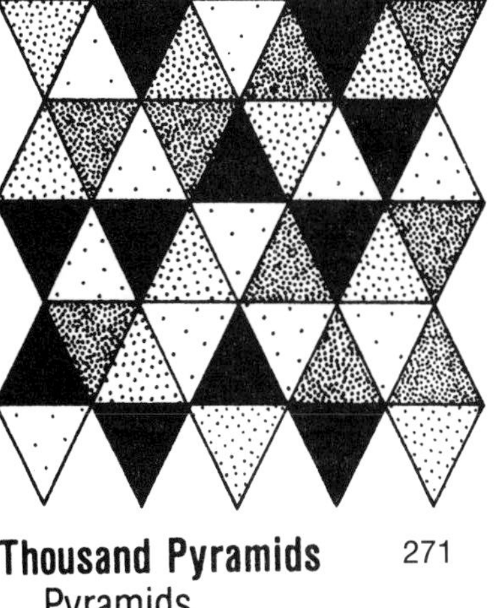

Thousand Pyramids 271
Pyramids
Triangles

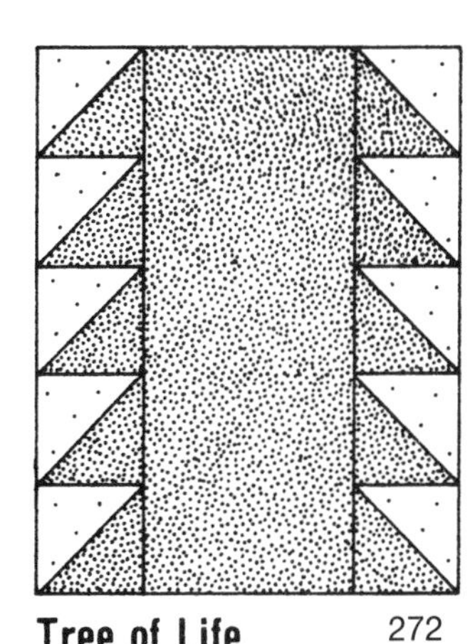

Tree of Life 272
Variation 2

Tree of Paradise
Variation 1

273

Tree of Paradise
Variation 2
274

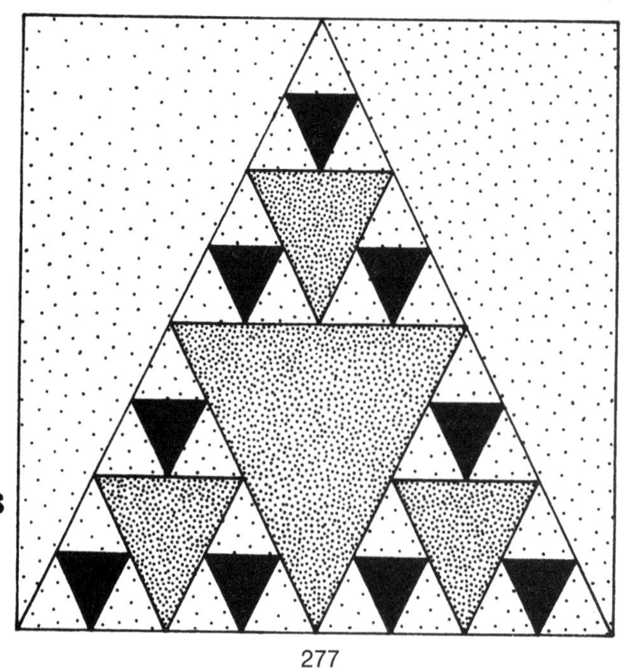

Triangular Triangles
277

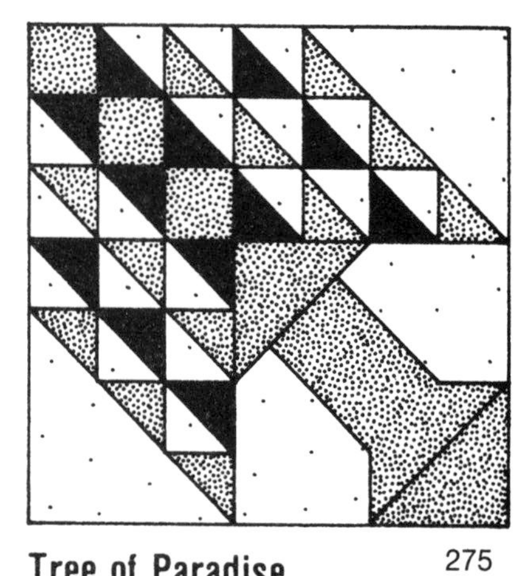

Tree of Paradise
Variation 3
275

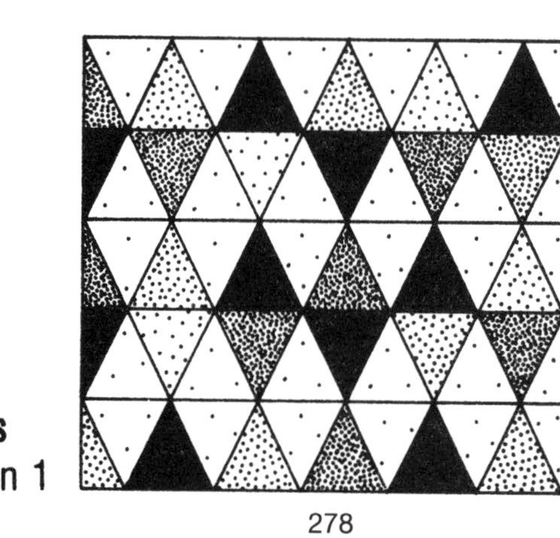

Tumblers
Variation 1
278

Triangle Puzzle
276

Twenty-four Triangles
279

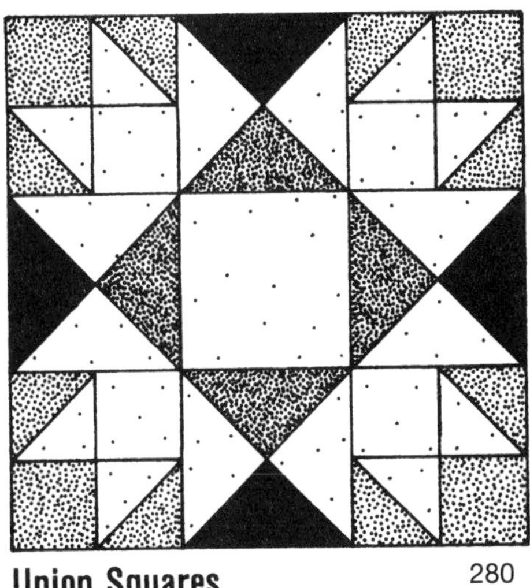

Union Squares 280

V-Block
Variation 2

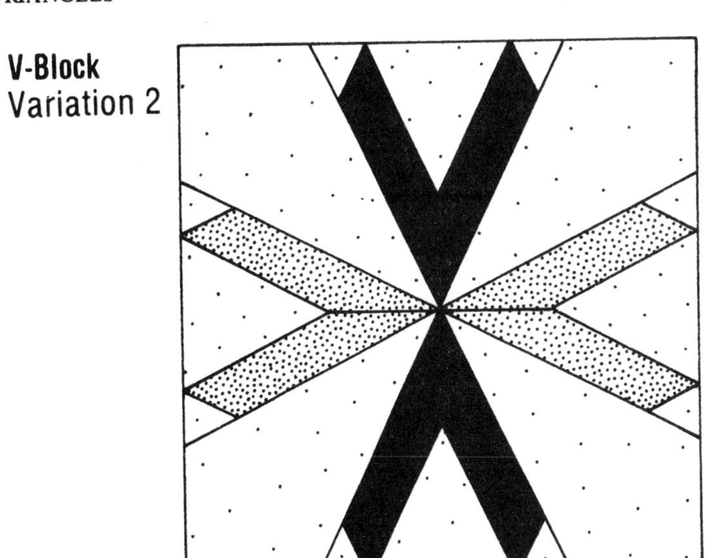

283

Water Wheel
Variation 2
Whirlwind

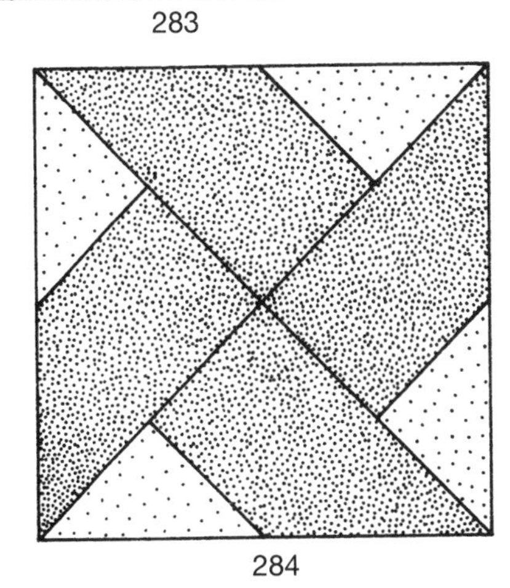

284

Unknown Four-Patch 281

Whirligig
Variation 2

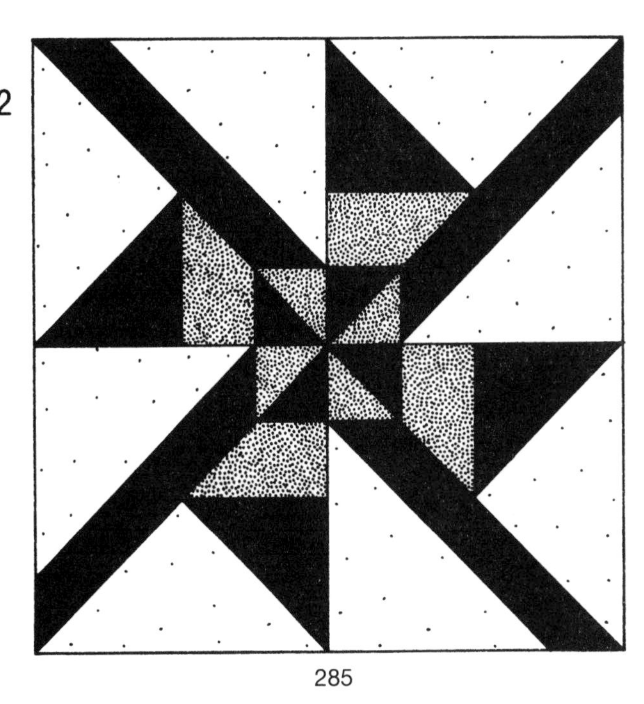

285

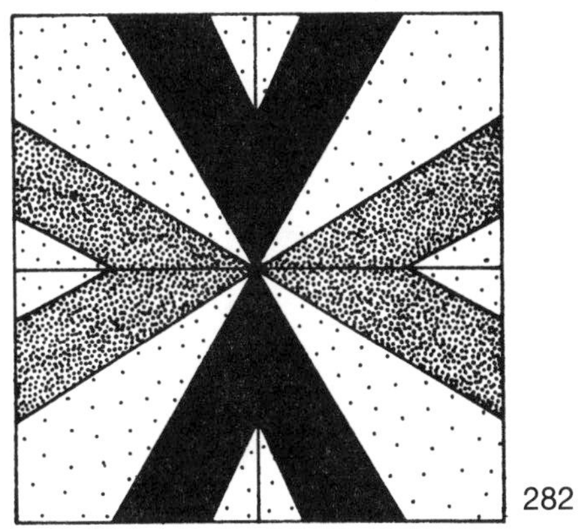

282

V-Block Variation 1

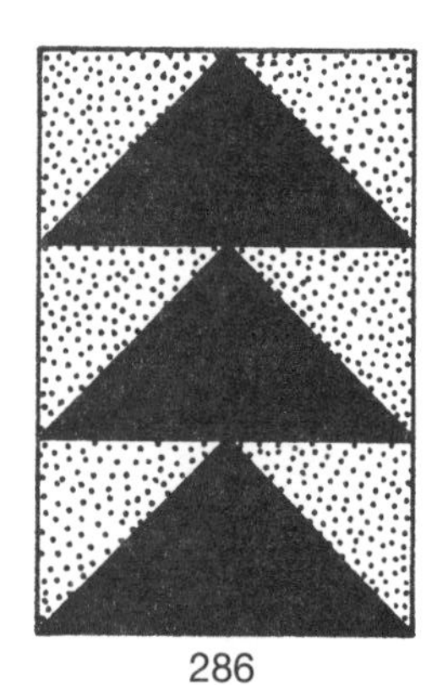
286

Wild Goose Chase
Variation 1

Windmill Variation 1
Crow's Foot, Var. 3
Fan Mill, Var. 1
Flutter Wheels, Var. 1
Fly, Var. 1
Honey's Choice
Kathy's Ramble, Var. 1
Mill Wheel, Var. 1
Old Windmill
Pinwheel, Var. 1
Slash Diagonal
Sugar Bowl, Var. 1
Water Mill
Water Wheel, Var. 1

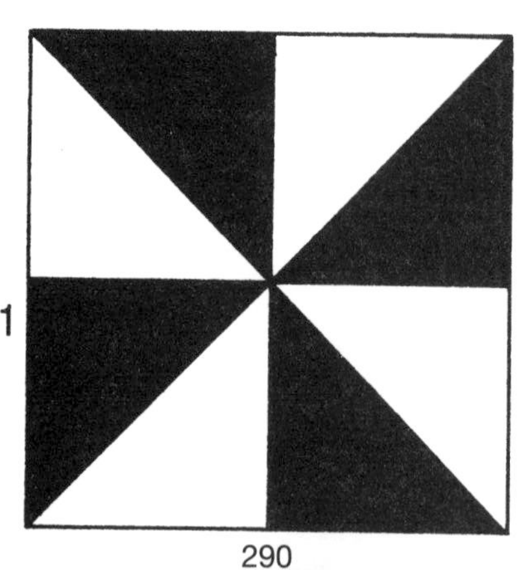
290

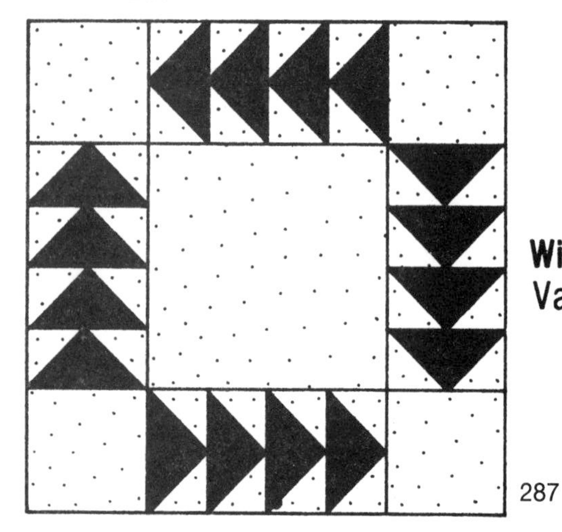
287

Wild Goose Chase
Variation 4

291

Windmill
Variation 4

288

Wild Goose Chase
Variation 5

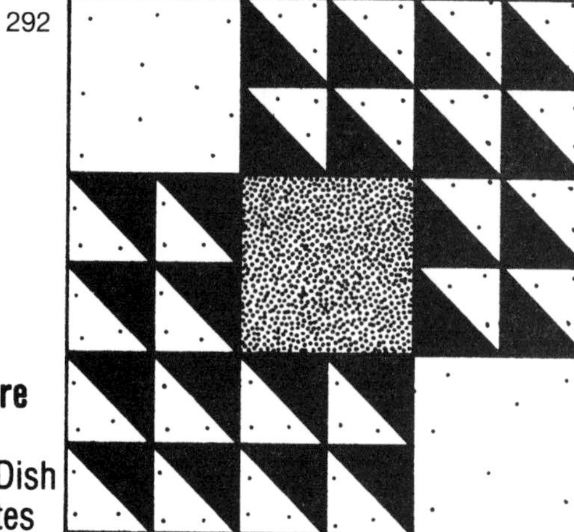
292

Winged Square
Variation 1
Cut Glass Dish
Golden Gates

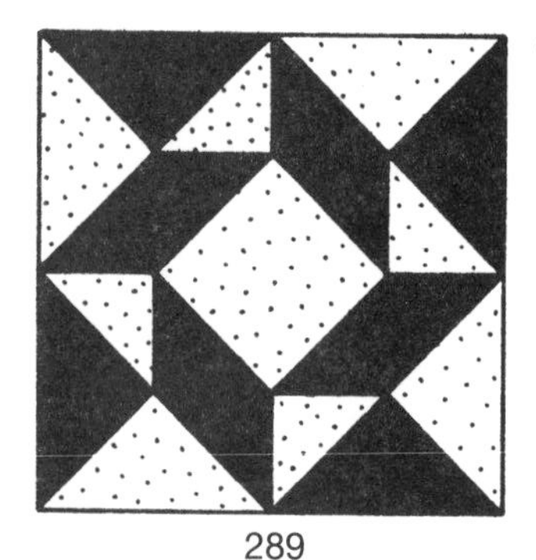
289

Windblown Square
Balkan Puzzle
Zigzag Tile

293

Yankee Puzzle
Variation 1
Hourglass, Var. 2

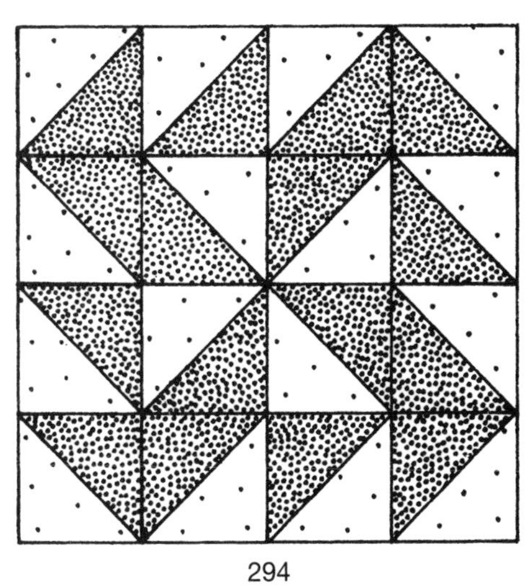

Yankee Puzzle Variation 2

294

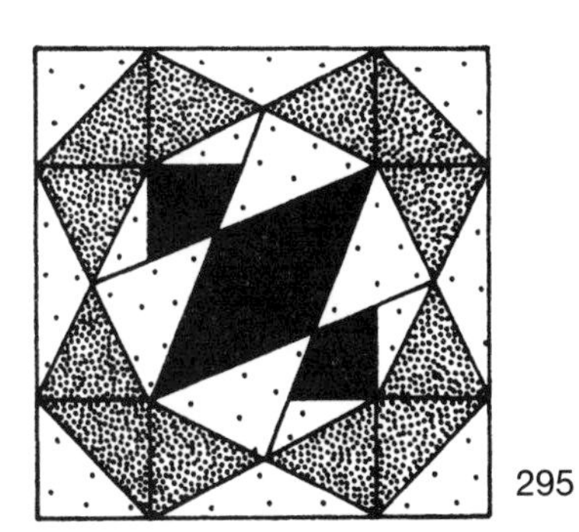

Indian Hatchet Variation 3 297

SUPPLEMENT

Dove in the Window Variation 3

295

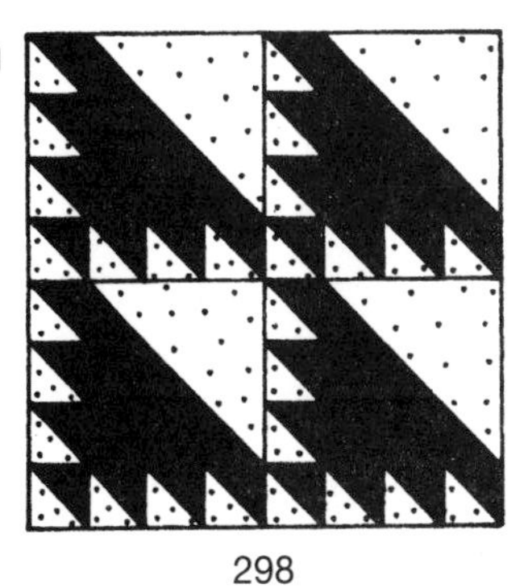

Rocky Glen Variation 4 Lost Ships, Var. 2

298

Free Trade Block

296

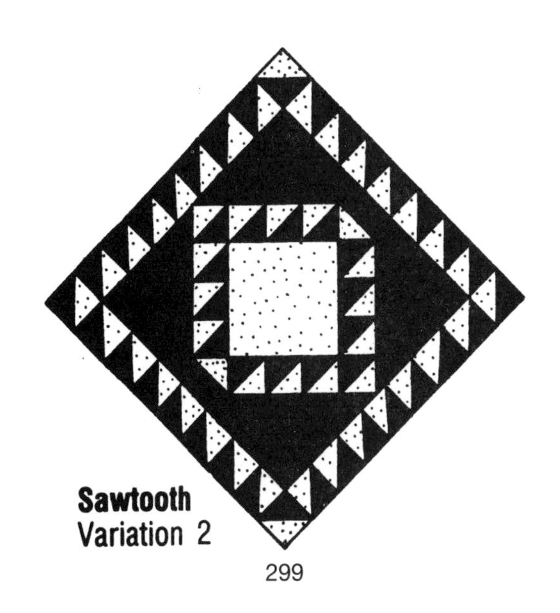

Sawtooth Variation 2

299

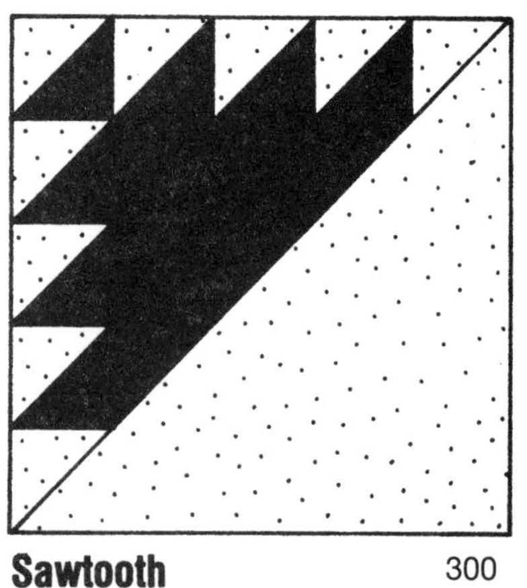

Sawtooth
Variation 4 300

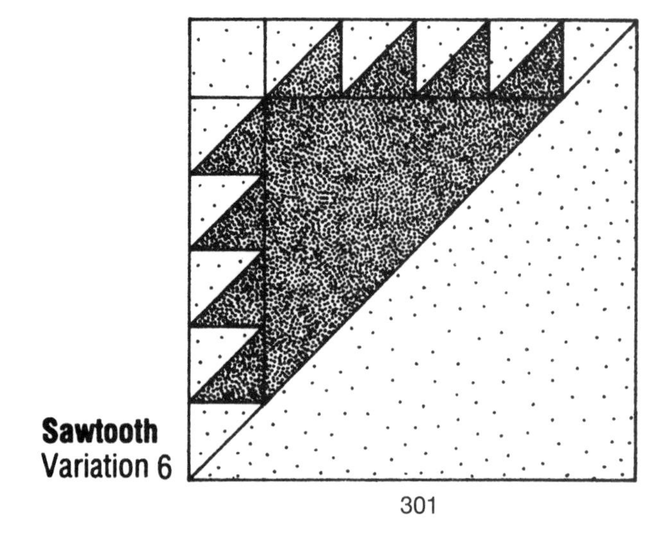

Sawtooth
Variation 6

301

Circles

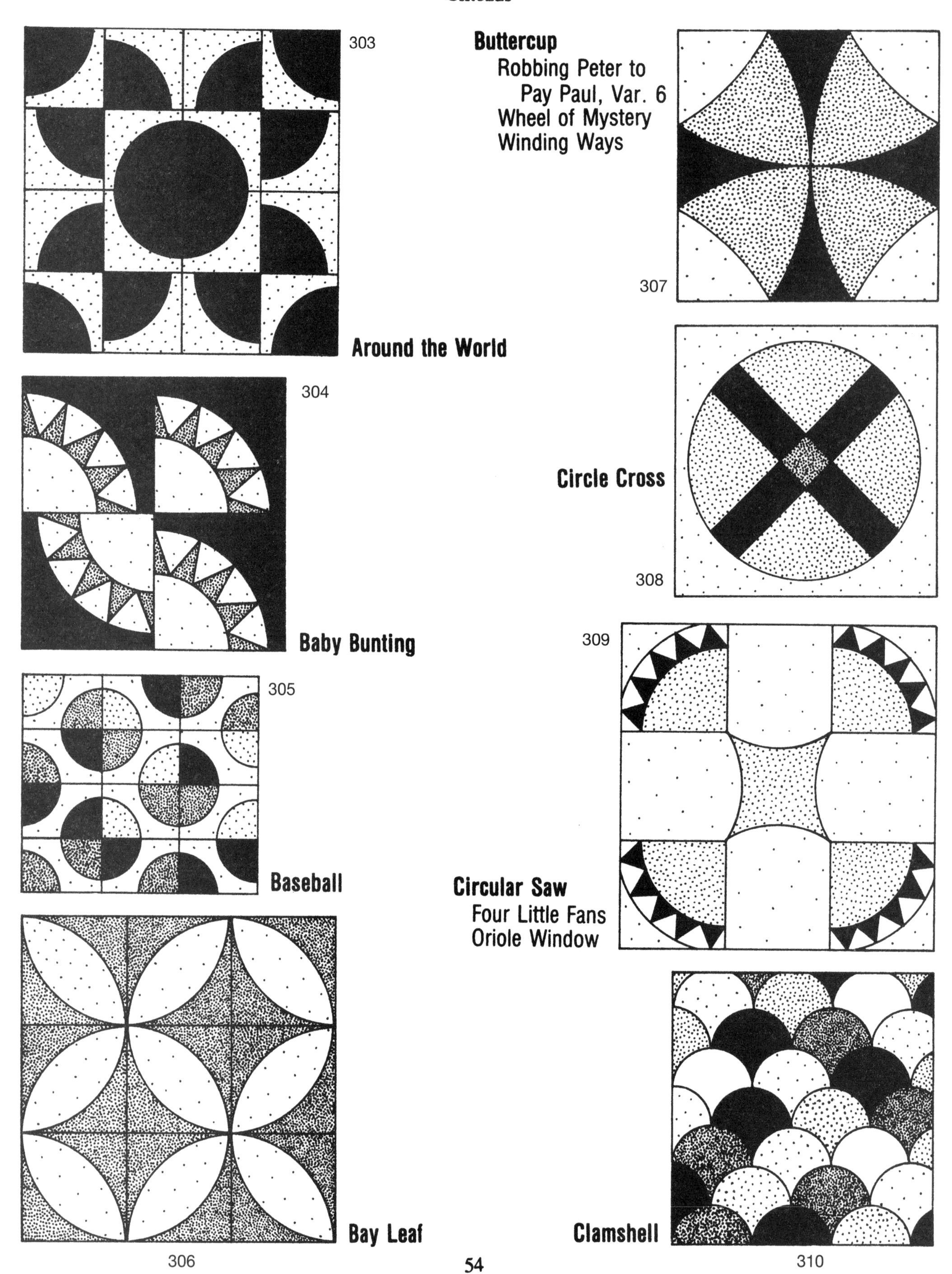
303
Around the World
304
Baby Bunting
305
Baseball
306
Bay Leaf
Buttercup
Robbing Peter to
Pay Paul, Var. 6
Wheel of Mystery
Winding Ways
307
Circle Cross
308
309
Circular Saw
Four Little Fans
Oriole Window
Clamshell
310

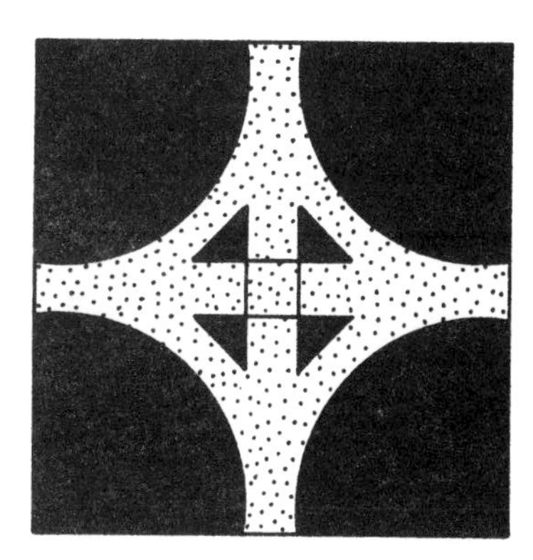

Country Crossroads

311

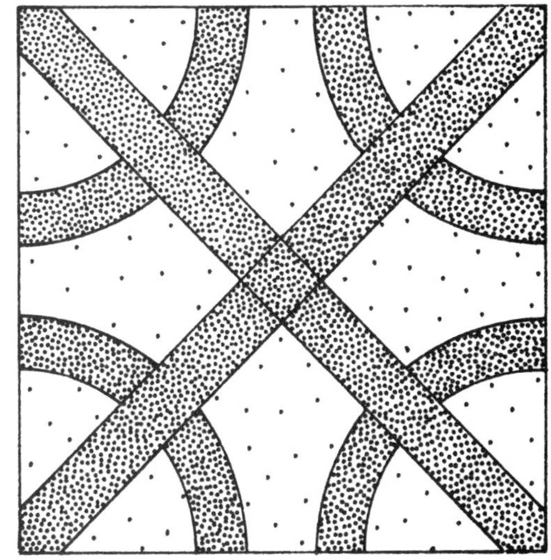

Crossroads

312

Double Wedding Ring
Wedding Ring

313

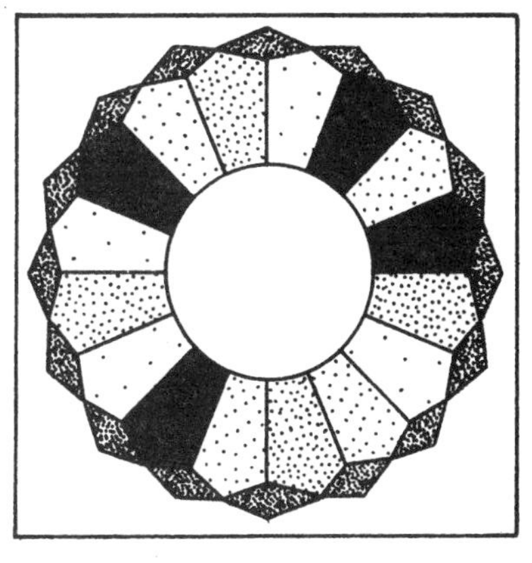

Dresden Plate
Variation 2

314

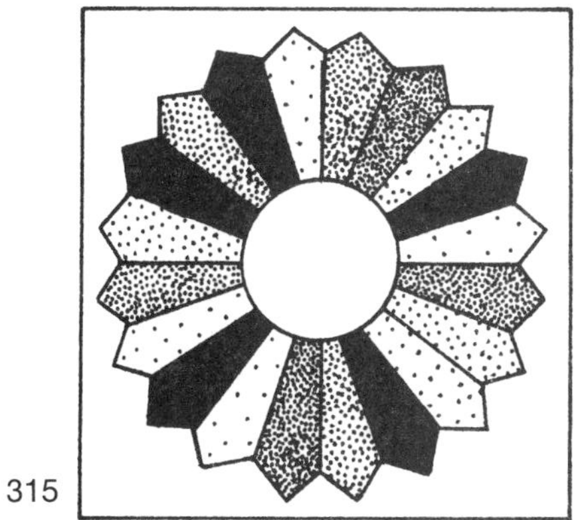

315

Dresden Plate Variation 3

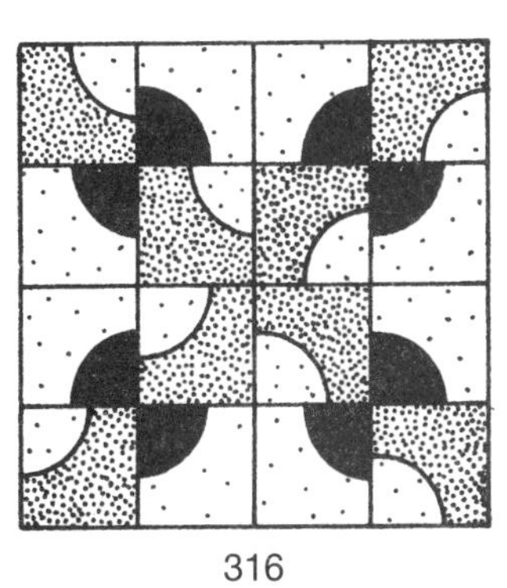

Drunkard's Path
Variation 1
Country Husband
Solomon's Puzzle
World's Puzzle

316

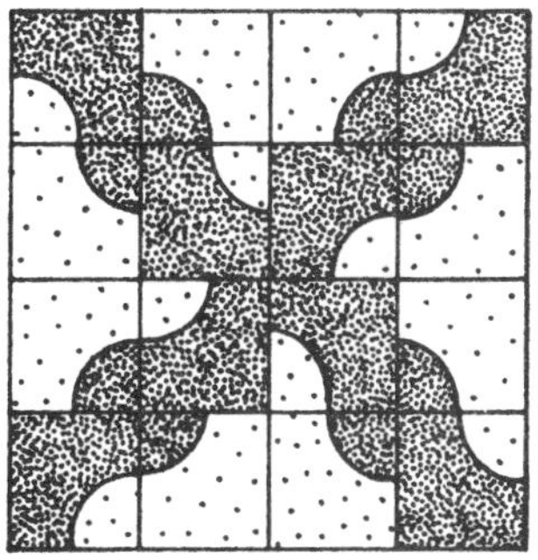

Drunkard's Path
Variation 2

317

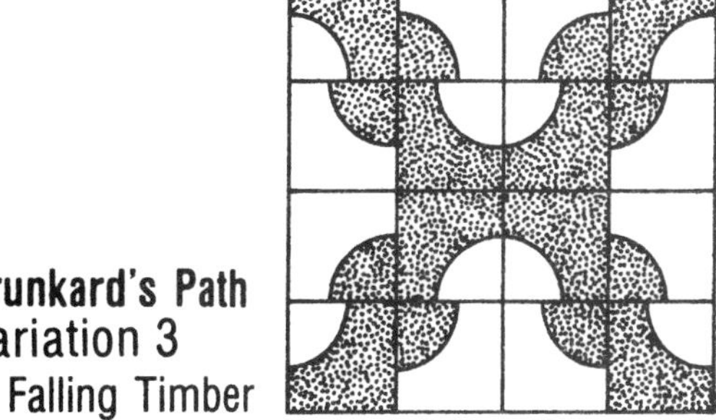

Drunkard's Path
Variation 3
Falling Timber

318

Drunkard's Path Variation 4 319

Flo's Fan 320

321

Fool's Puzzle Variation 1

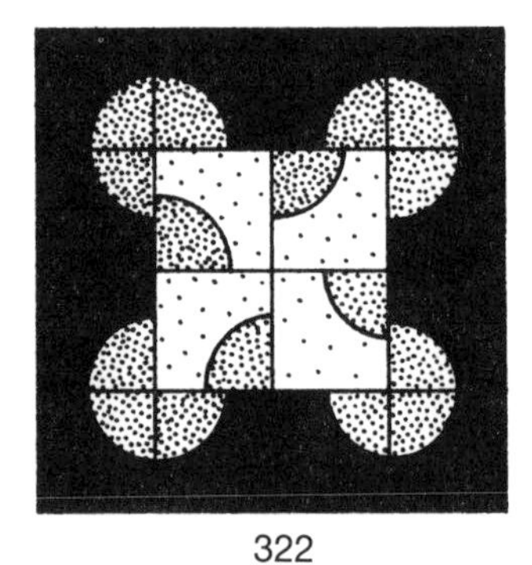

322

Fool's Puzzle Variation 2

Friendship Ring
Aster
Dresden Plate, Var. 1

323

Full-blown Tulip Variation 2

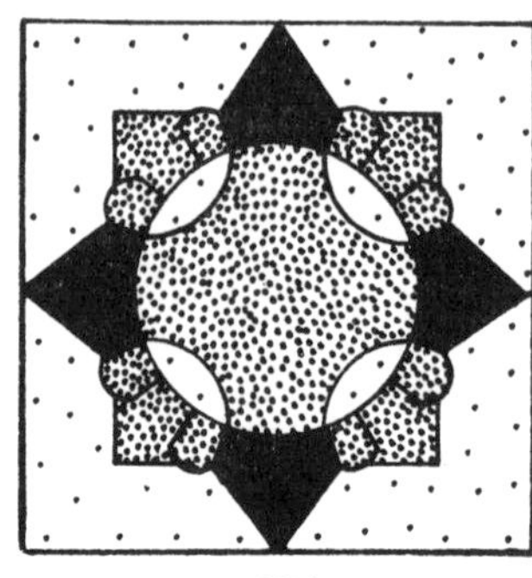

324

Grandmother's Fan
Fan
Fanny's Fan, Var. 1

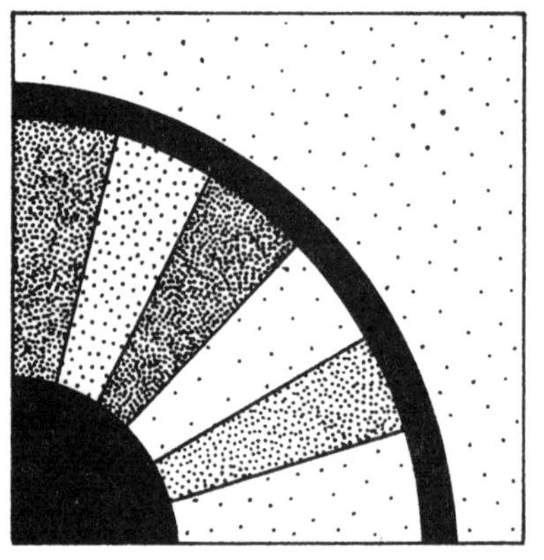

325

Hearts and Gizzards
Lazy Daisy, Var. 1
Petal Quilt
Pierrot's Pom-pon
Springtime Blossom
Wheel of Fortune, Var. 1
Windmill, Var. 2

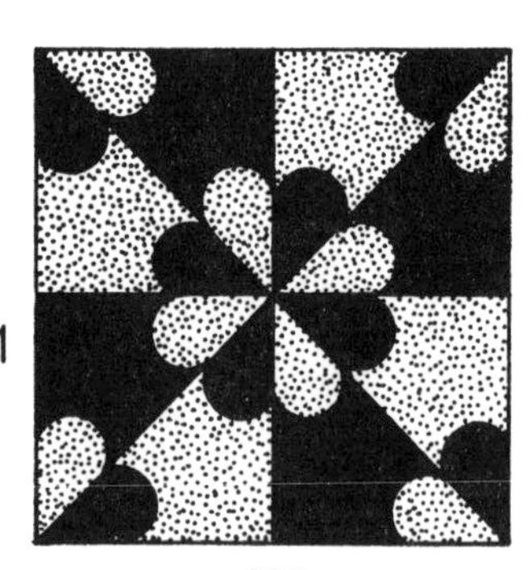

326

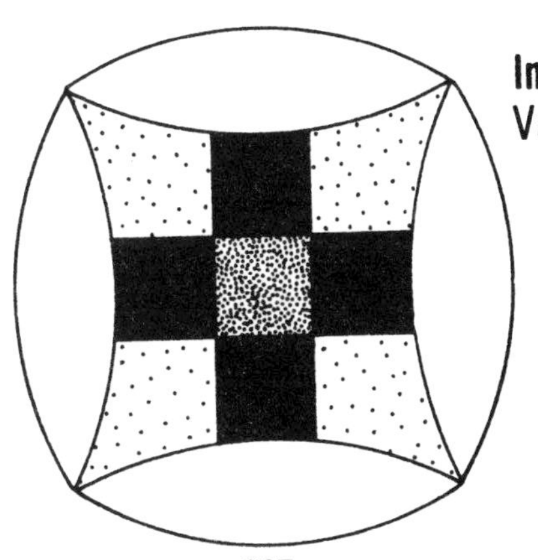

327

Improved Nine-patch
Variation 1
Bailey Nine-Patch
Glorified Nine-Patch

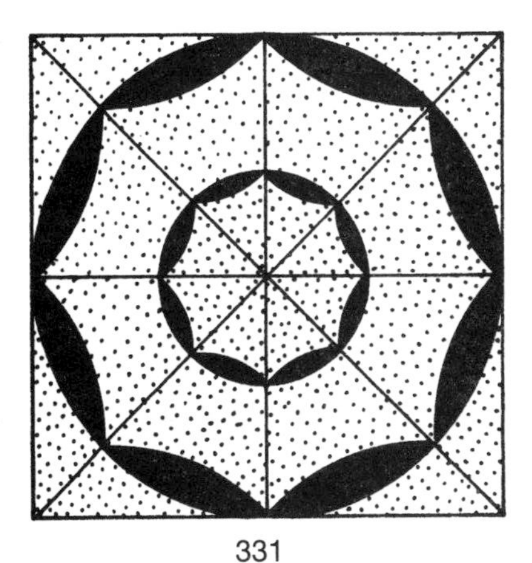

Odds and Ends

331

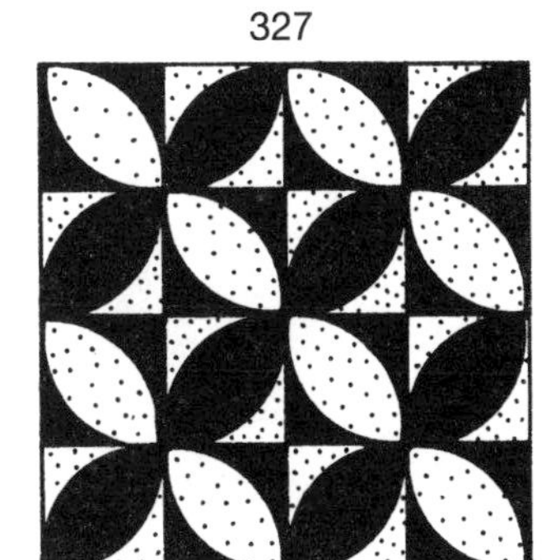

328

Lafayette Orange Peel
Melon Patch
Orange Peel, Var. 2

Orange Peel
Variation 1

332

Compass, Var. 2
Dolly Madison's Workbox, Var. 2
Robbing Peter to Pay Paul, Var. 4

329

Love Ring
Lone Ring
Nonesuch

330

Missouri Beauty

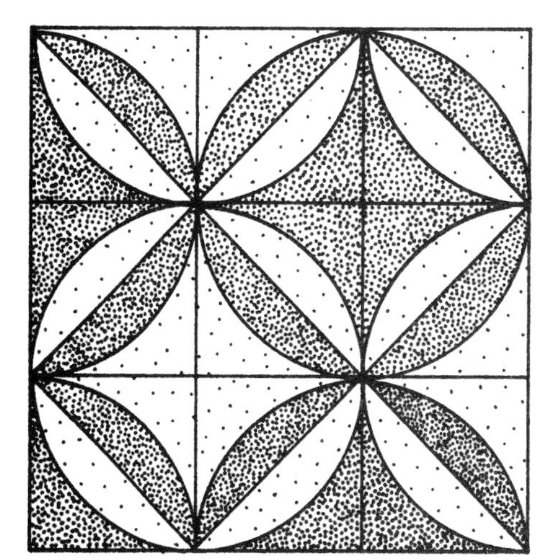

Orange Peel
Variation 3

333

Dolly Madison's Workbox, Var. 1
Rob Peter to Pay Paul, Var. 2

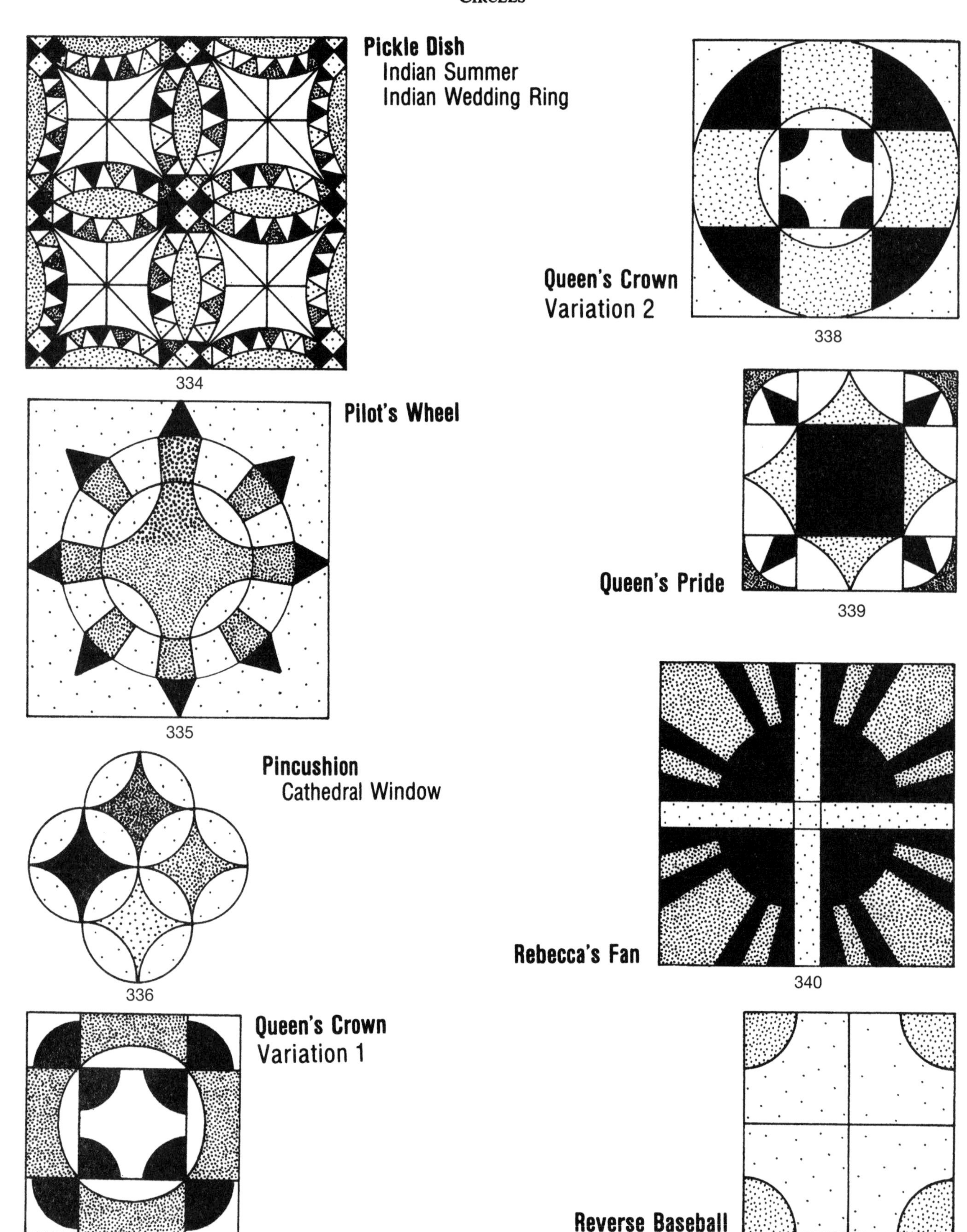
Pickle Dish
Indian Summer
Indian Wedding Ring
334
Queen's Crown
Variation 2
338
Pilot's Wheel
335
Queen's Pride
339
Pincushion
Cathedral Window
336
Rebecca's Fan
340
Queen's Crown
Variation 1
337
Reverse Baseball
341

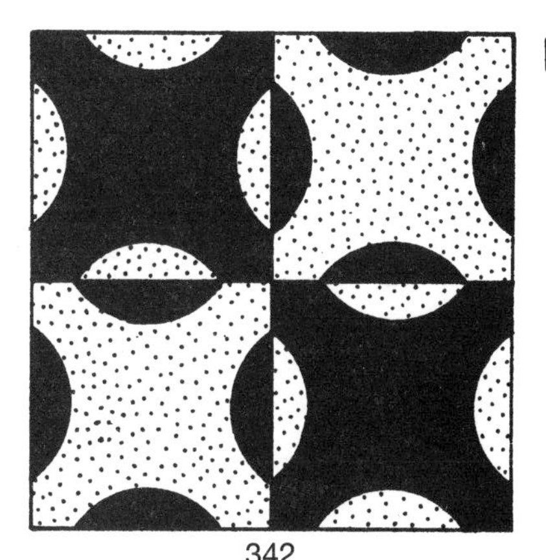

Robbing Peter to Pay Paul
Variation 2

342

Signature

346

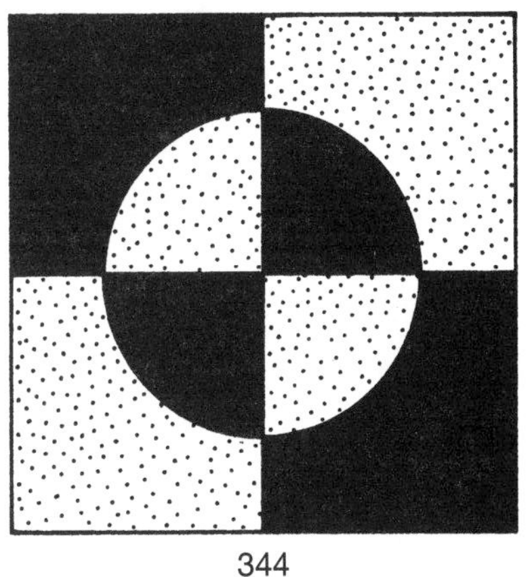

Robbing Peter to Pay Paul
Variation 3
Falling Timbers
Vine of Friendship

343

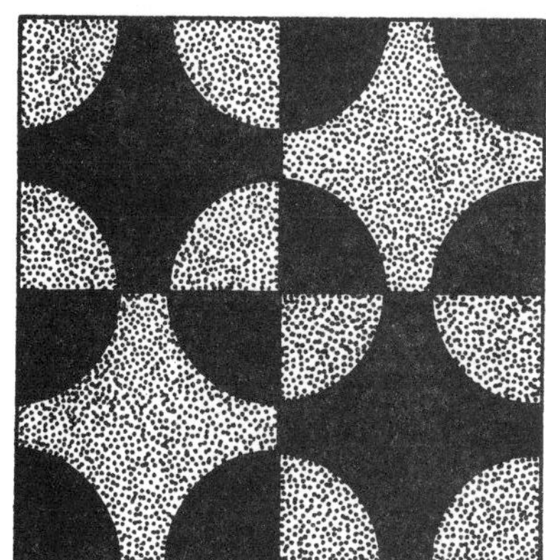

Snowball Variation 1
Mill Wheel, Var. 2
Old Mill Wheel
Pullman Puzzle

347

Rob Peter to Pay Paul
Variation 1

344

Snowball Variation 2
Compass, Var. 3

348

Rocky Road to Dublin

345

Snowball
Variation 4

349

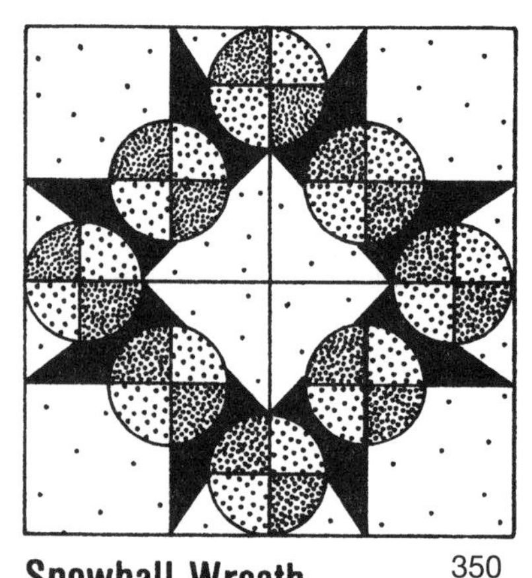

Snowball Wreath 350

Steeplechase
Bows and Arrows

353

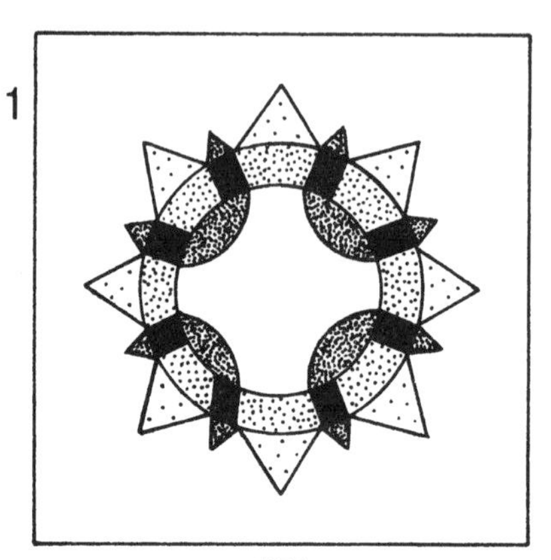

Strawberry
Full-Blown Tulip, Var. 1
Oriental Star, Var. 2

354

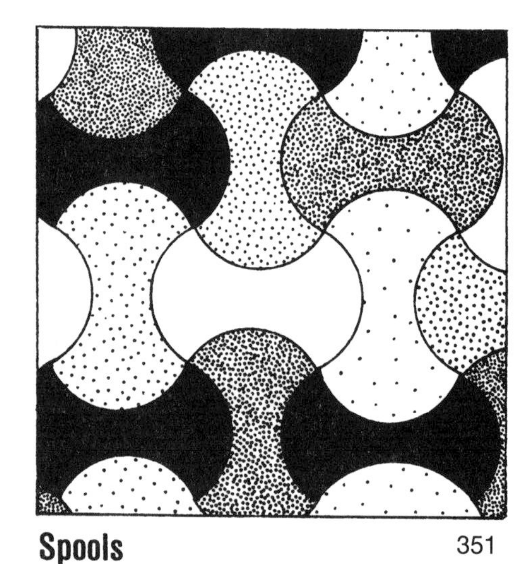

Spools 351
Always Friends
Friendship Chain

Turkey Tracks
Variation 1
Wandering Foot

355

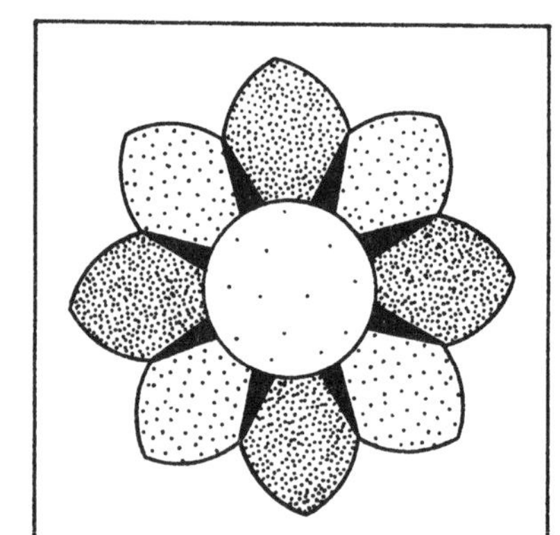

352

Star Flower Variation 1
Golden Glow, Var. 1

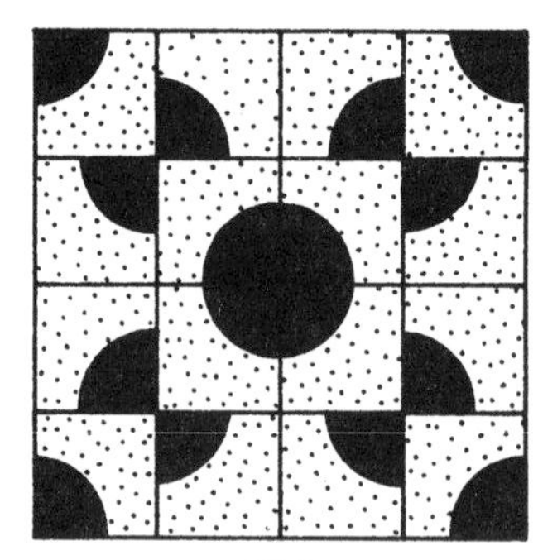

Unnamed
Variation 1

356

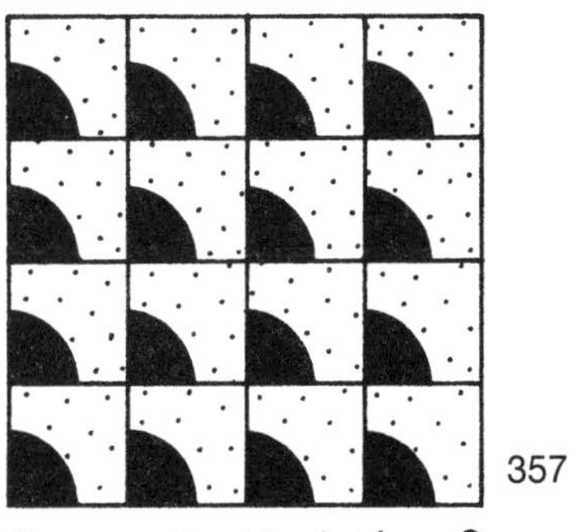

357

Unnamed Variation 2

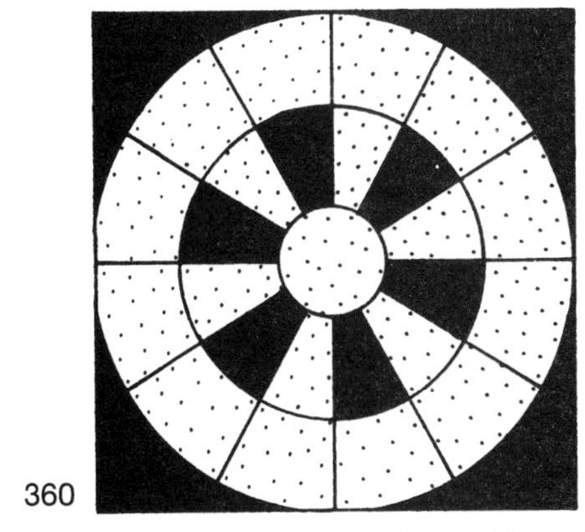

360

Wheel of Fortune Variation 4

Victoria's Crown 358

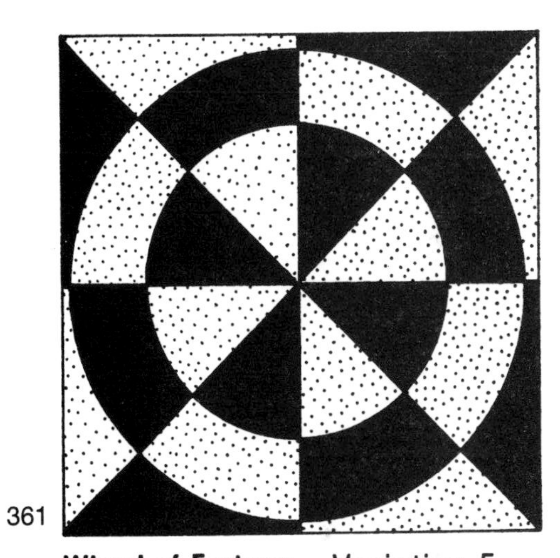

361

Wheel of Fortune Variation 5

359

Wheel of Chance
True Lover's Buggy Wheel

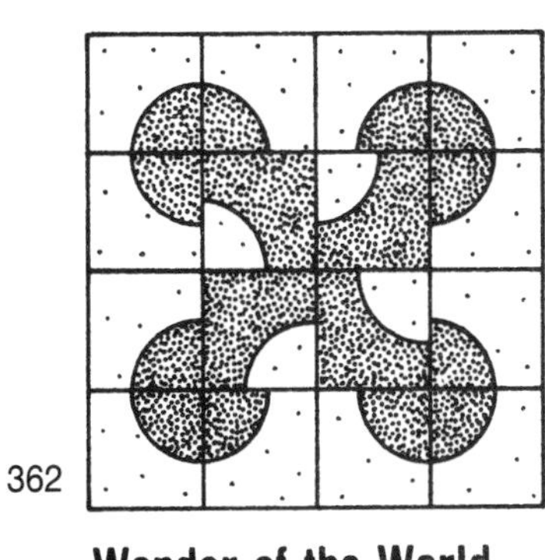

362

Wonder of the World

SUPPLEMENT

Reel

363

Combinations

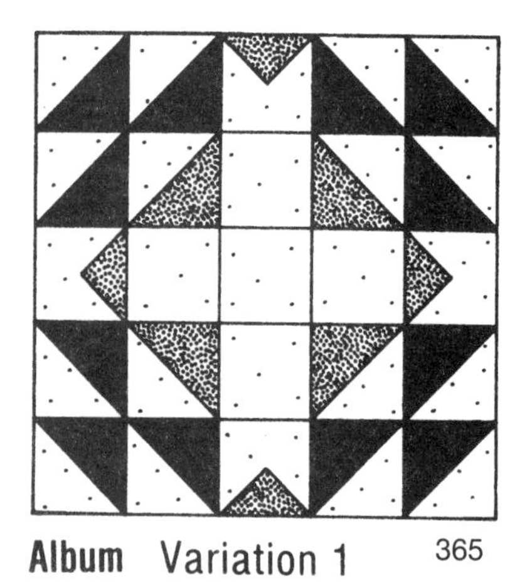

Album Variation 1 365

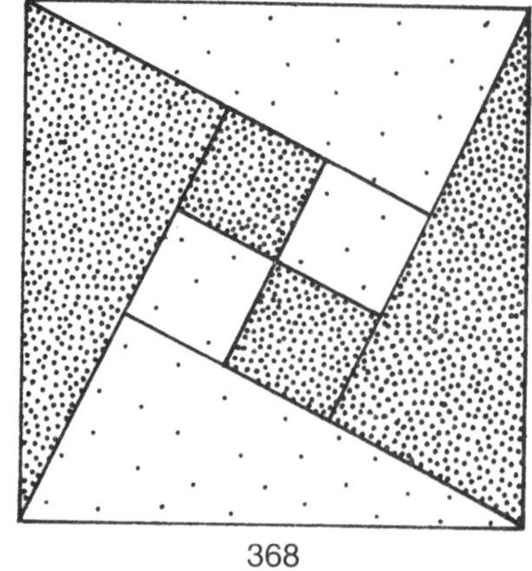

Arabic Lattice 368

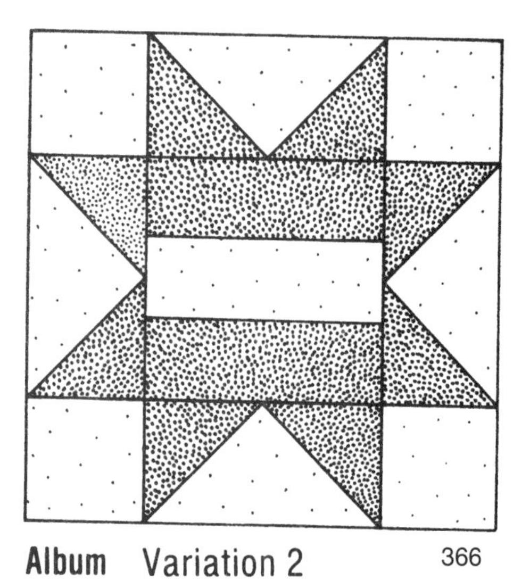

Album Variation 2 366

Arrowheads Variation 1 369

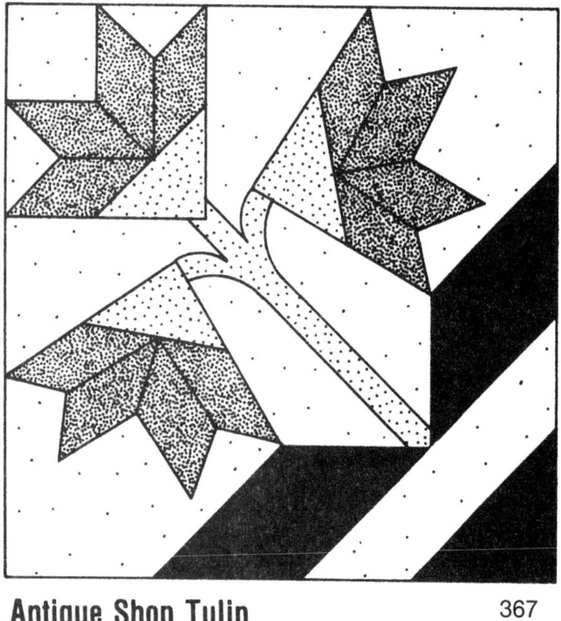

Antique Shop Tulip
Double Tulip 367

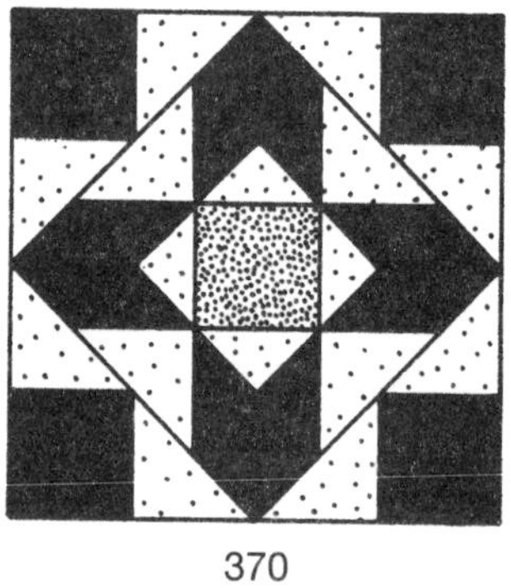

Aunt Sukey's Choice
Puss 'n' Boots 370

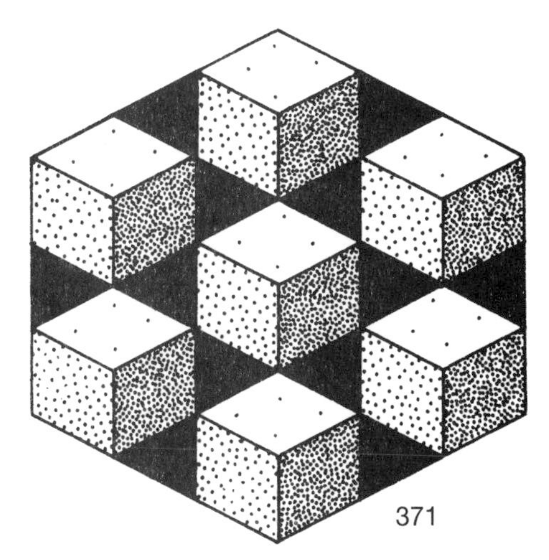

371

Baby Blocks
Variation 2

Baskets

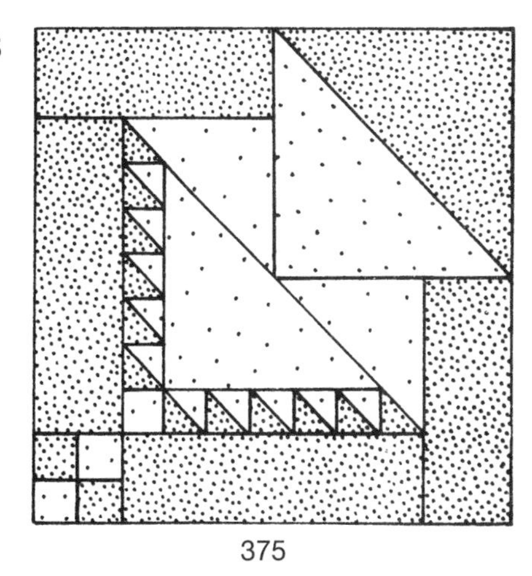

375

Bear Tracks Variation 1
Bear's Foot
Bear's Paw, Var. 3
Bear's Track, Var. 1
Cross and Crown, Var. 3
Duck's Foot in the Mud, Var. 2
Goose Tracks, Var. 1
Hand of Friendship, Var. 2
Illinois Turkey Track
Lily Design

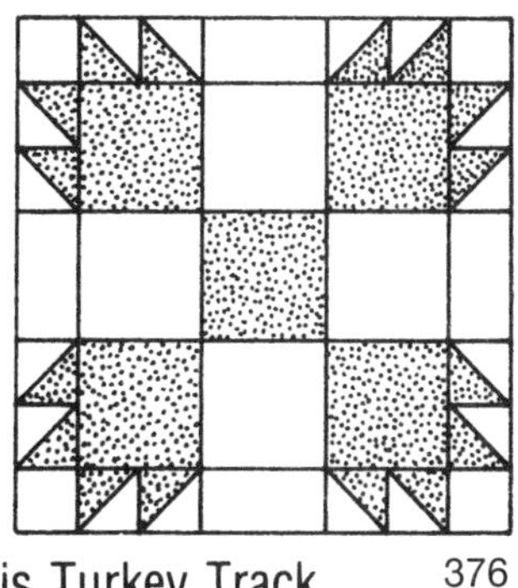

376

372

Basket of Lillies
Variation 2
Basket of Tulips, Var. 2

373

Basket of Scraps
Cactus Basket, Var. 2
Desert Rose, Var. 2
Texas Rose, Var. 2
Texas Treasure, Var. 2

Bear Tracks
Variation 2
Bear's Track, Var. 2

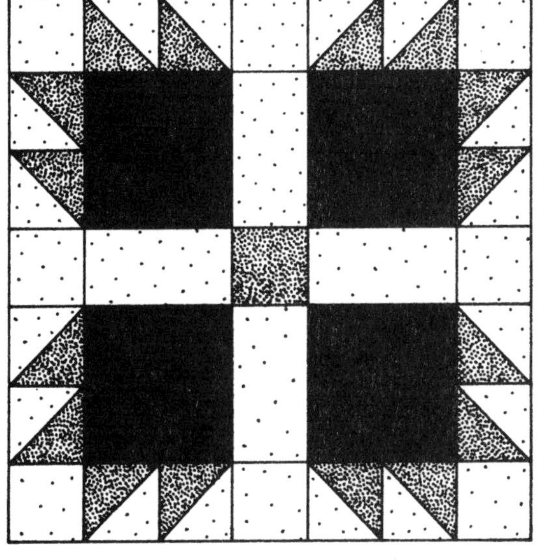

377

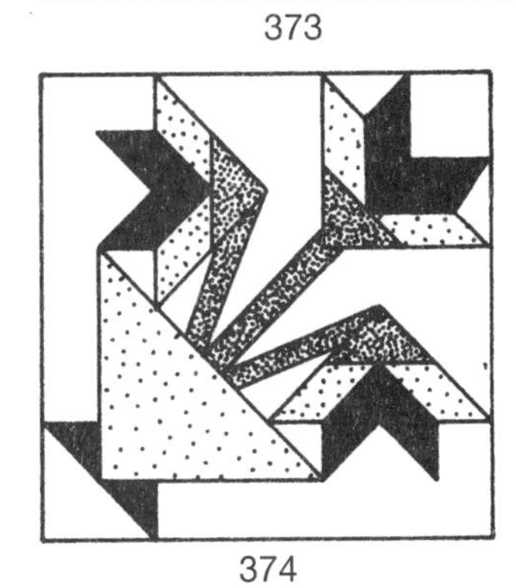

374

Basket of Tulips
Variation 1
Basket of Lilies, Var. 1

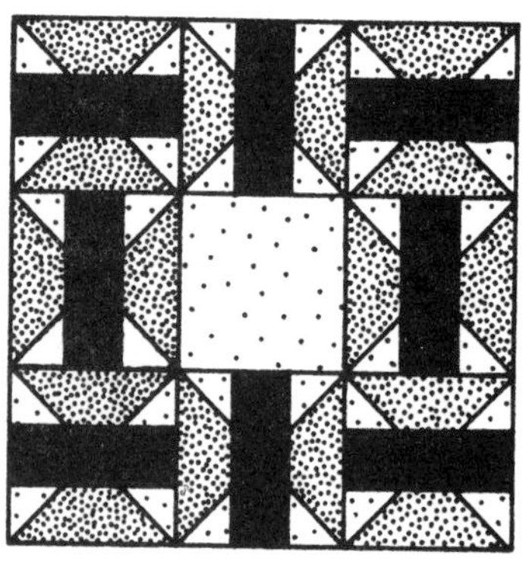

378

Beggar's Block
Cats and Mice, Var. 2

379

Bird's Nest

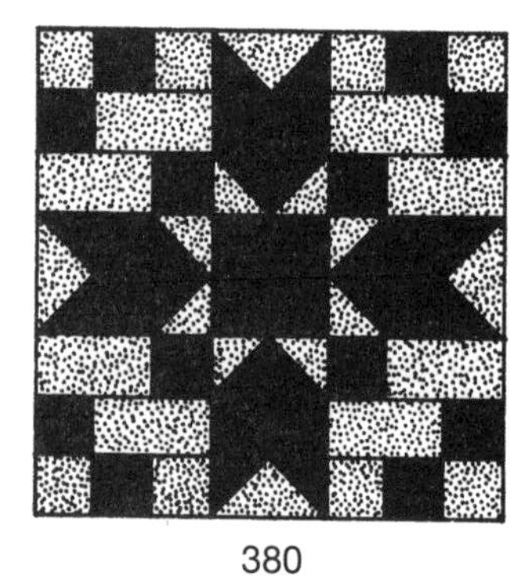

380

Blackford's Beauty

381

Blocks and Stars

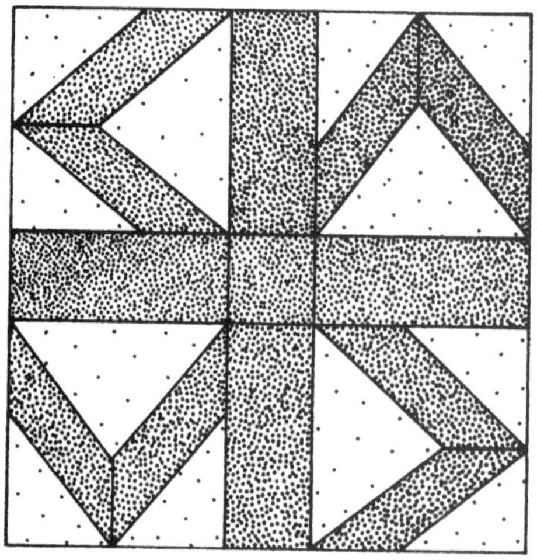

382

Bow Knot
Farmer's Puzzle
Swastika, Var. 1

Boxed Ts 383

Braced Star 384

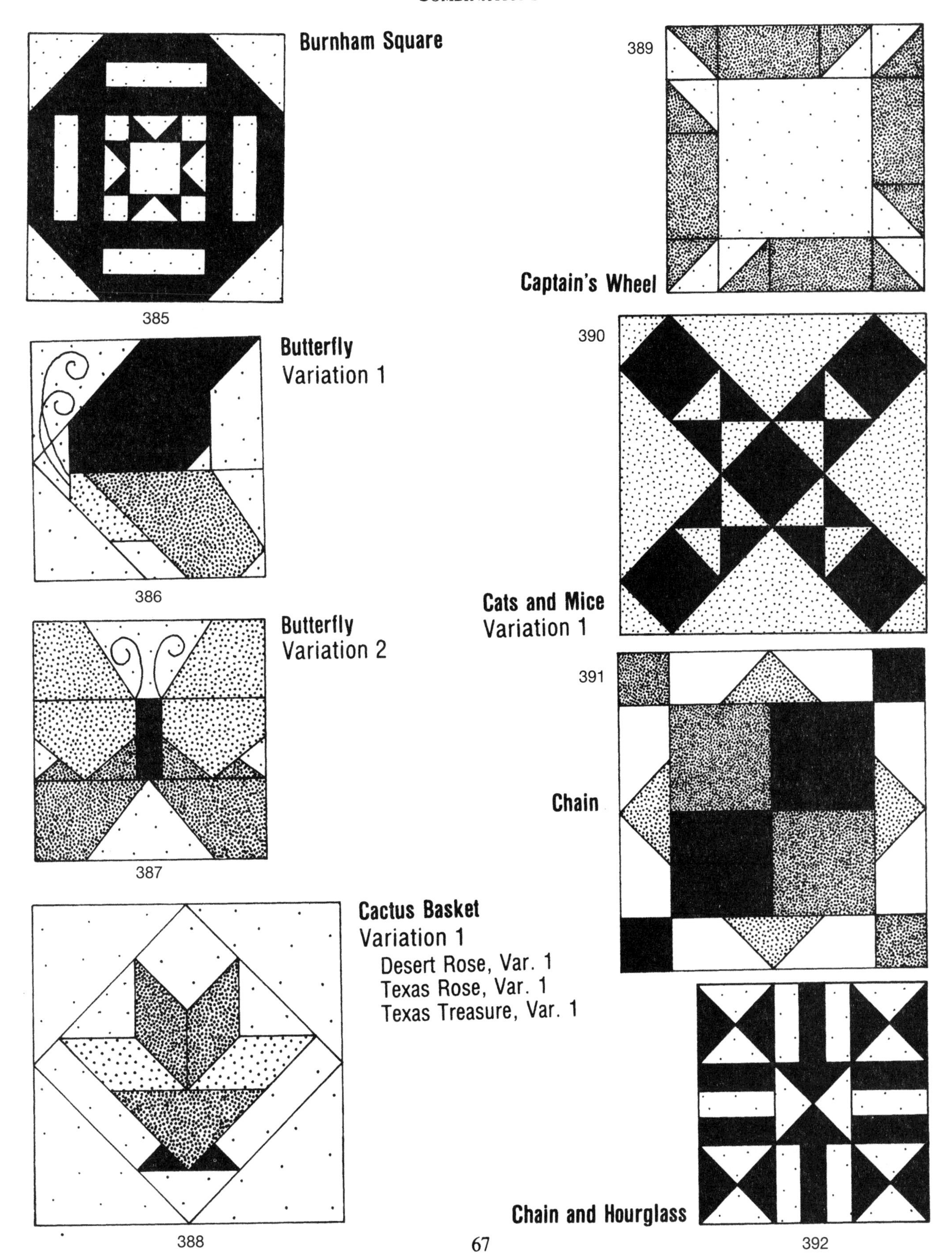
Burnham Square
385
Butterfly
Variation 1
386
Butterfly
Variation 2
387
Cactus Basket
Variation 1
Desert Rose, Var. 1
Texas Rose, Var. 1
Texas Treasure, Var. 1
388
389
Captain's Wheel
390
Cats and Mice
Variation 1
391
Chain
Chain and Hourglass
392

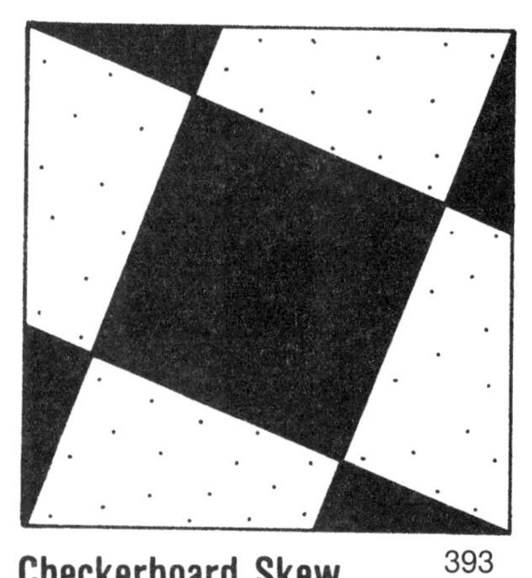
Checkerboard Skew 393

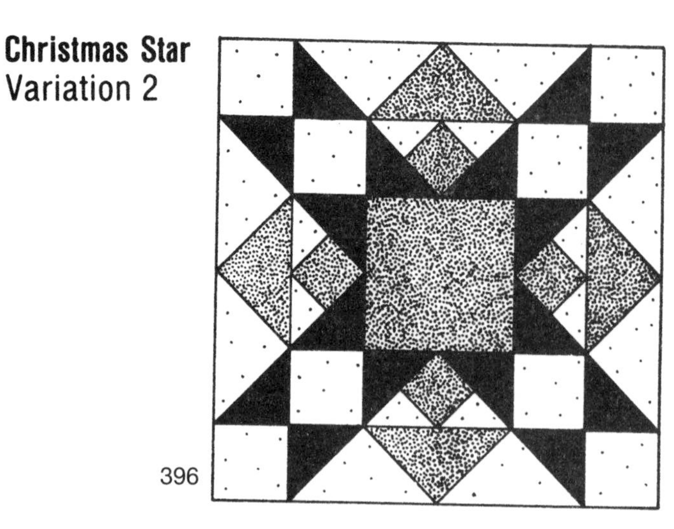
Christmas Star Variation 2 396

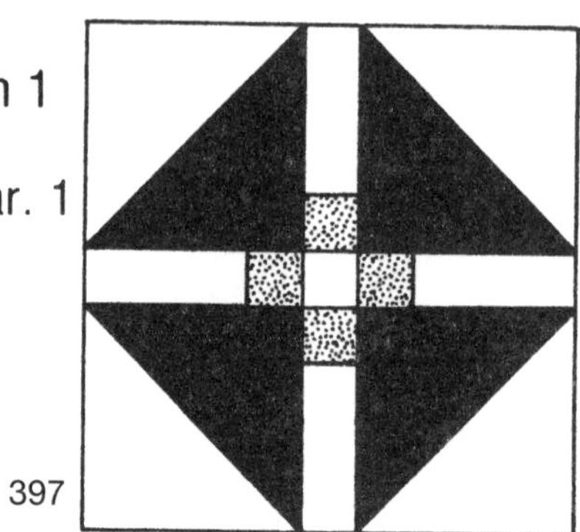
Churn Dash Variation 1
Lover's Knot
Monkey Wrench, Var. 1
397

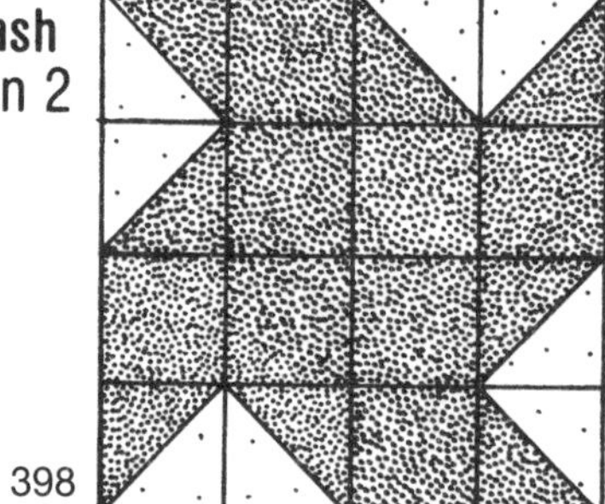
Churn Dash Variation 2 398

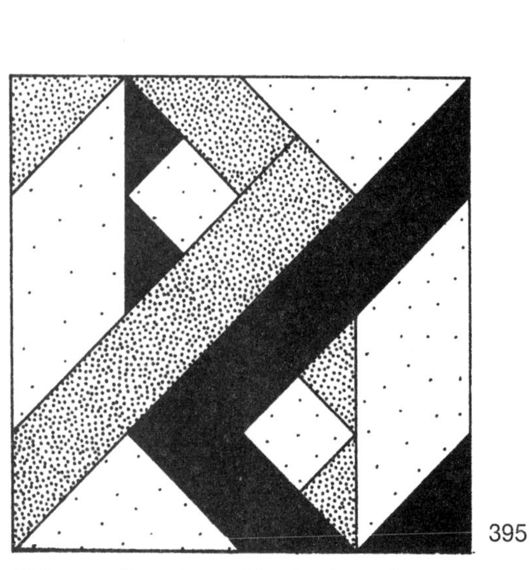
Chinese Puzzle Variation 1 395

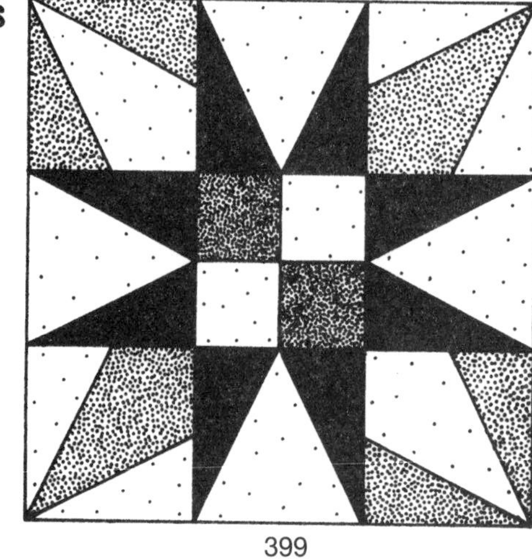
Claws 399

Children of Israel 394

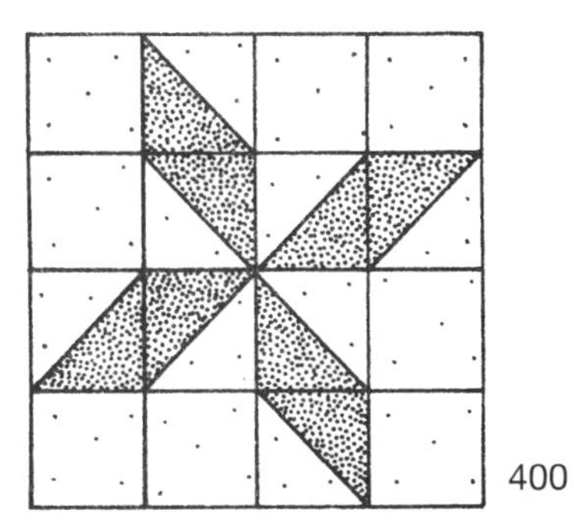
400

Clay's Choice
Harry's Star
Henry of the West
Jackson's Star, Var. 2
Star of the West, Var. 3

Crazy Ann Variation 2
403

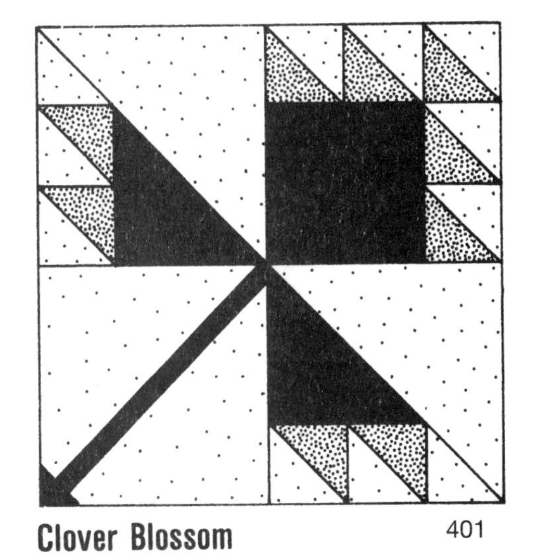
Clover Blossom
English Ivy
401

Crazy House
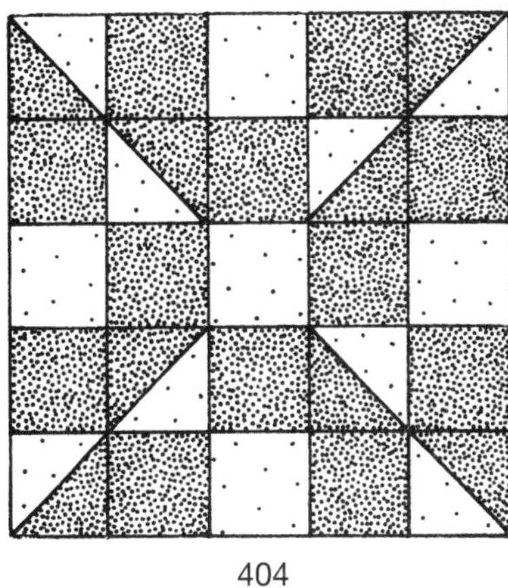
404

Combination star figure, 402

Combination Star
Ornate Star

Cross and Crown
Variation 1
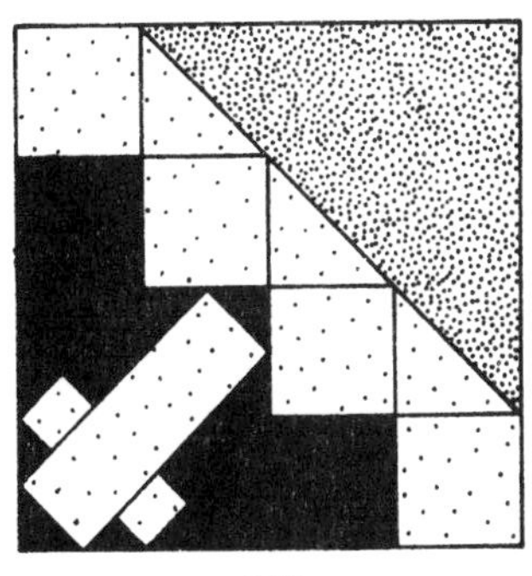
405

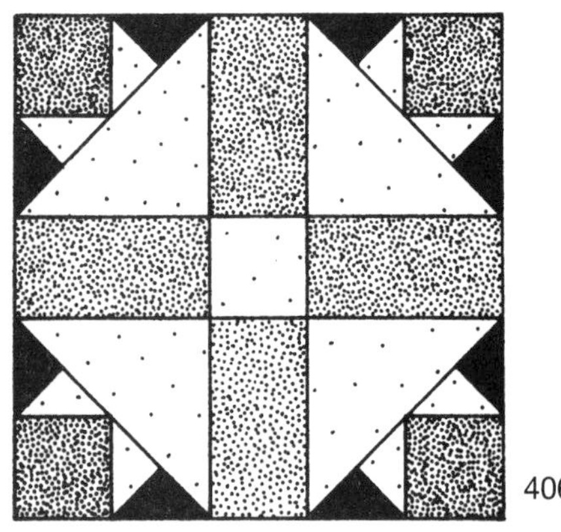
406

Cross and Crown Variation 4

407

Cross Upon a Cross
Cross and Crown, Var. 2
Crown and Cross
Crowned Cross, Var. 1
Golgotha, Var. 2
Three Crosses, Var. 2

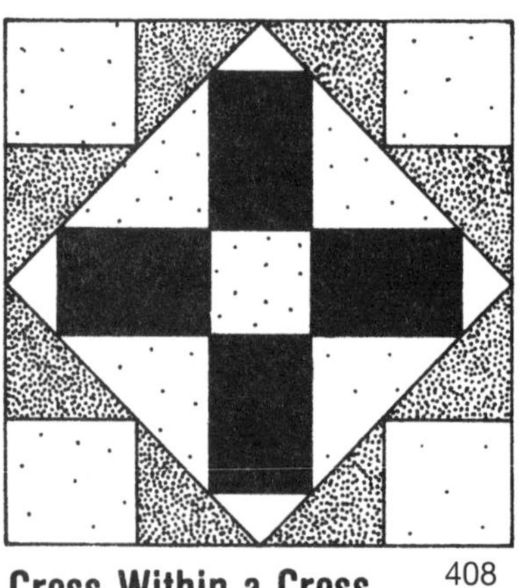
408

Cross Within a Cross

Crow Foot
Devil's Claws, Var. 2

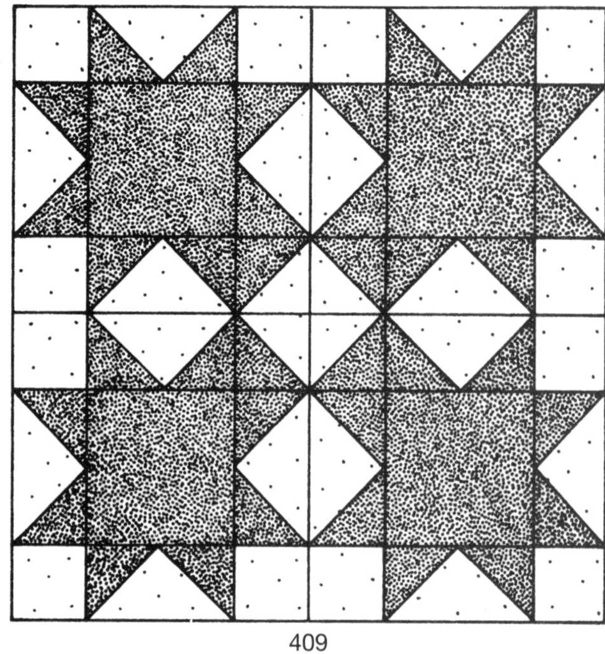
409

Crown and Thorns
Crown of Thorns
Georgetown Circle, Var. 1
Memory Wreath
Single Wedding Ring, Var. 1

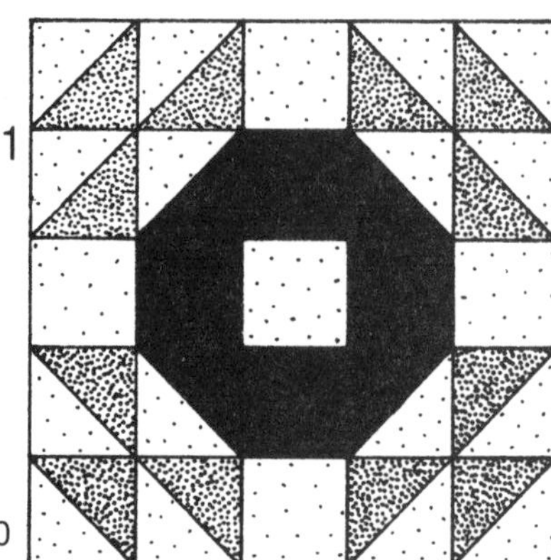
410

Crow's Foot
Variation 4

411

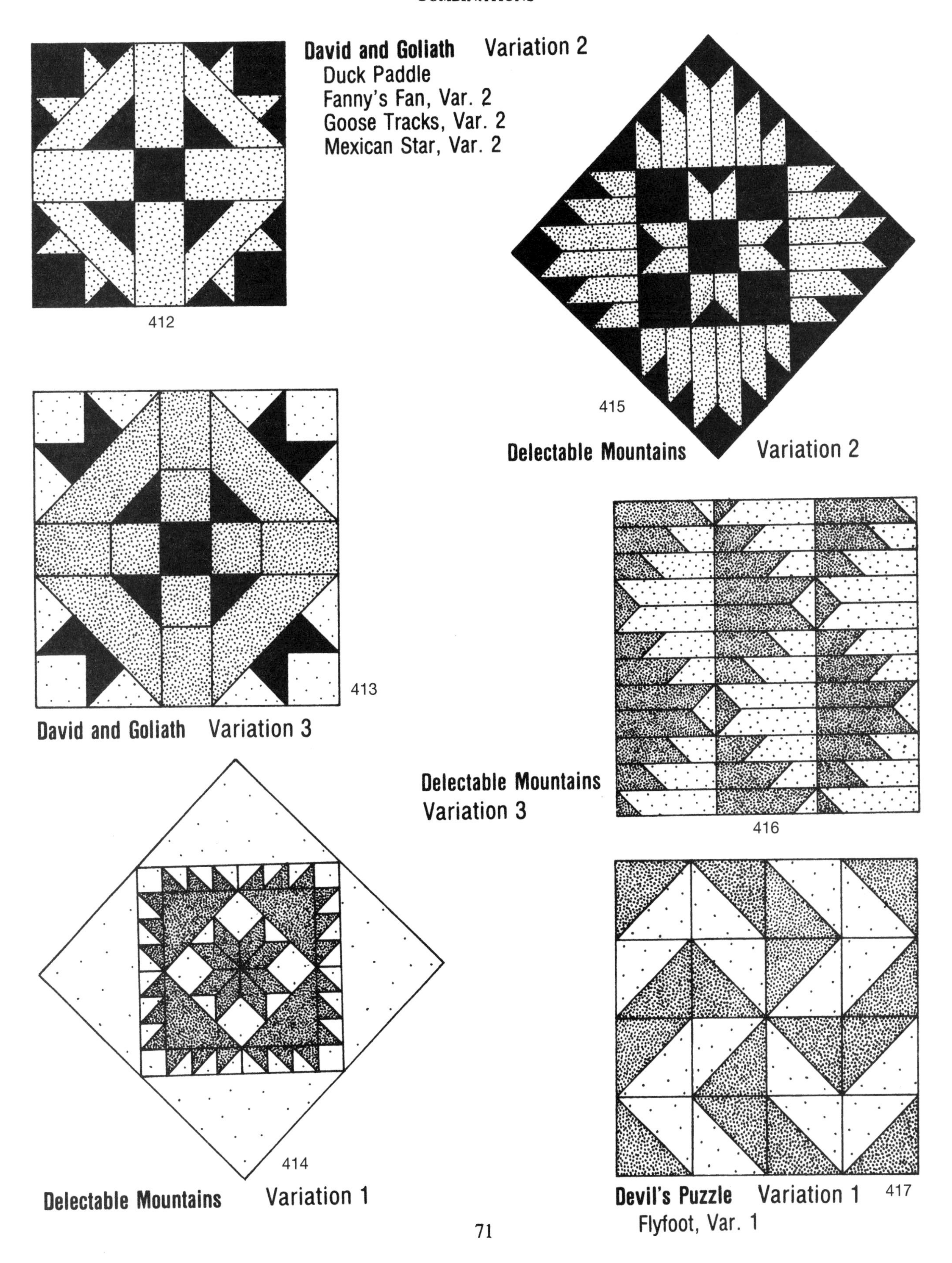

412

David and Goliath Variation 2
Duck Paddle
Fanny's Fan, Var. 2
Goose Tracks, Var. 2
Mexican Star, Var. 2

413

David and Goliath Variation 3

414

Delectable Mountains Variation 1

415

Delectable Mountains Variation 2

416

Delectable Mountains Variation 3

417

Devil's Puzzle Variation 1
Flyfoot, Var. 1

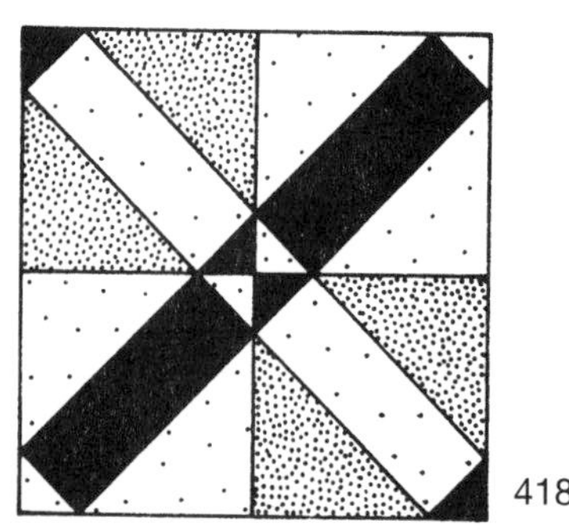

418

Devil's Puzzle Variation 2
Flyfoot, Var. 2

Double Square Variation 1

421

Dogwood Blossoms 419

Double X Variation 1

422

Domino and Squares 420

423

Dove in the Window Variation 2

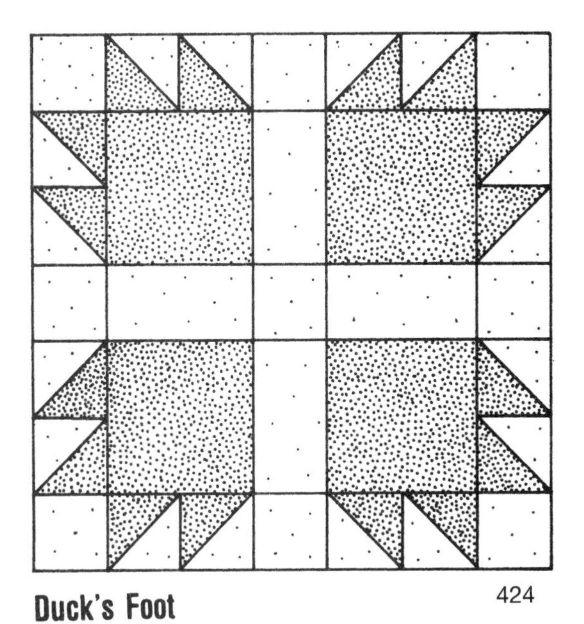
Duck's Foot 424

425 **Duck's Foot in the Mud** Variation 1
Bear's Paw, Var. 1
Crow's Foot, Var. 1
Hand of Friendship, Var. 1

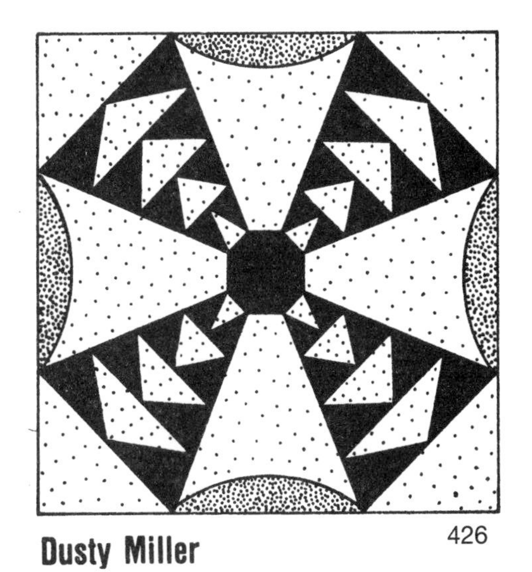
Dusty Miller 426

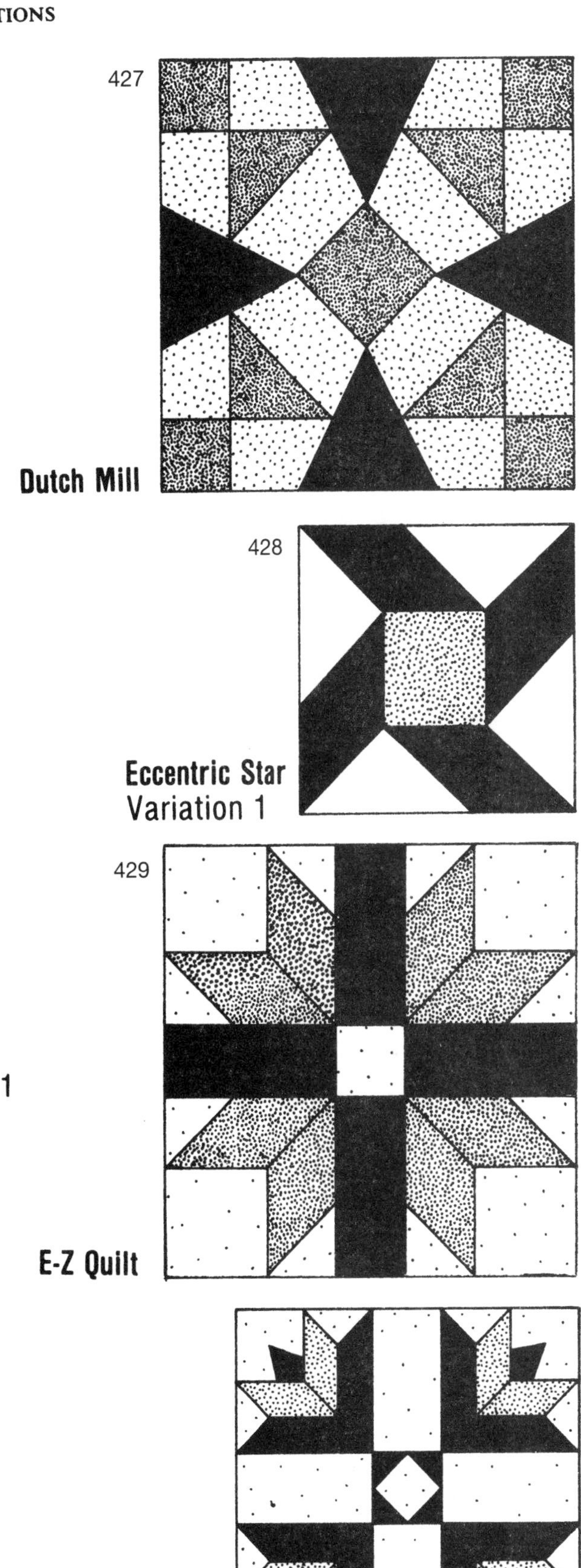
427 Dutch Mill

428 Eccentric Star Variation 1

429 E-Z Quilt

Fannie's Fan Variation 1 430

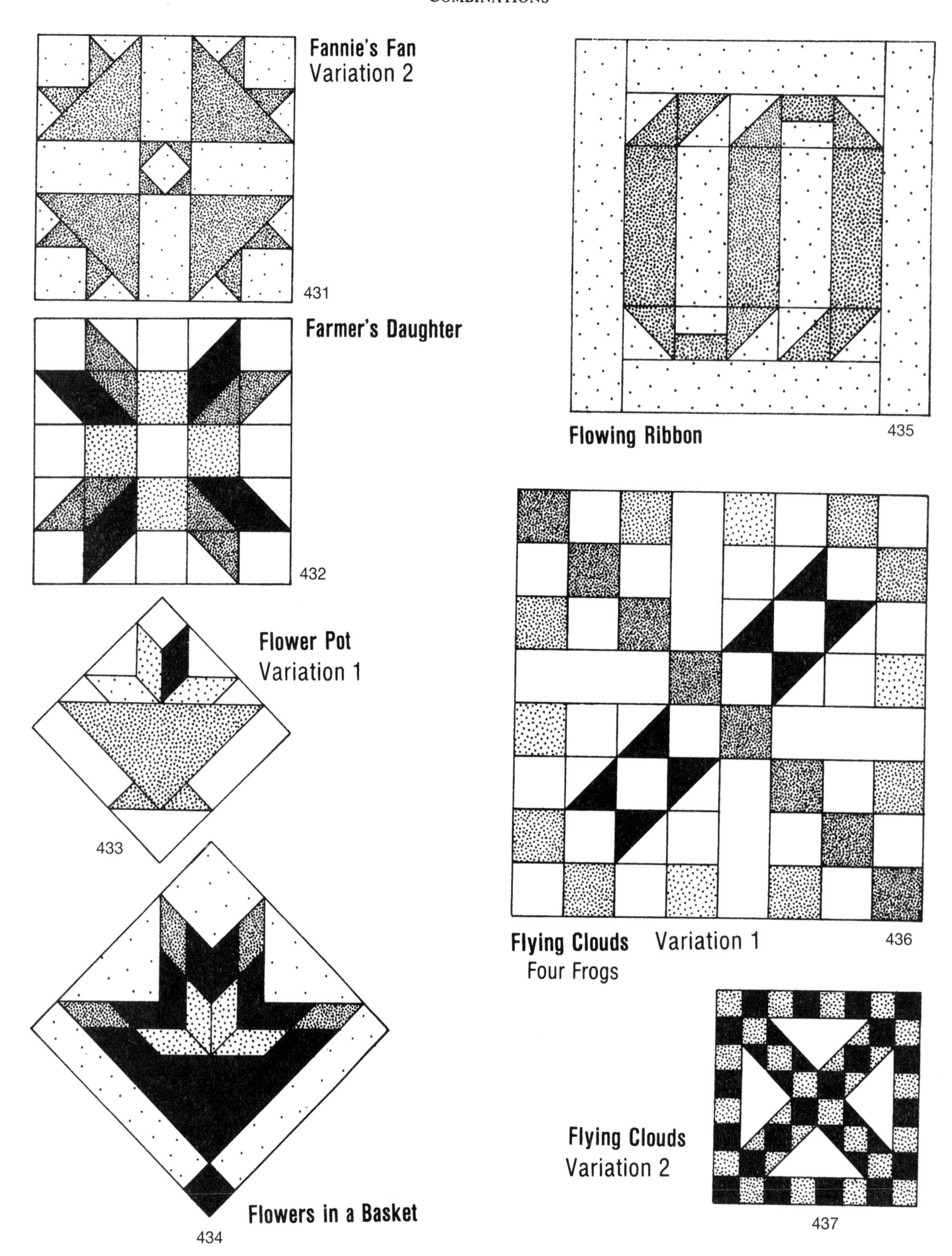

Fannie's Fan
Variation 2
431
Farmer's Daughter
432
Flower Pot
Variation 1
433
Flowers in a Basket
434
Flowing Ribbon
435
Flying Clouds Variation 1
Four Frogs
436
Flying Clouds
Variation 2
437

438

Flying Dutchman Variation 1

Four Little Baskets

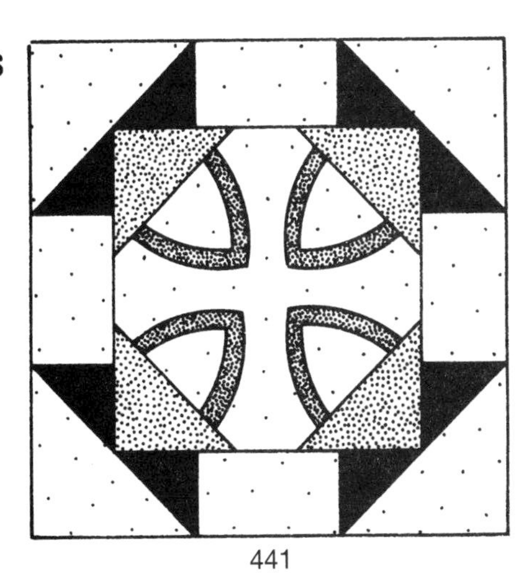

441

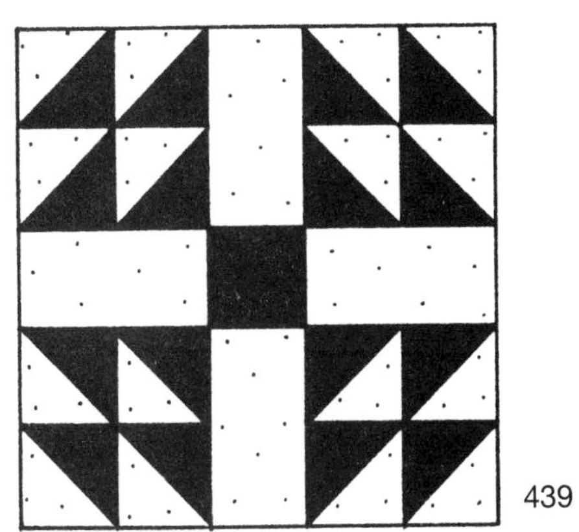

439

Flying Geese Variation 2
Handy Andy, Var. 6

Friendship Knot

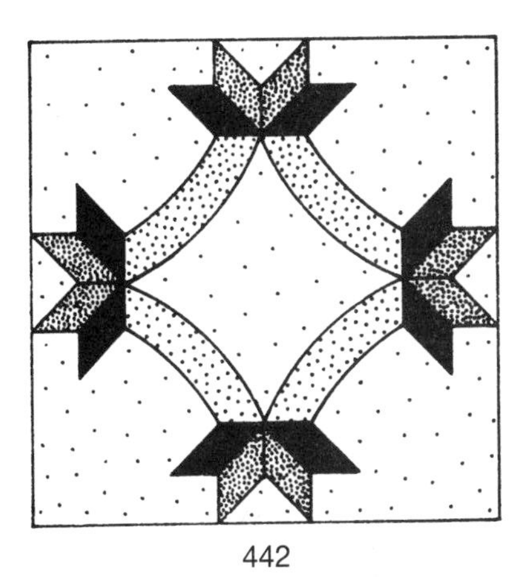

442

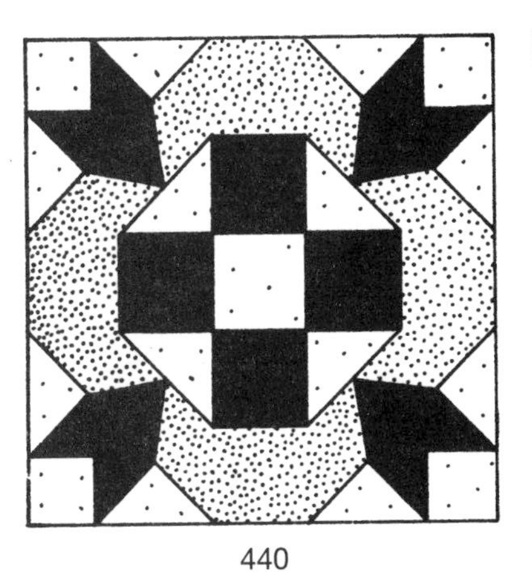

440

Four Darts
Bull's Eye
David and Goliath, Var. 1
Doe and Darts
Flying Darts

Garden of Eden Variation 1

443

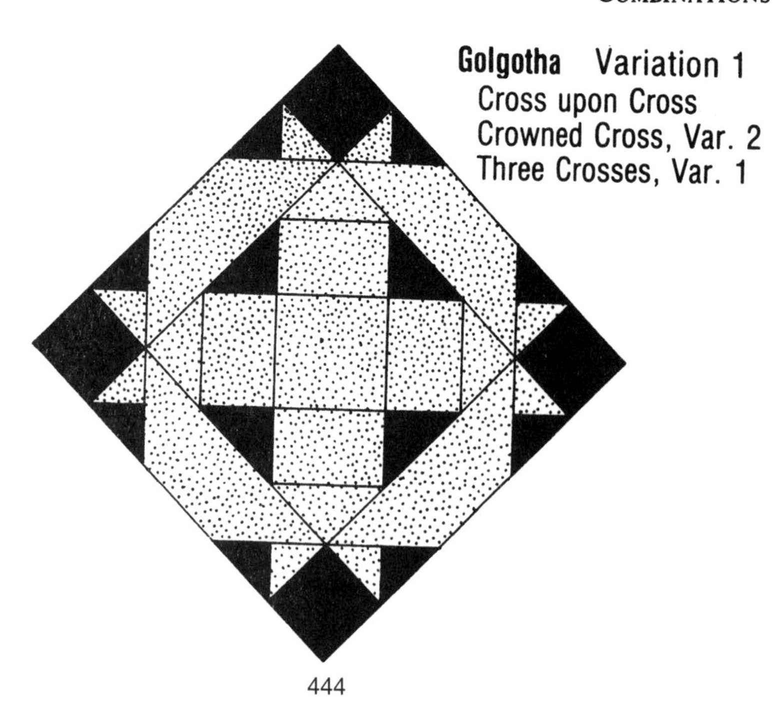

Golgotha Variation 1
Cross upon Cross
Crowned Cross, Var. 2
Three Crosses, Var. 1

444

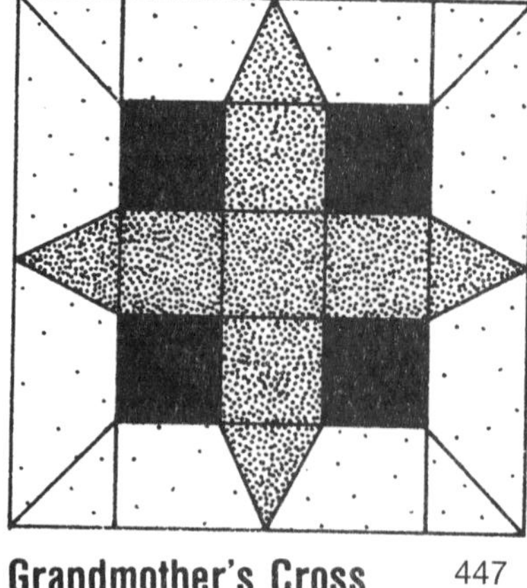

Grandmother's Cross 447

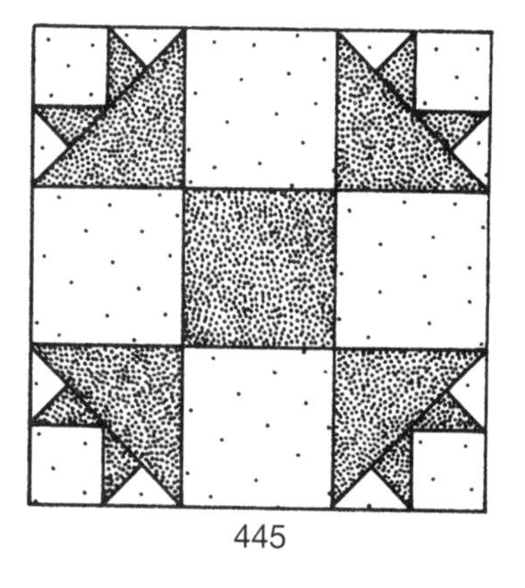

Goose Tracks
Variation 3

445

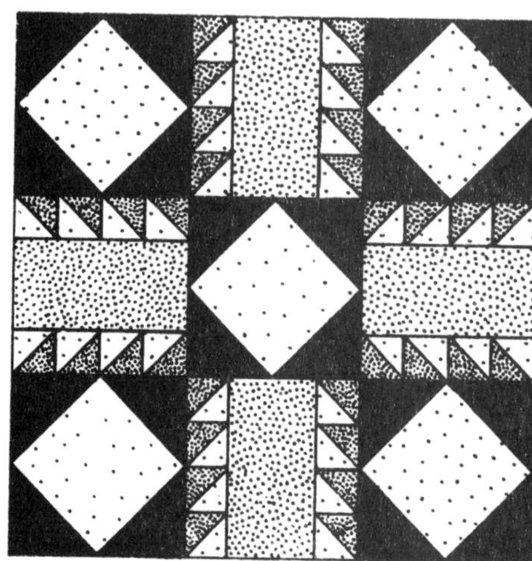

Grandmother's Dream 448
Mother's Dream

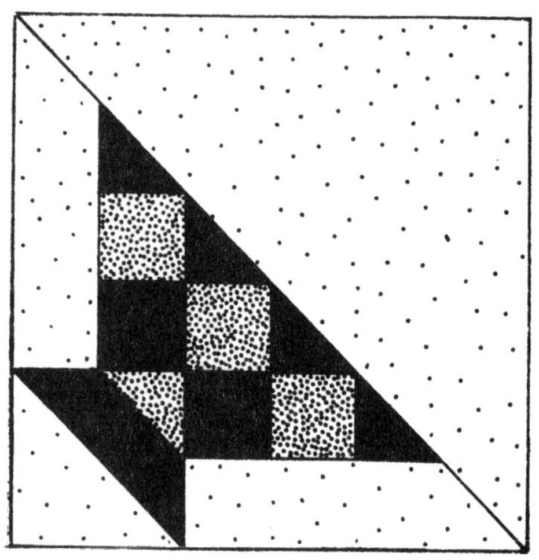

Grandmother's Basket 446

Greek Cross Variation 2 449

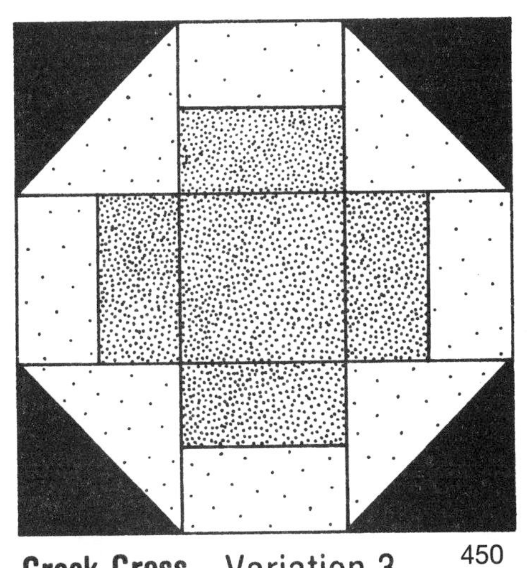

Greek Cross Variation 3 450
Grecian
Grecian Design

Hayes' Corner

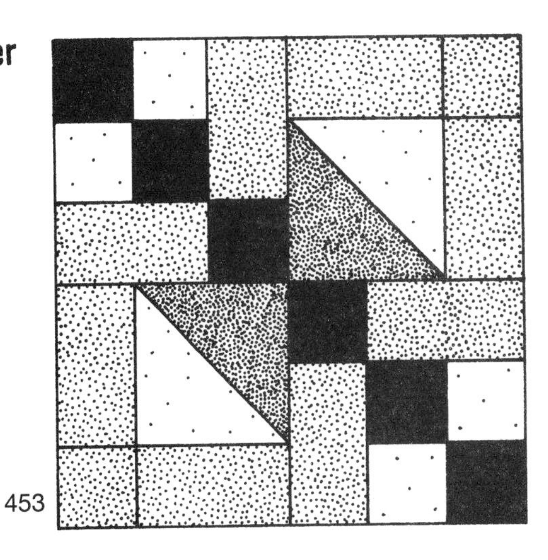

453

Heart's Desire

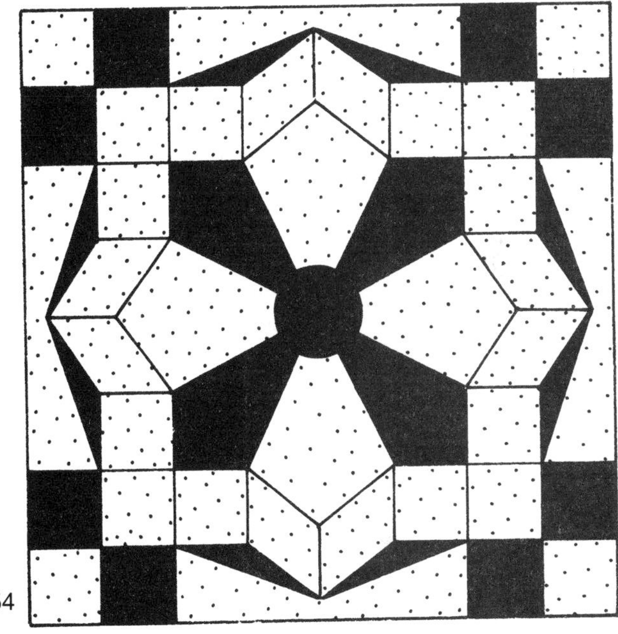

454

Handy Andy Variation 2 451

Hen and Chickens
Variation 2

455

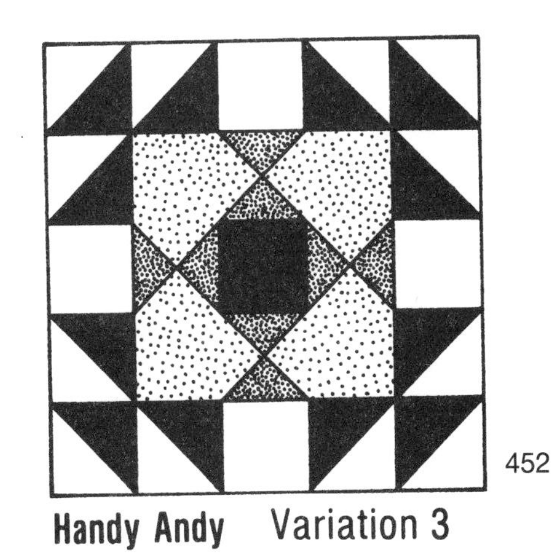

452

Handy Andy Variation 3

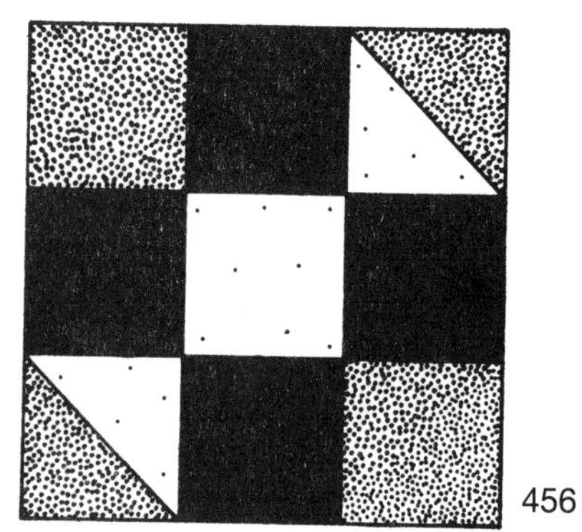

456

Hourglass Variation 1

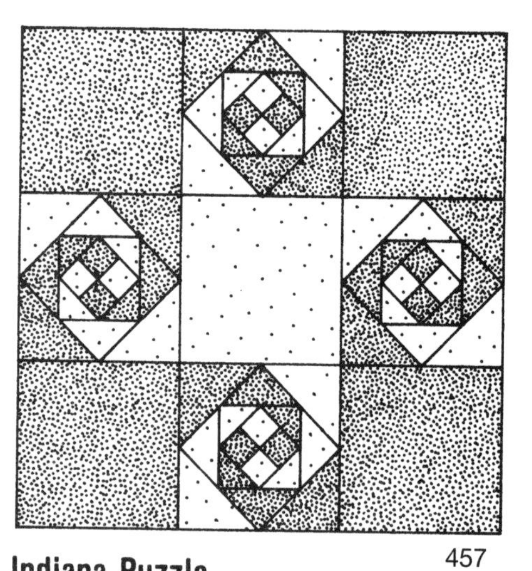

457

Indiana Puzzle
Monkey Wrench, Var. 3

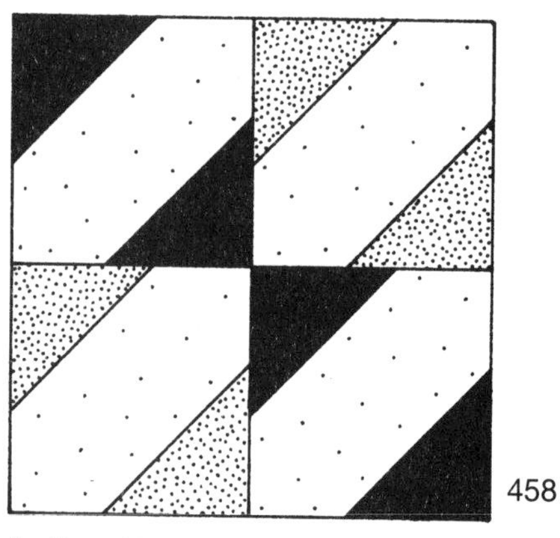

458

Indian Hatchet Variation 1

Indian Hatchet
Variation 2

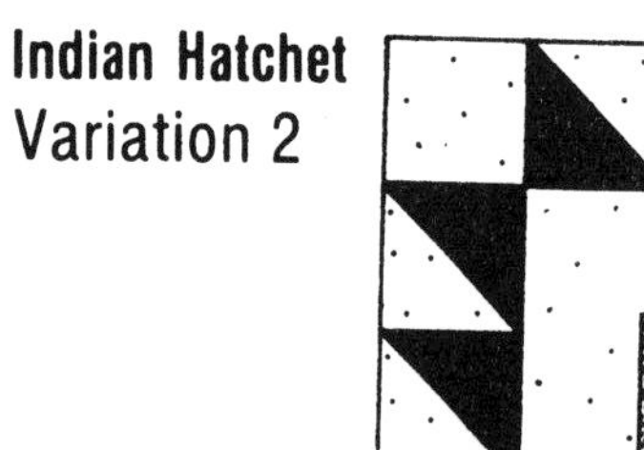

459

Indian Meadows Variation 1
Mountain Meadows
Queen Charlotte's Crown,
Var. 1

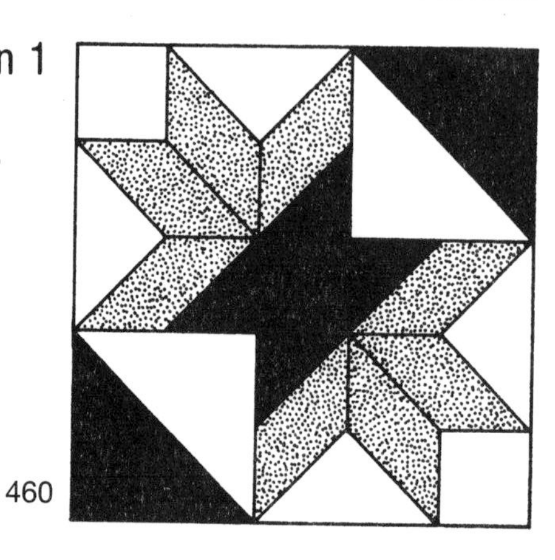

460

Irish Chain
Variation 1

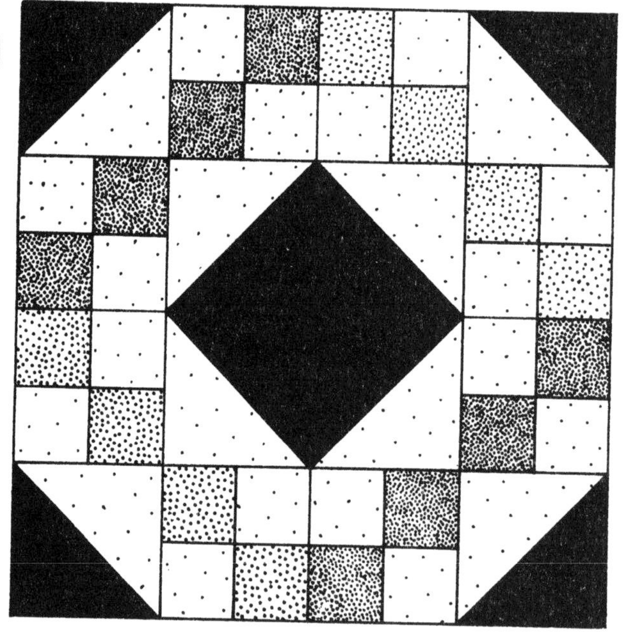

461

462

Jack in the Box
Whirligig, Var. 1

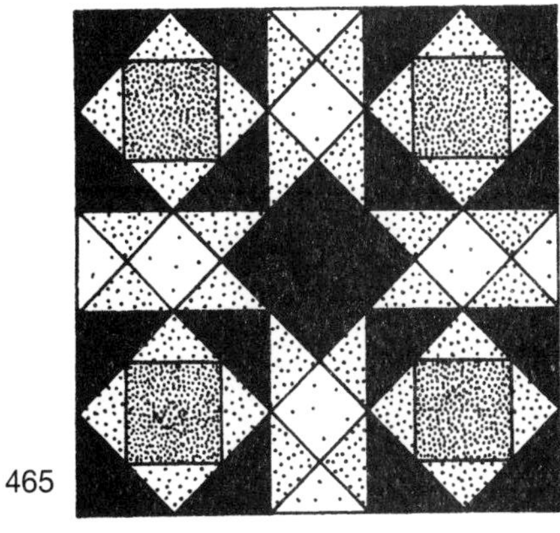

465

Joseph's Coat Variation 1
Scrap-Bag

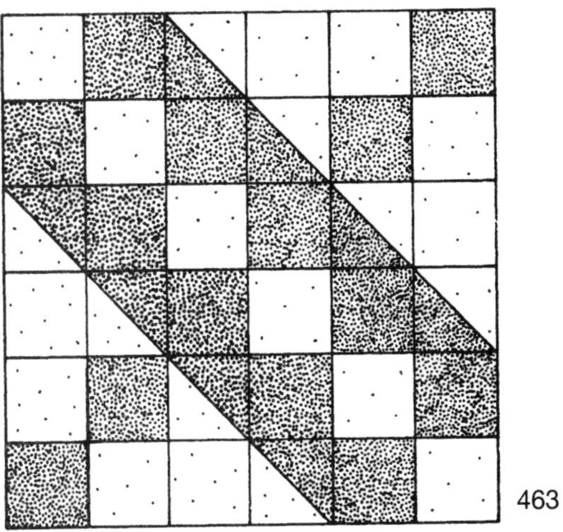

463

Jacob's Ladder Variation 1

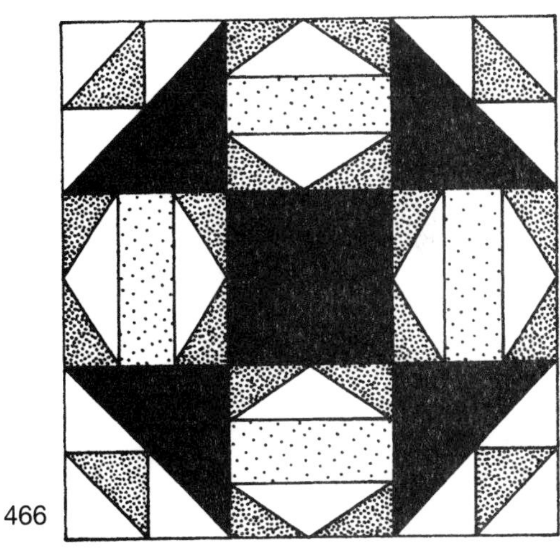

466

Joseph's Coat Variation 2
Mollie's Choice

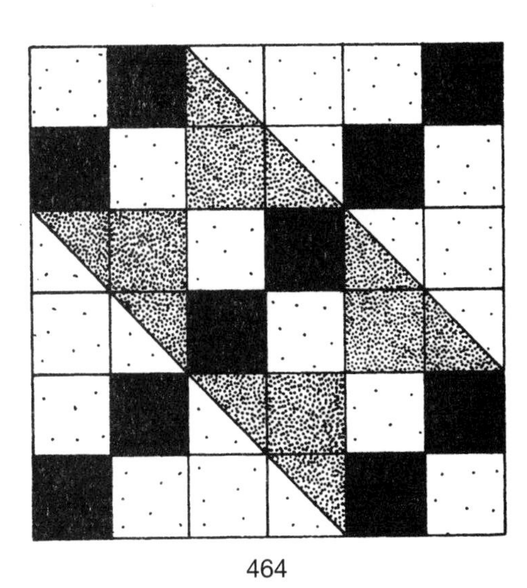

464

Jacob's Ladder Variation 2
Road to California, Var. 1
Rocky Road to California
Stepping Stones, Var. 1
Tail of Benjamin's Kite
Trail of the Covered Wagon
Underground Railroad
Wagon Tracks

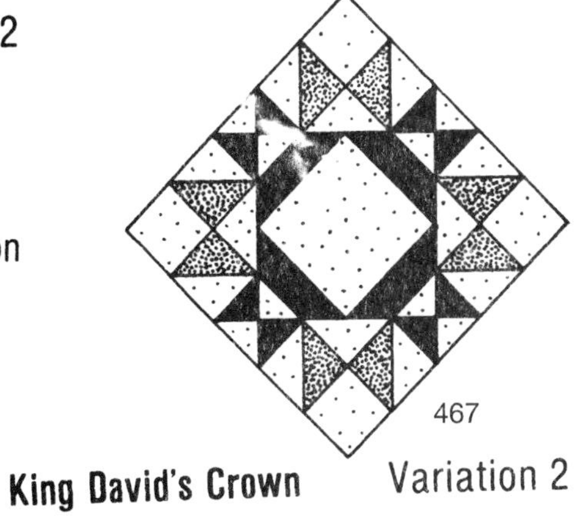

467

King David's Crown Variation 2

King's Crown Variation 1 468

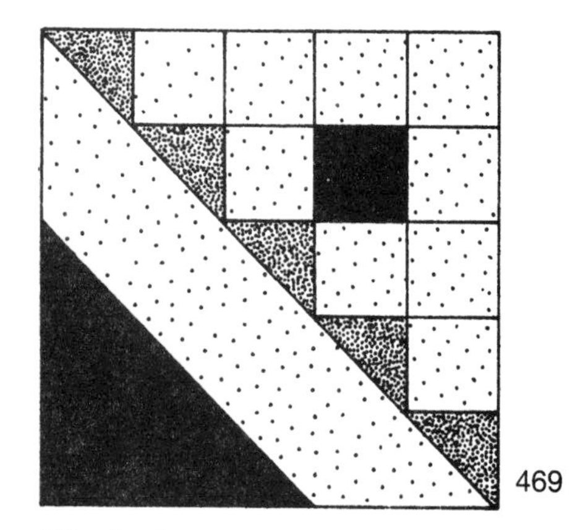

469

King's Crown Variation 2
Greek Cross, Var. 1

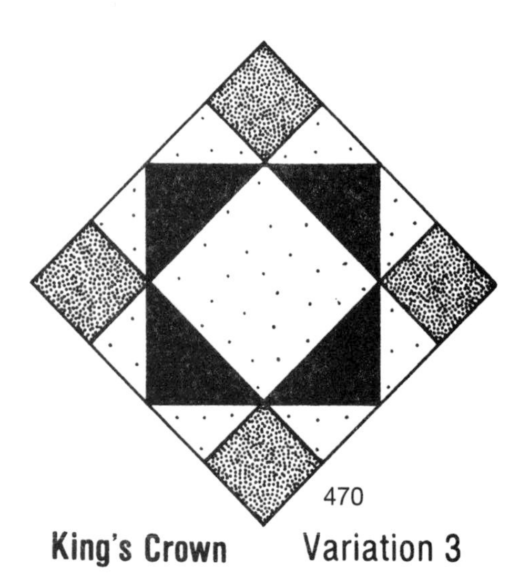

470

King's Crown Variation 3

Ladies' Delight

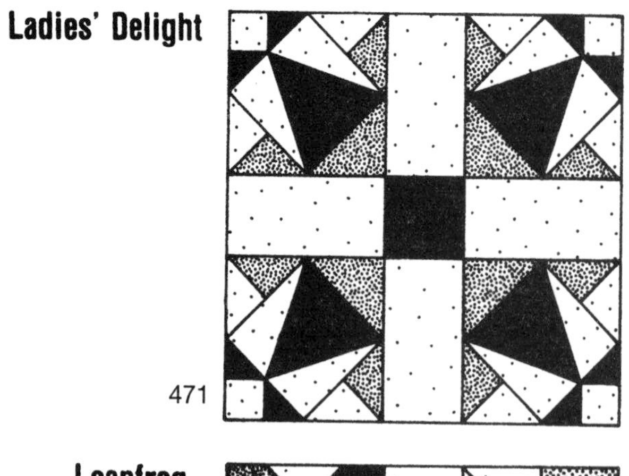

471

Leapfrog

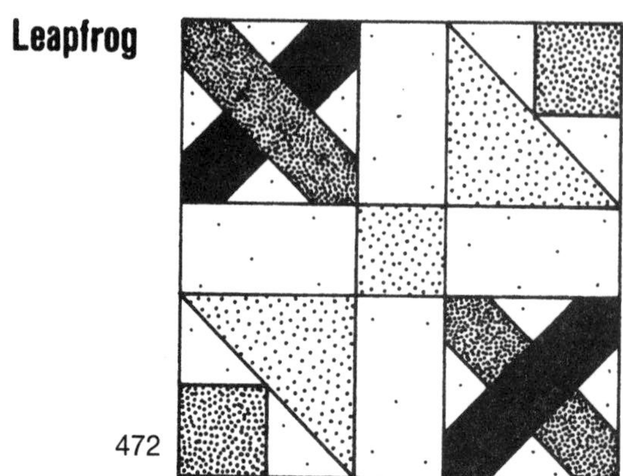

472

Lily

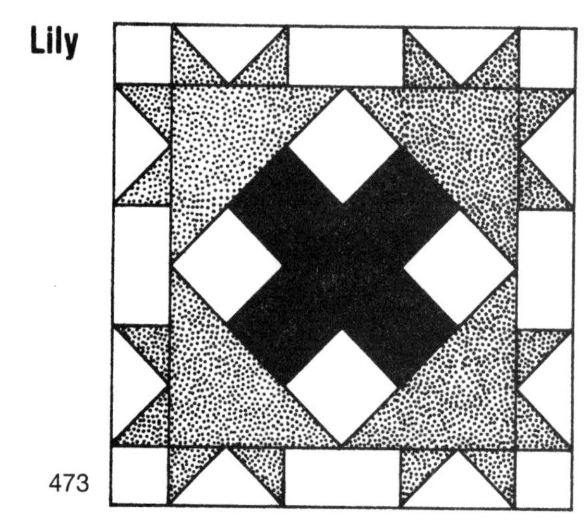

473

Lily of the Field

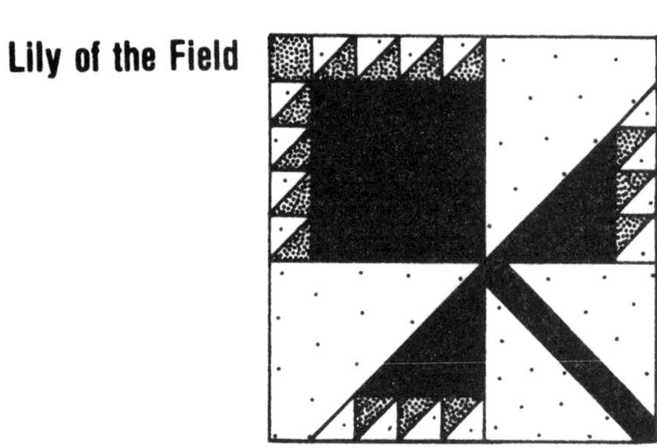

474

Little Giant 475

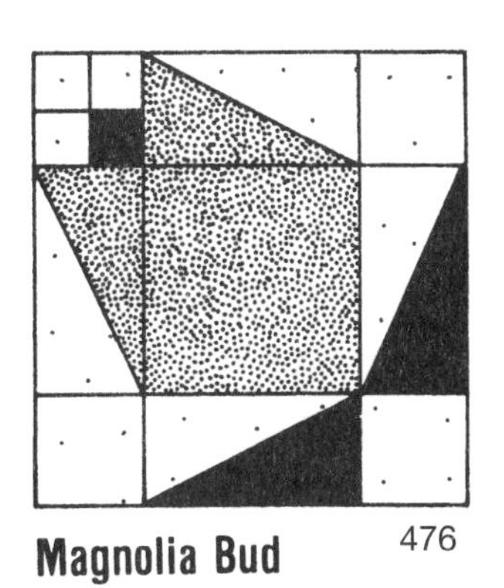

Magnolia Bud 476

Maple Leaf Variation 1 477

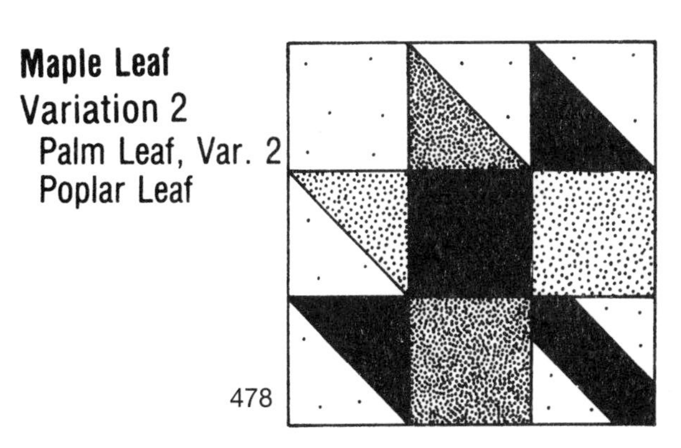

Maple Leaf
Variation 2
Palm Leaf, Var. 2
Poplar Leaf
478

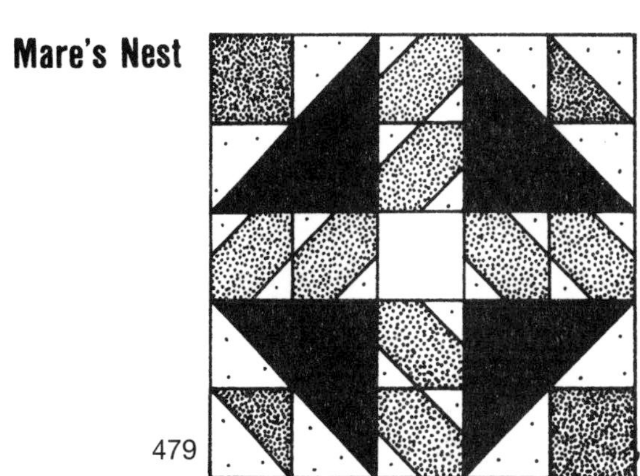

Mare's Nest 479

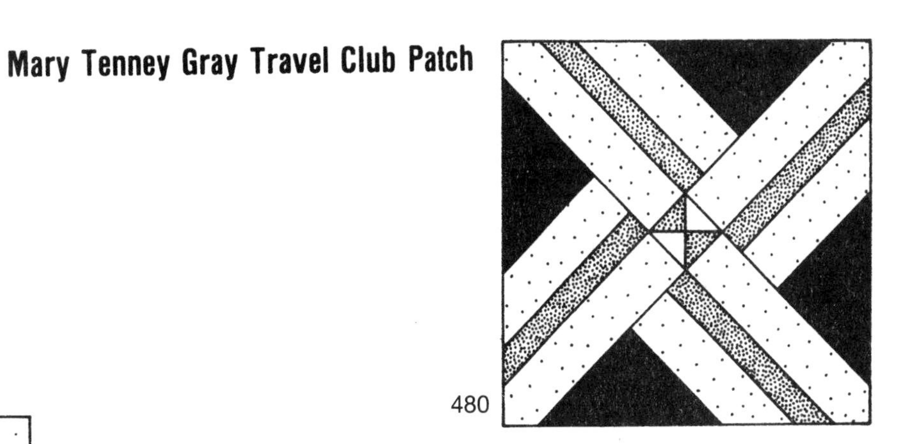

Mary Tenney Gray Travel Club Patch 480

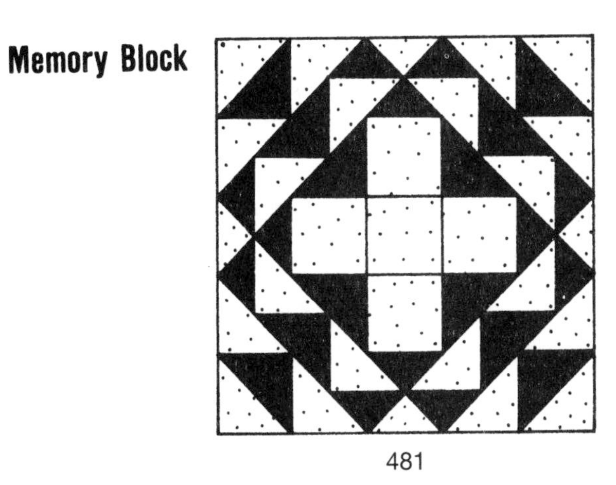

Memory Block 481

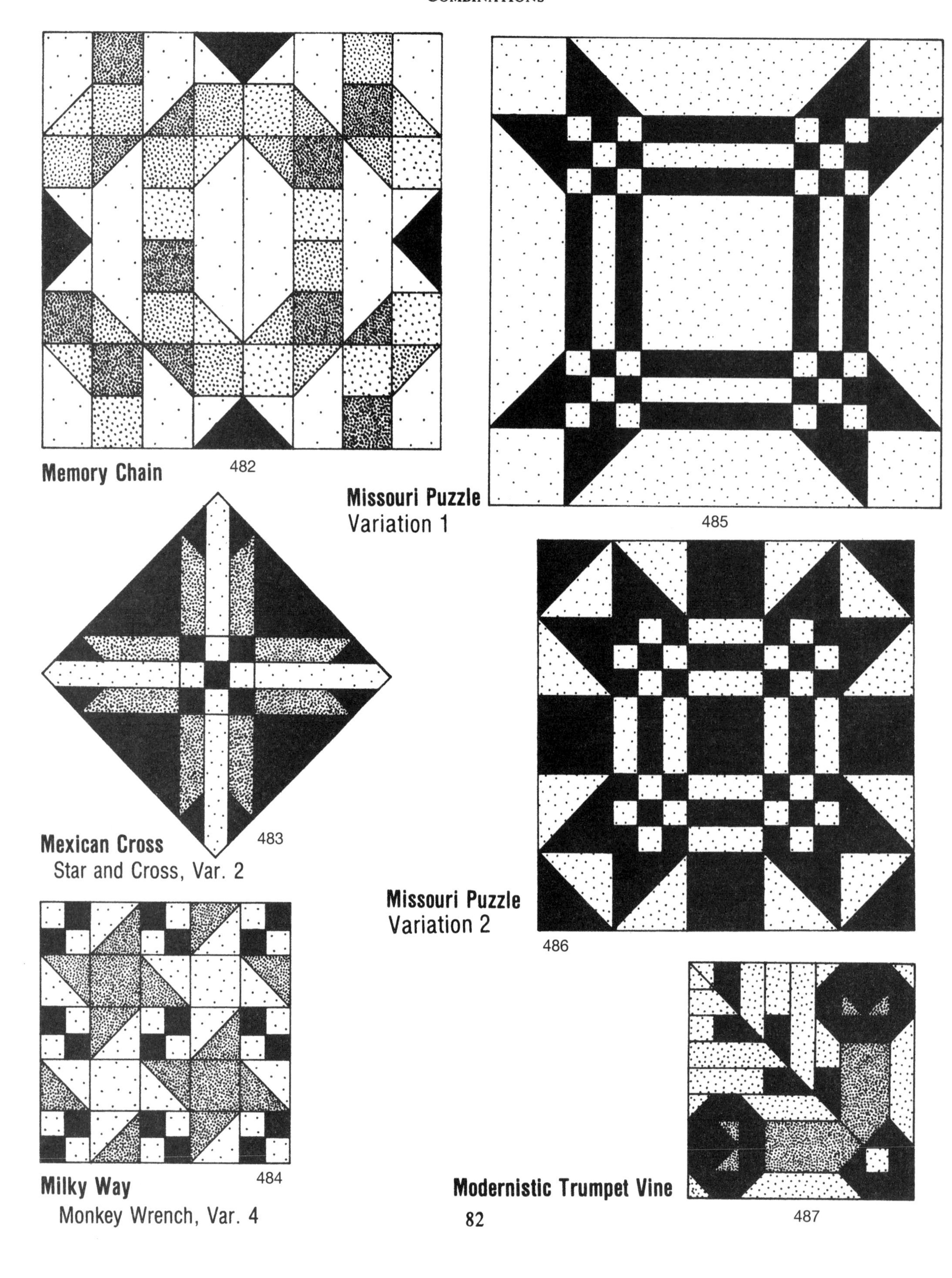

Memory Chain 482

Mexican Cross 483
Star and Cross, Var. 2

Milky Way 484
Monkey Wrench, Var. 4

Missouri Puzzle
Variation 1 485

Missouri Puzzle
Variation 2 486

Modernistic Trumpet Vine 487

Mother's Fancy Star

488

Mrs. Cleveland's Choice
County Fair

489

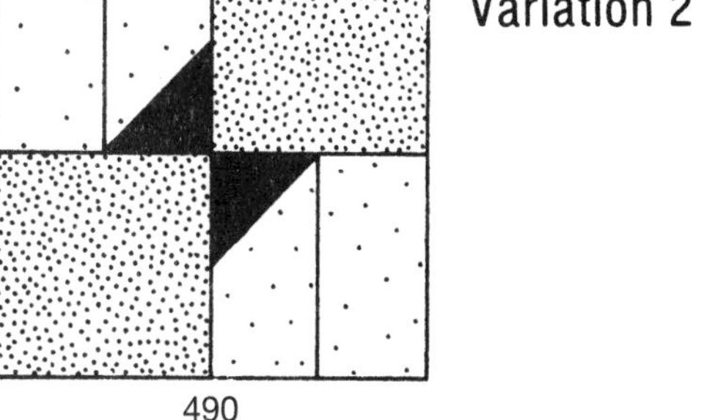

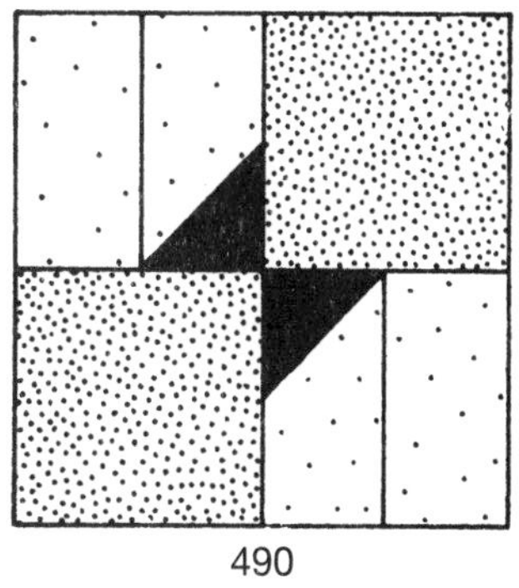

Necktie
Variation 2

490

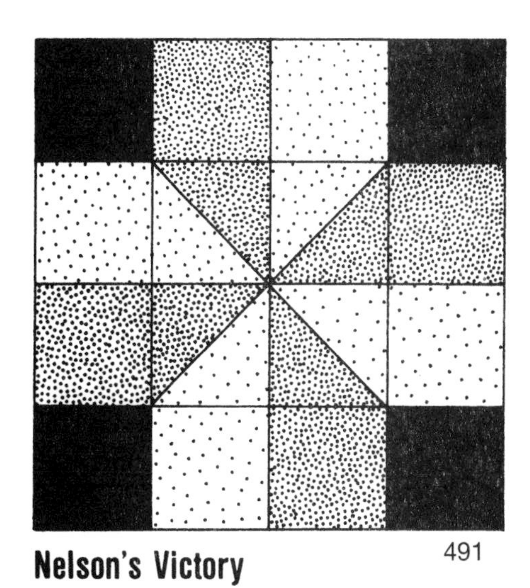

Nelson's Victory

491

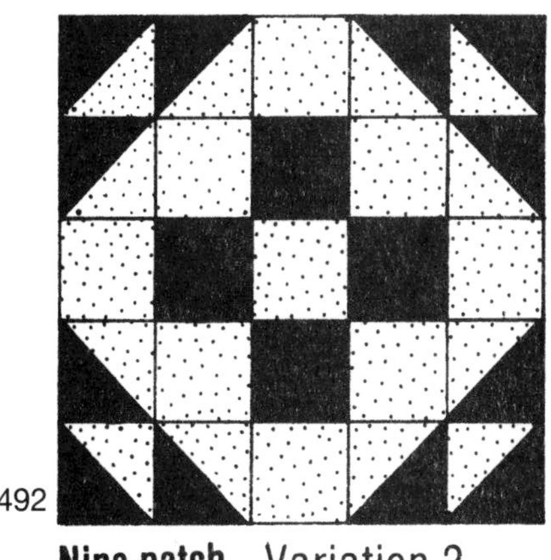

492

Nine-patch Variation 2

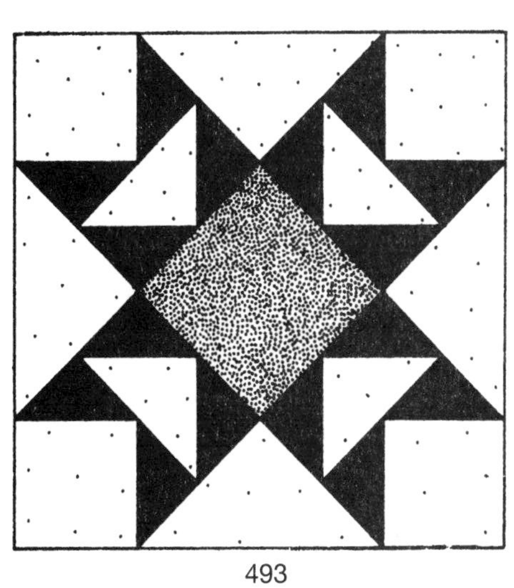

Northumberland Star
Variation 1

493

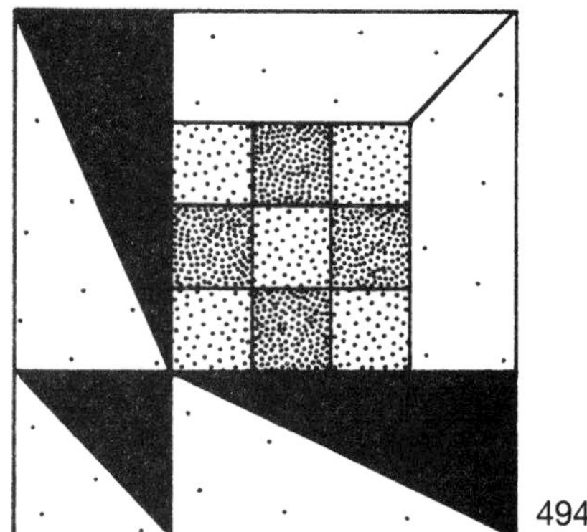
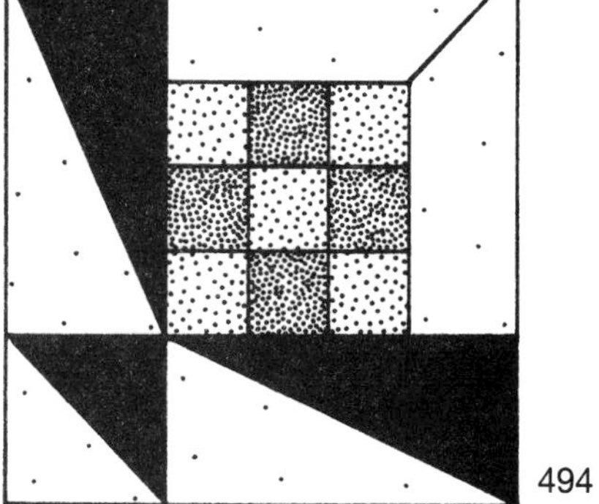
494

Nosegay Variation 2

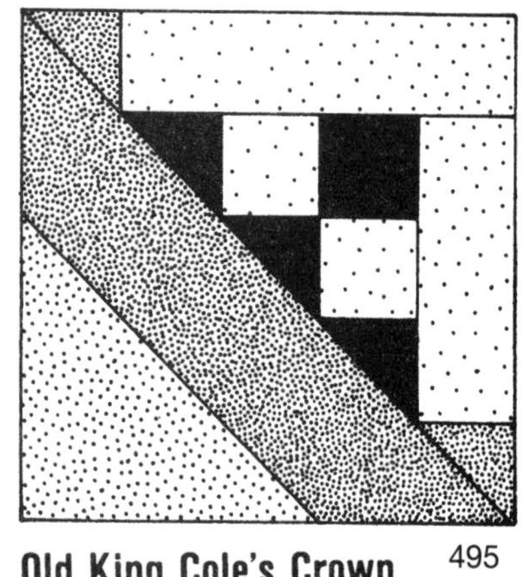

Old King Cole's Crown 495

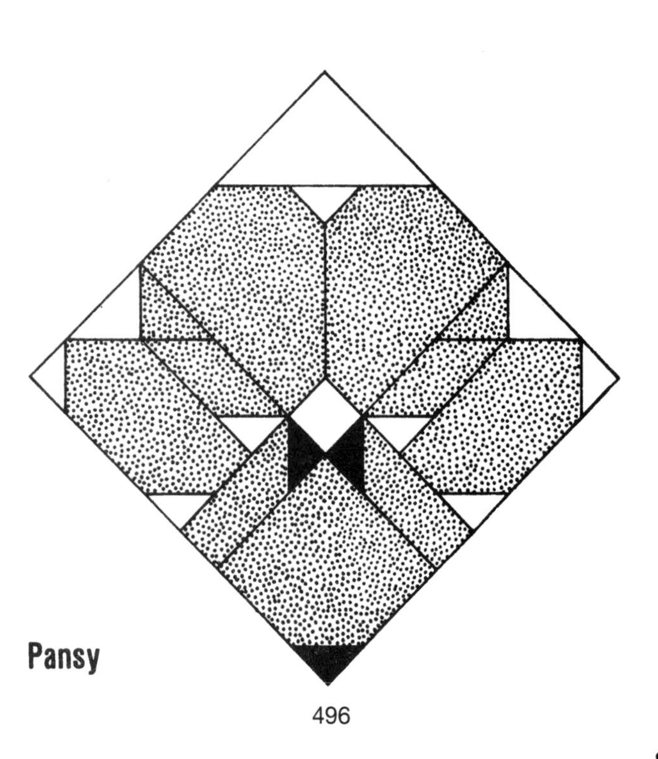

Pansy

496

Philadelphia Pavement

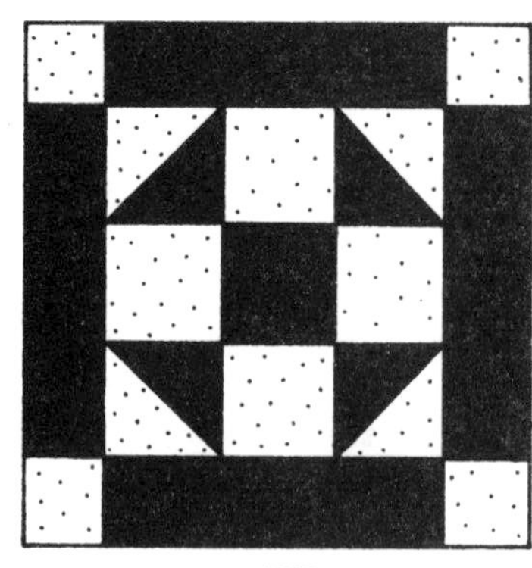
497

Pieced Pyramids

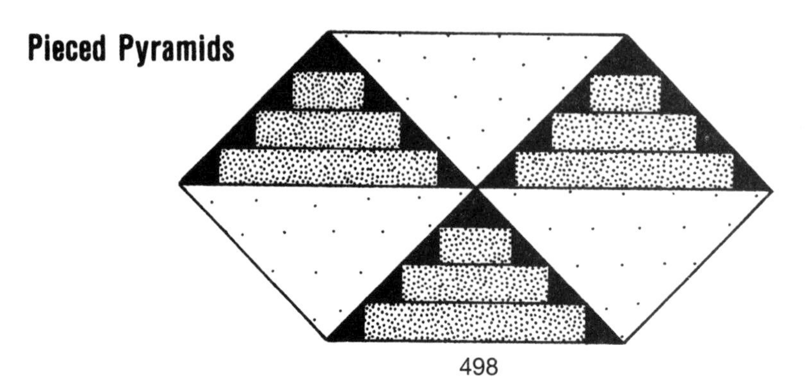
498

Pieced Star Variation 2
Octagonal Star, Var. 2

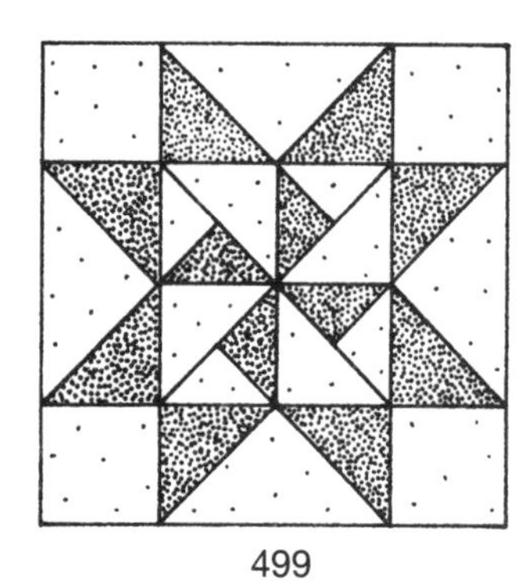
499

Pigeon Toes

500

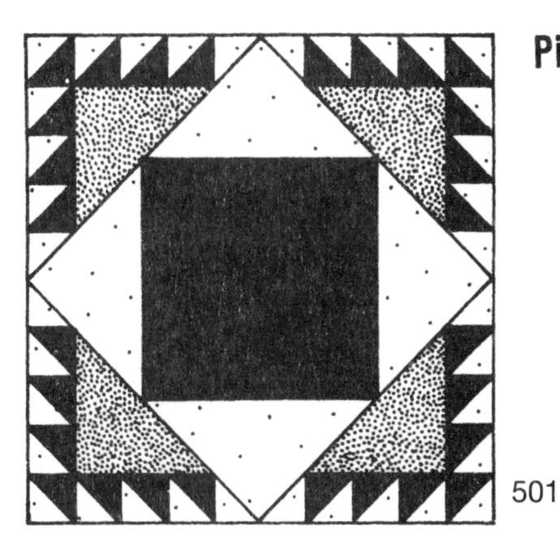

Pine Burr

501

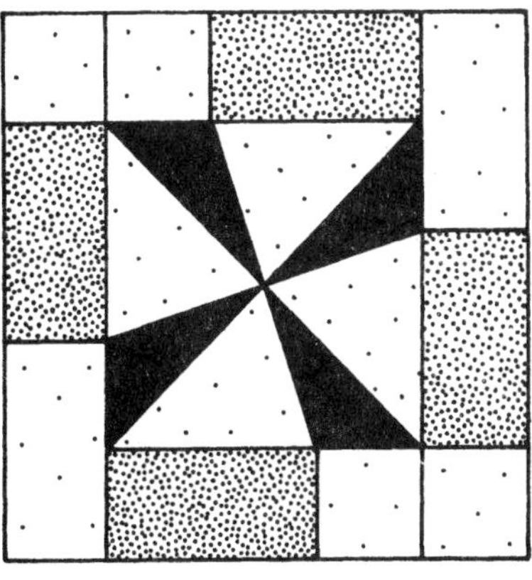

Pinwheel Skew 504

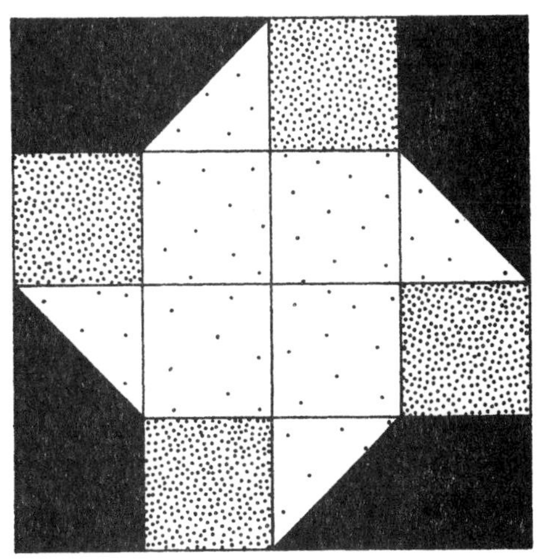

502

Pinwheel Variation 2
Crow's Foot, Var. 2
Fan Mill, Var. 2
Flutter Wheels, Var. 2
Fly, Var. 2
Foot
Kathy's Ramble, Var. 2
Sugar Bowl, Var. 2

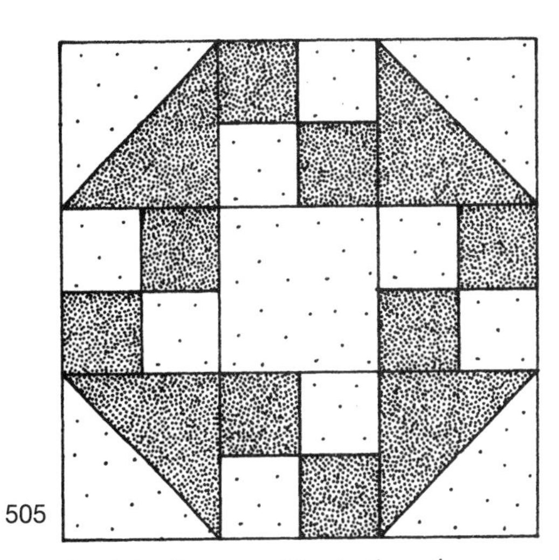

505

Prairie Queen Variation 1

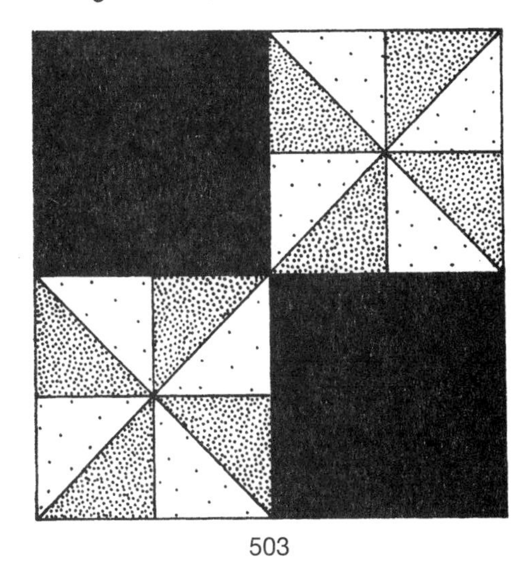

Pinwheels

503

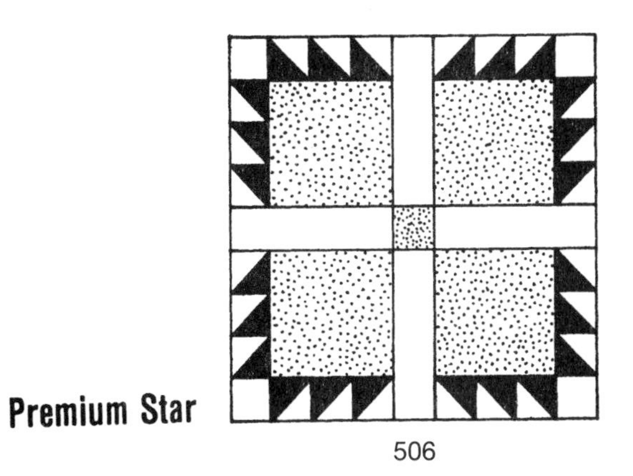

Premium Star

506

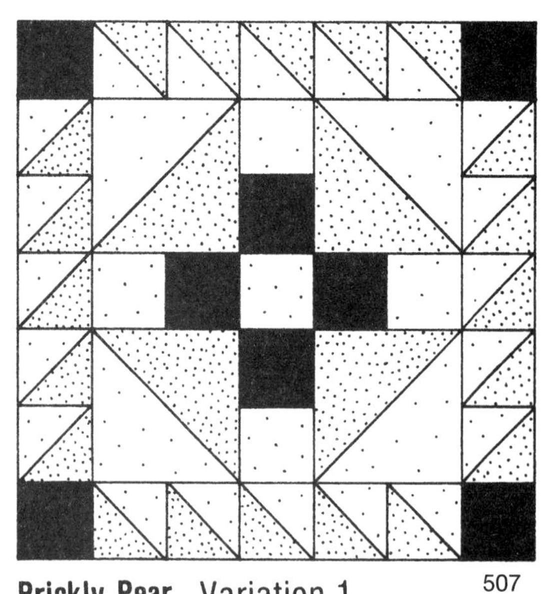

Prickly Pear Variation 1 507

Puss in the Corner
Variation 1
Kitty Corner, Var. 2
Tic Tac Toe, Var. 2

510

Primrose Path 508

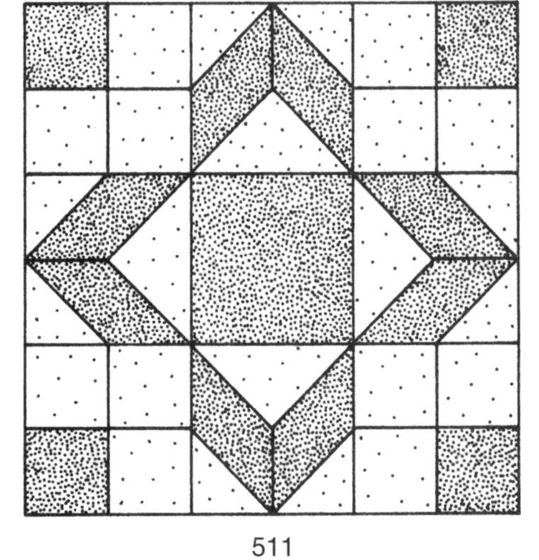

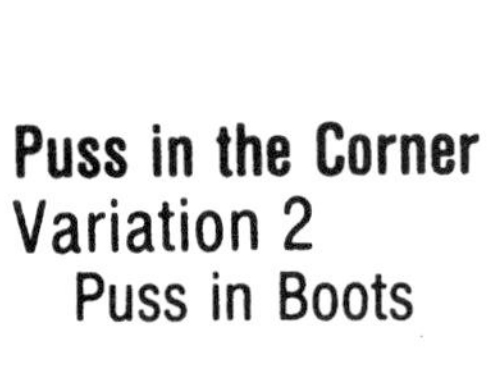

Puss in the Corner
Variation 2
Puss in Boots

511

Propellor

509

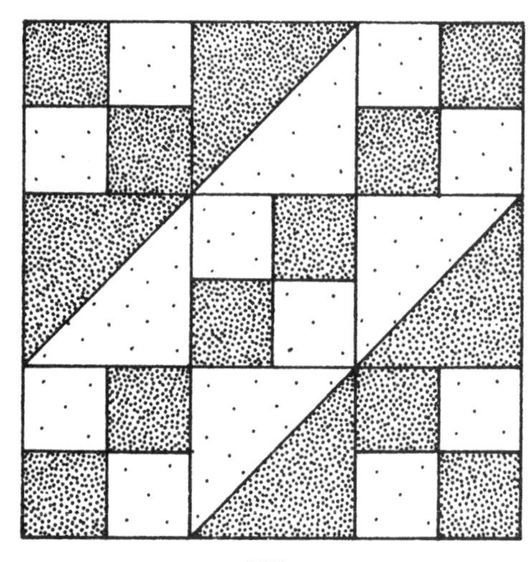

Railroad

512

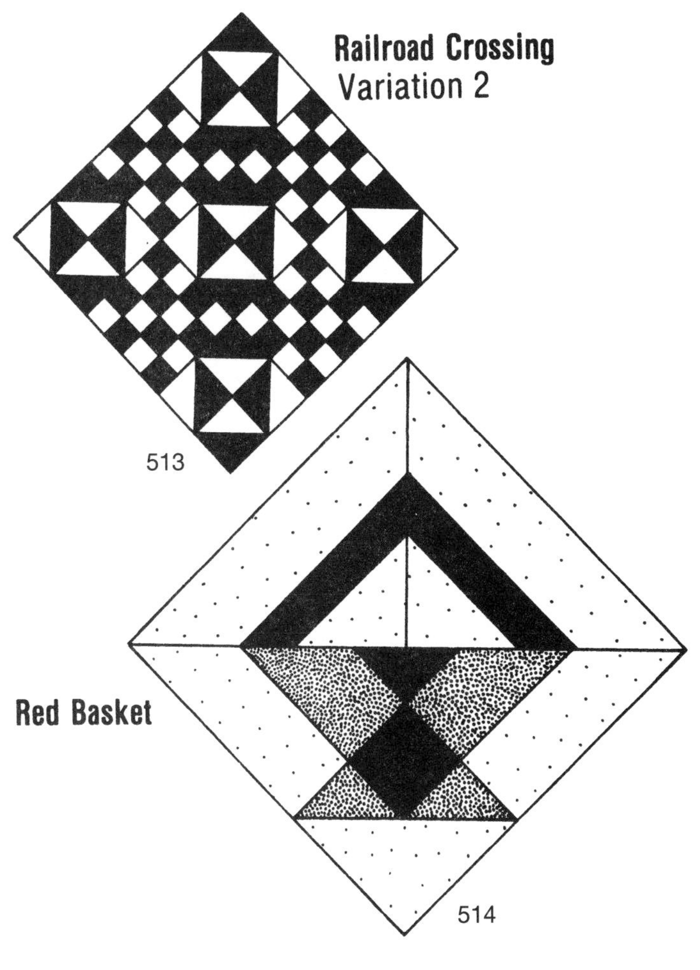

Railroad Crossing
Variation 2

513

Red Basket

514

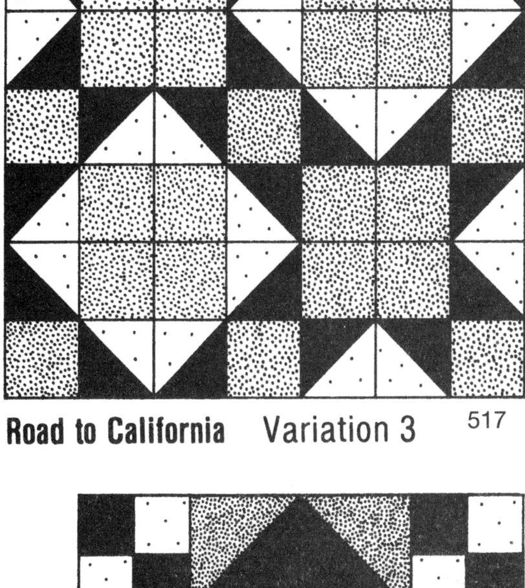

Road to California Variation 3

517

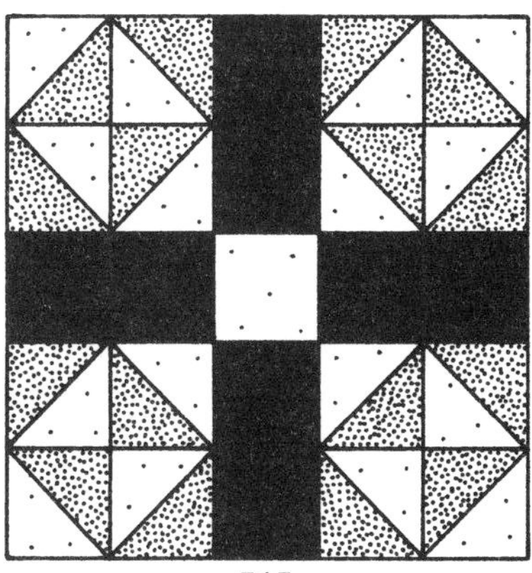

Red Cross
Variation 1

515

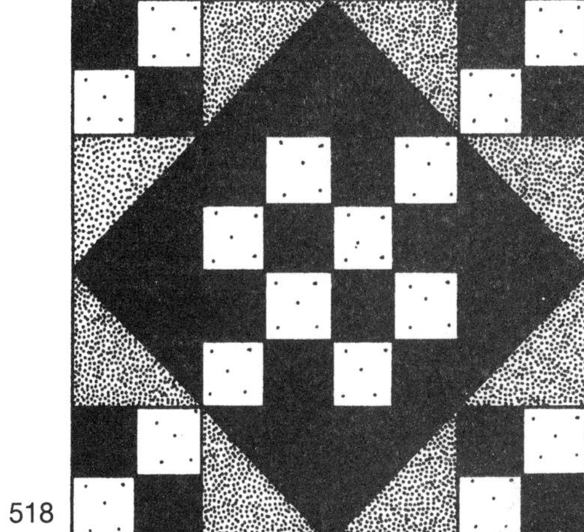

518

Road to California Variation 4

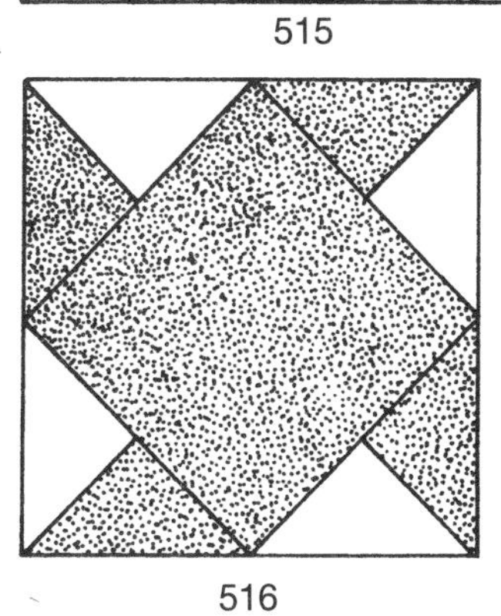

Right and Left

516

Robbing Peter to Pay Paul
Variation 1

519

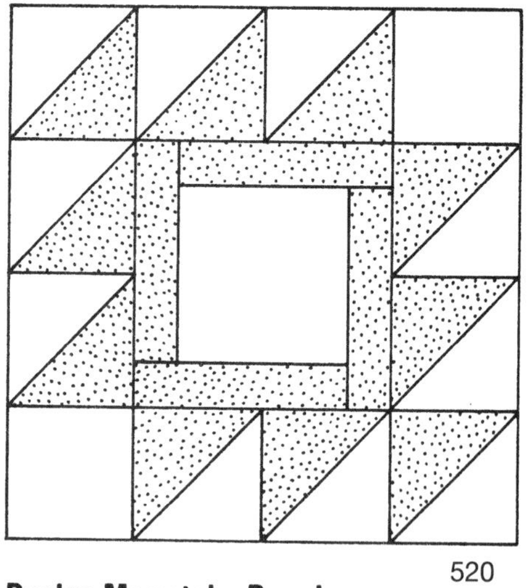

520

Rocky Mountain Puzzle

Sawtooth Variation 3

523

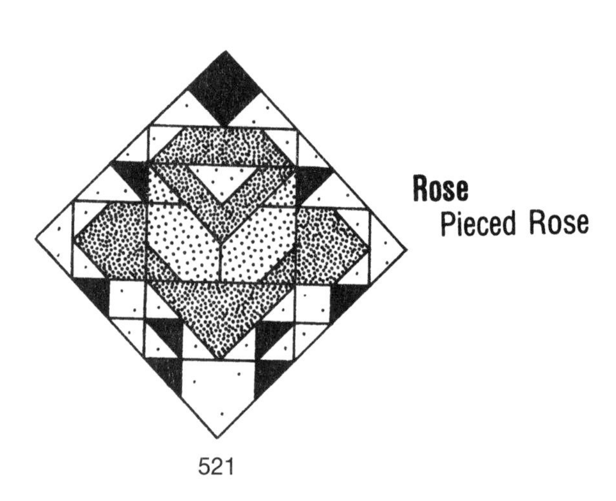

Rose Pieced Rose

521

Secret Drawer

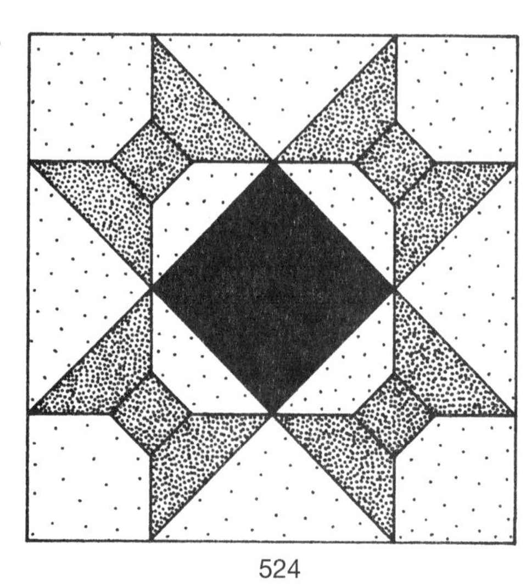

524

Shadows

522

Royal Cross

525

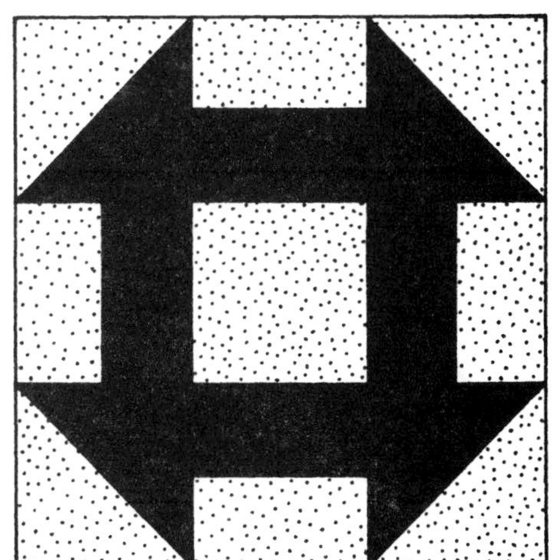
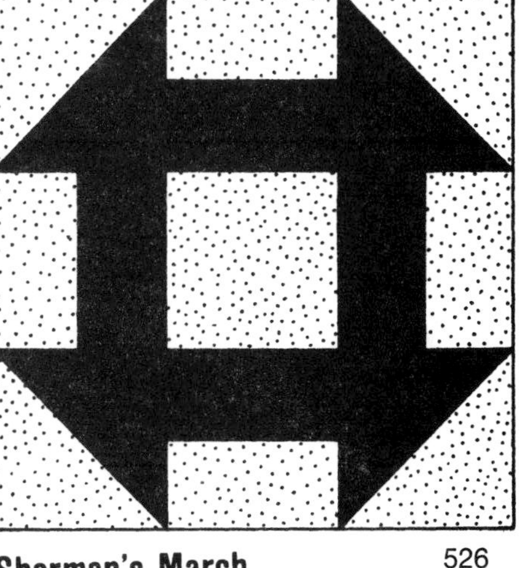

526

Sherman's March
Barn Door
Double Monkey Wrench
Hole in the Barn Door
Lincoln's Platform
Love Knot
Monkey Wrench, Var. 2
Quail's Nest

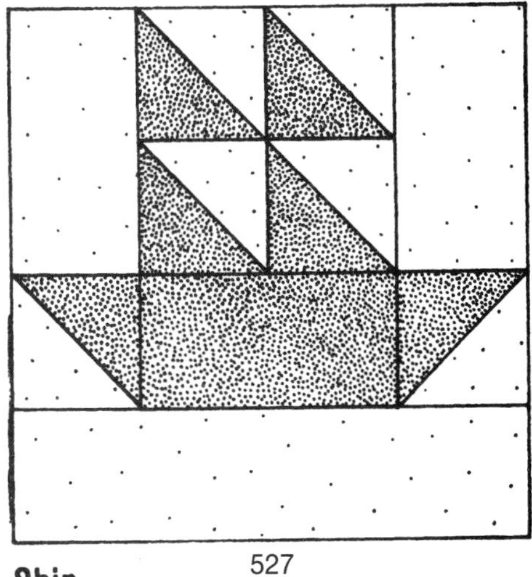

527

Ship

528

Shoofly Variation 1
Chinese Coin
Grandmother's Choice, Var. 2
Star Spangled Banner

Sister's Choice
Five-Patch Star
Four-X Star

529

Square and a Half

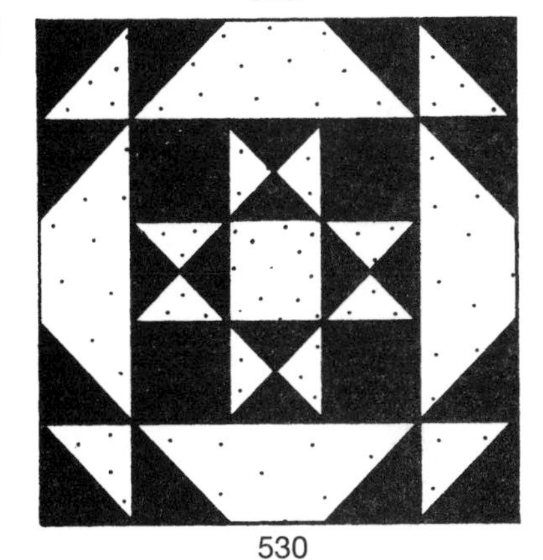

530

Square Within Squares

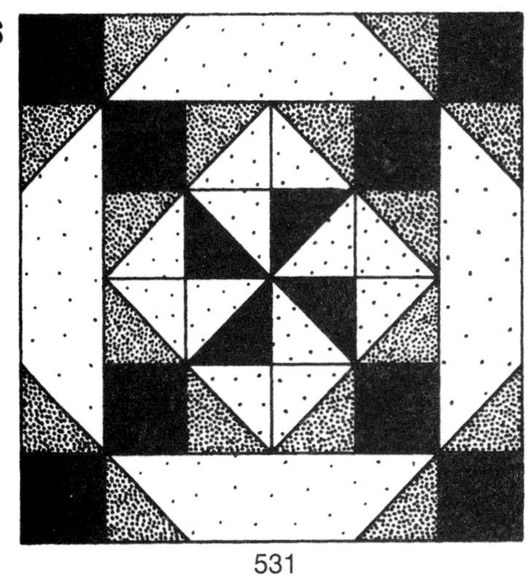

531

Star of Hope
Variation 1

532

Starry Lane

533

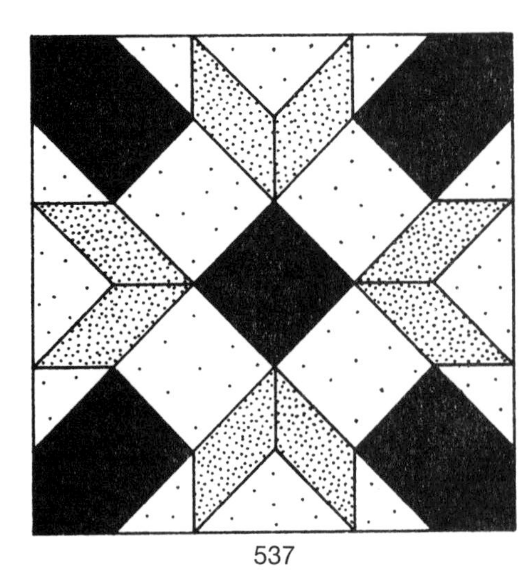

Swing in the Center
Variation 1

537

Stepping Stones
Variation 3

534

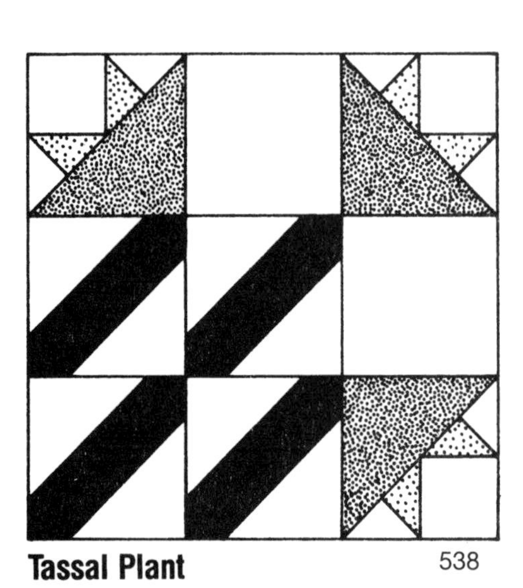

Tassal Plant

538

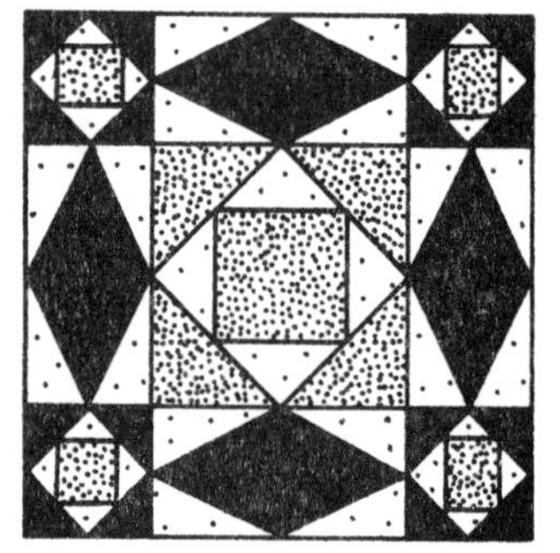

Storm at Sea Variation 2
Rolling Stone, Var. 1

535

T-Blocks Variation 2

539

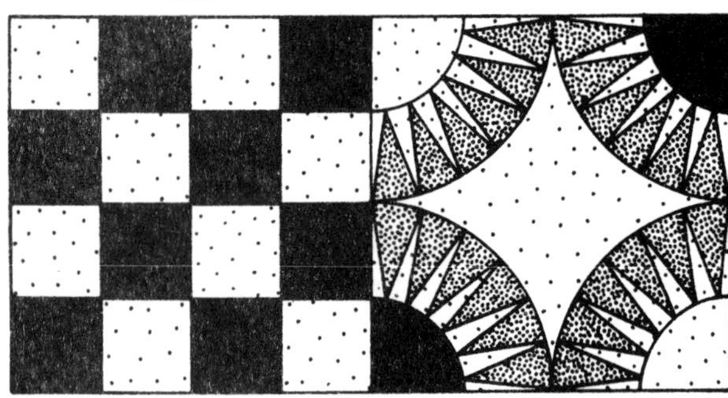

Suspension Bridge

536

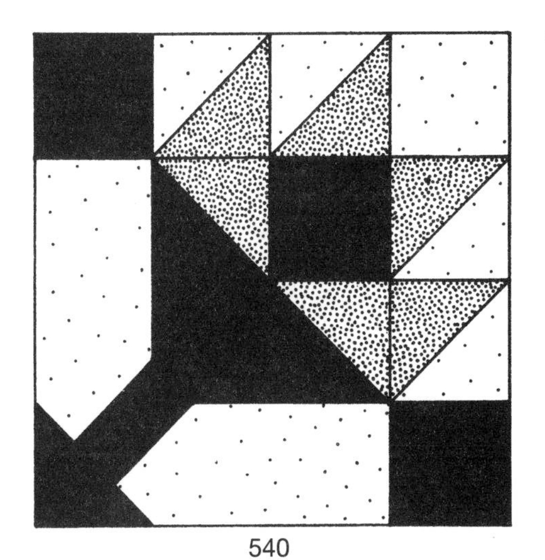
540

Tea Basket

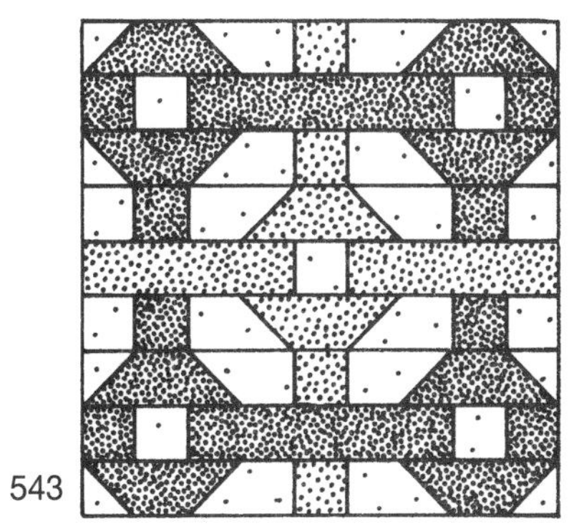
543

Tile Puzzle Variation 2

Thelma's Choice

541

Toad in the Puddle Variation 1

544

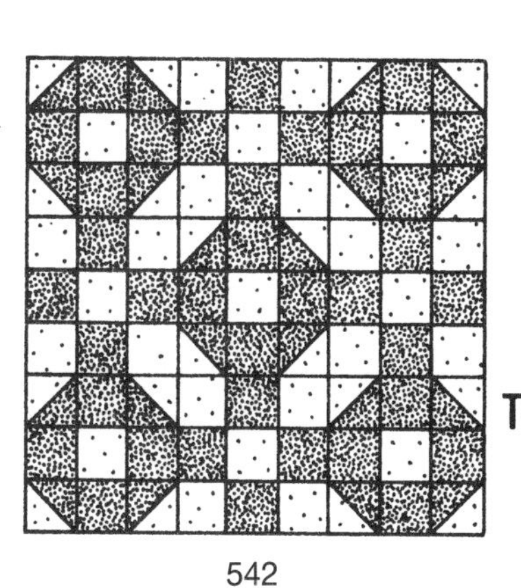

Tile Puzzle Variation 1
Improved Nine-Patch, Var. 2
Puzzled Tile

542

Toad in the Puddle
Variation 2
Double Square, Var. 2
Jack in the Pulpit

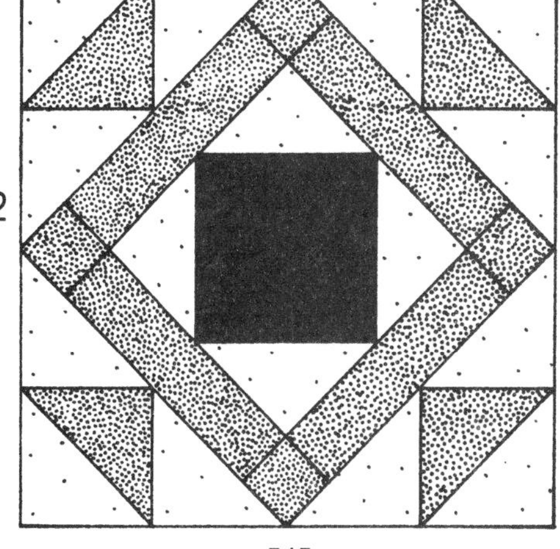
545

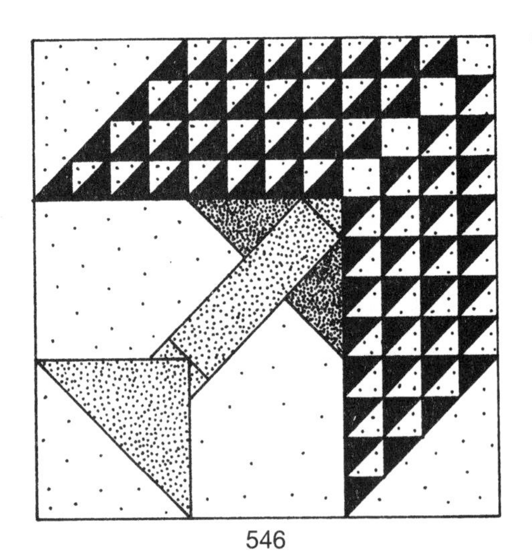
546

Tree of Life Variation 1
Pine Tree, Var. 1

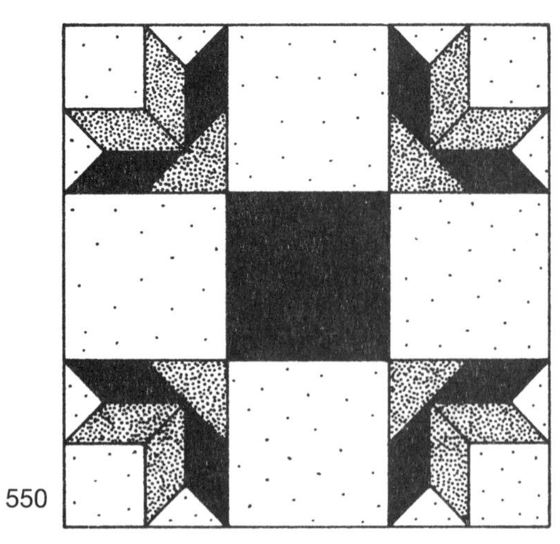
550

Turkey Tracks Variation 2
Sage Bud

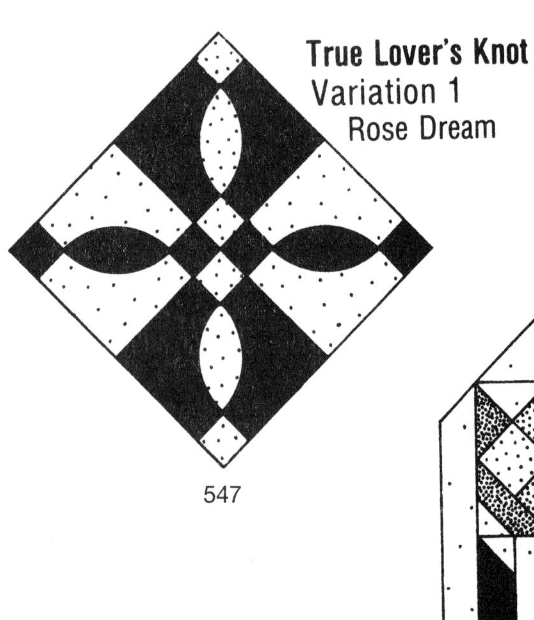
547

True Lover's Knot Variation 1
Rose Dream

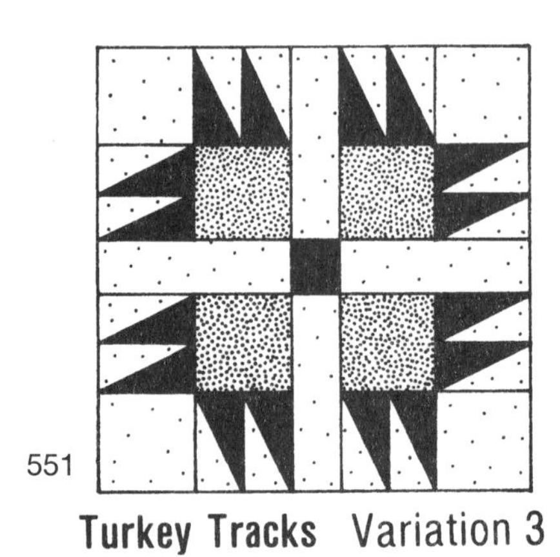
551

Turkey Tracks Variation 3

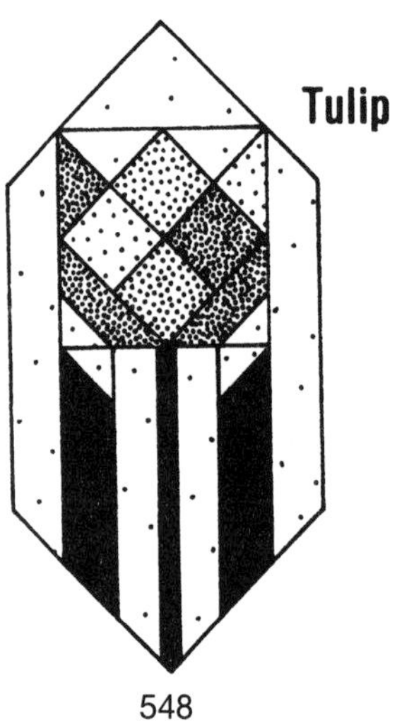
548

Tulip

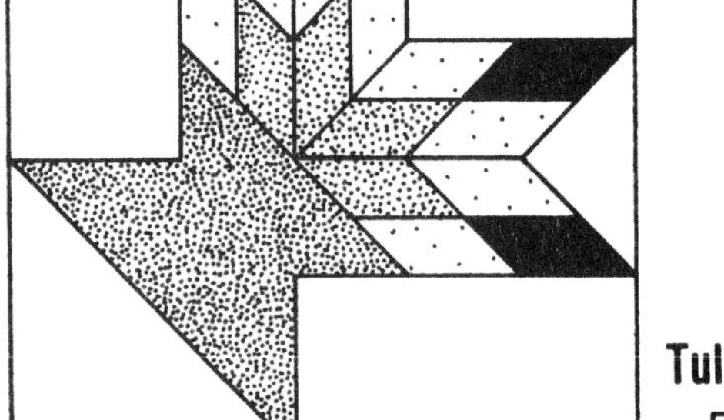
549

Tulip Basket
Flower Pot, Var. 2

552

Turnabout T

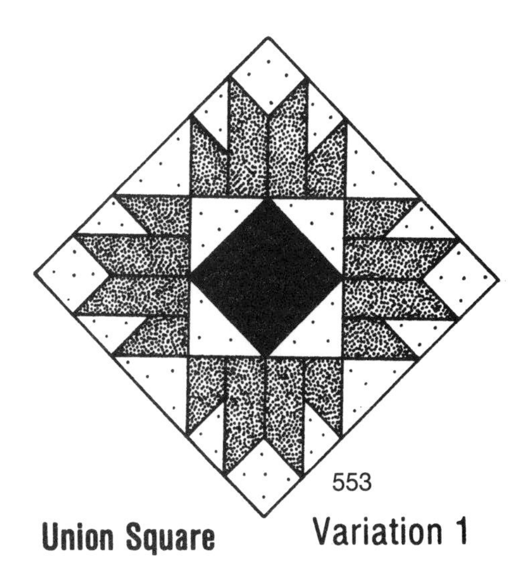
553

Union Square Variation 1

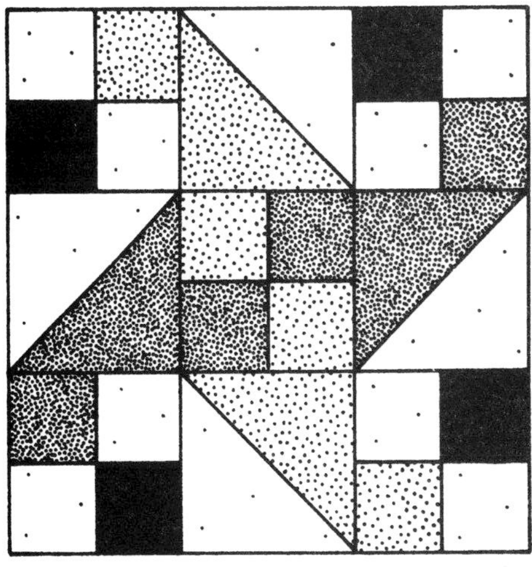
Water Wheel Variation 3 556

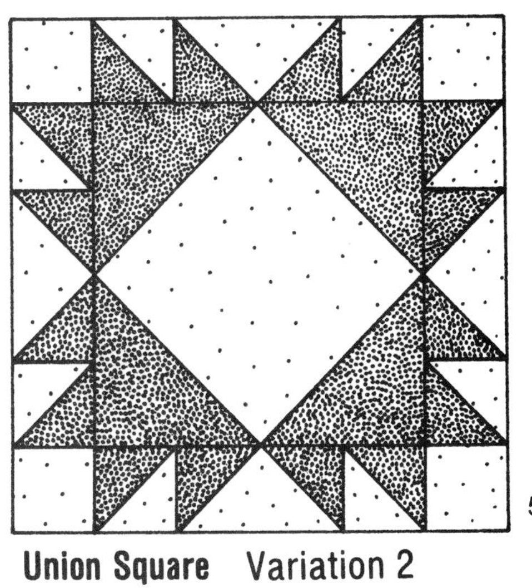
554

Union Square Variation 2

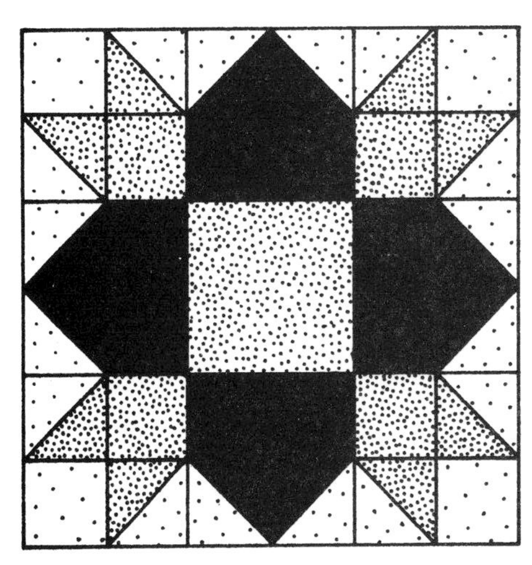
Weather Vane Variation 2 557

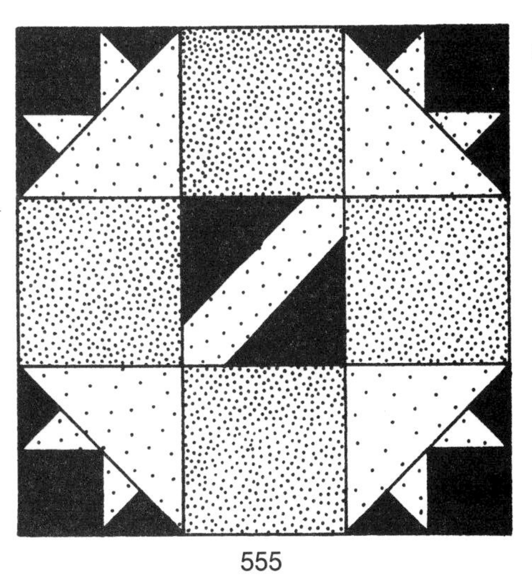
W.C.T.U.

555

Weather Vane Variation 3

558

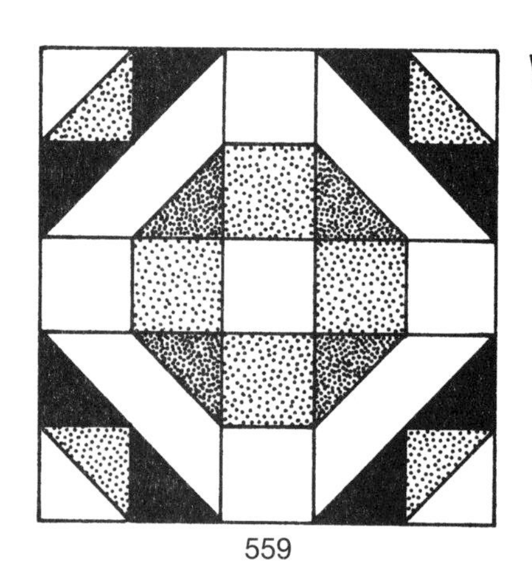

Wedding Rings

559

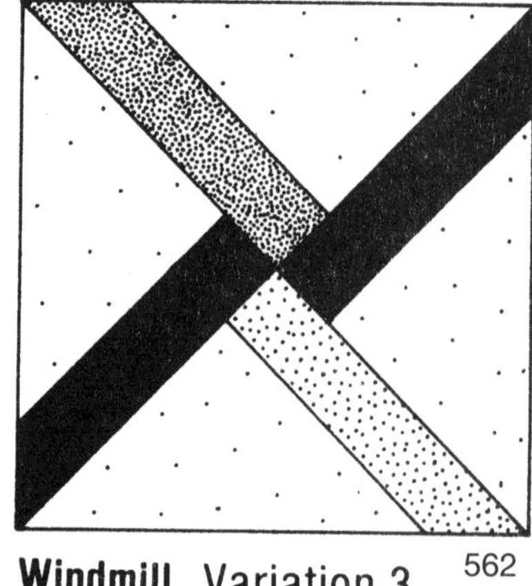

Windmill Variation 3 562

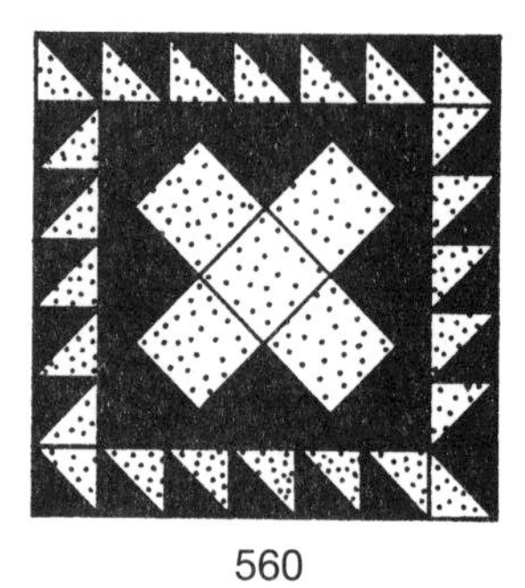

White Cross

560

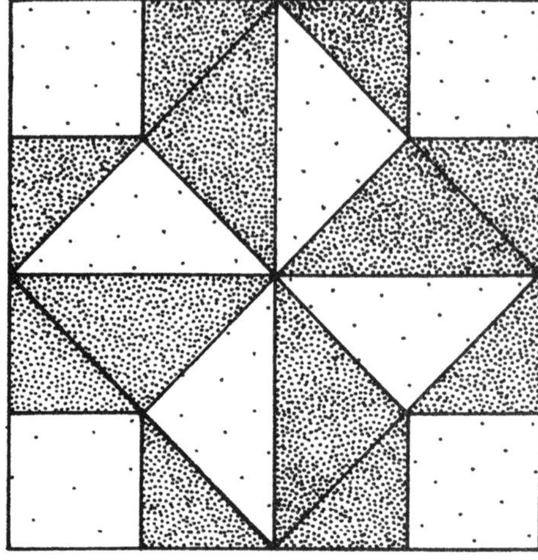

Windmill Variation 5

563

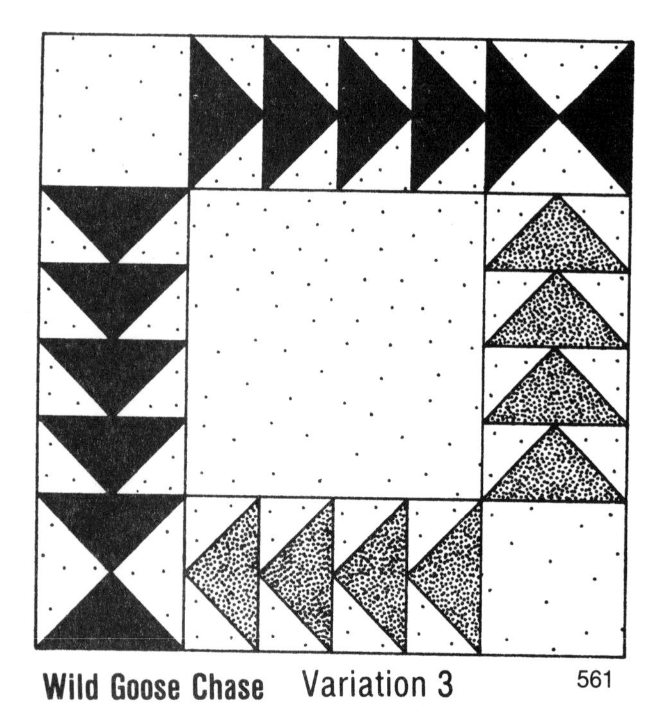

Wild Goose Chase Variation 3 561

Wishing Ring 564

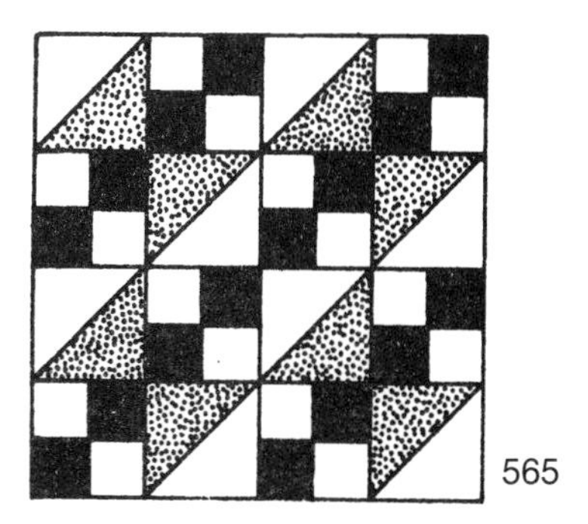

565

World's Fair Variation 1

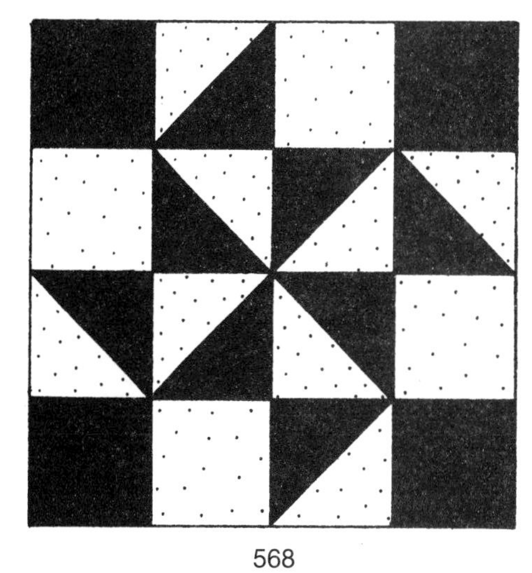

X-Quartet

568

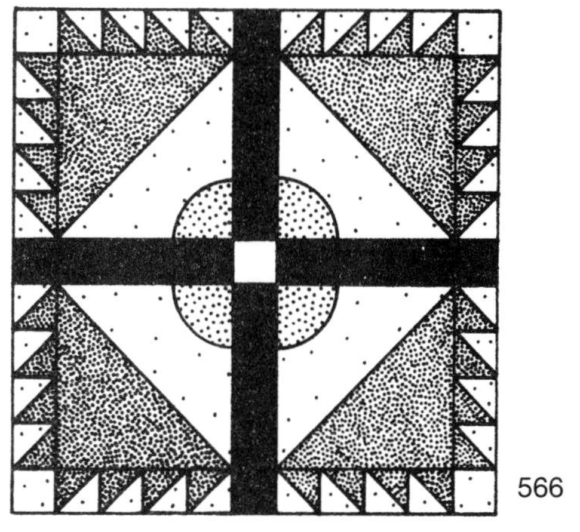

566

World's Fair Variation 2

X-Quisite

569

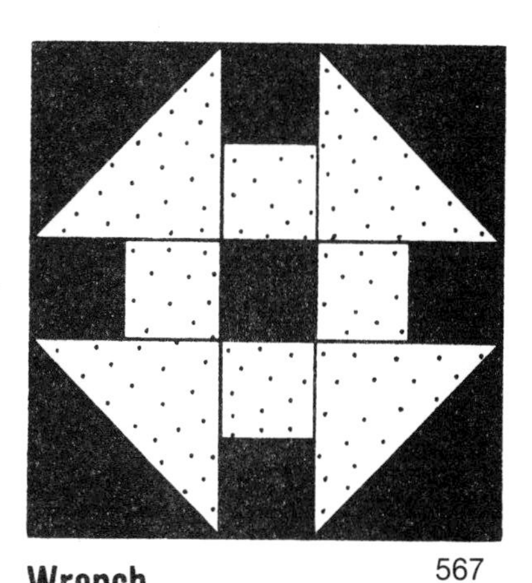

Wrench

567

Young Man's Fancy

Goose in the Pond, Var. 2

Mrs. Wolf's Red Beauty

570

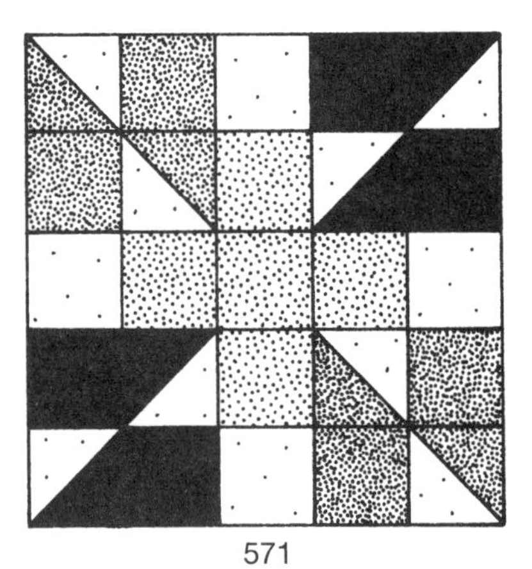

Z-Cross

571

Grandmother's Choice
Variation 1

574

SUPPLEMENT

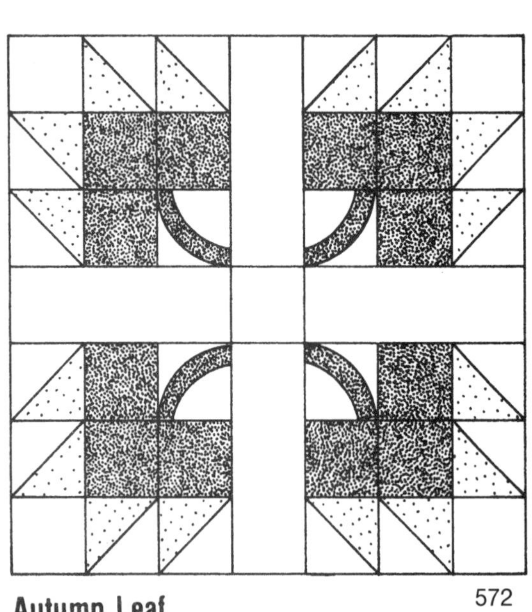

Autumn Leaf

572

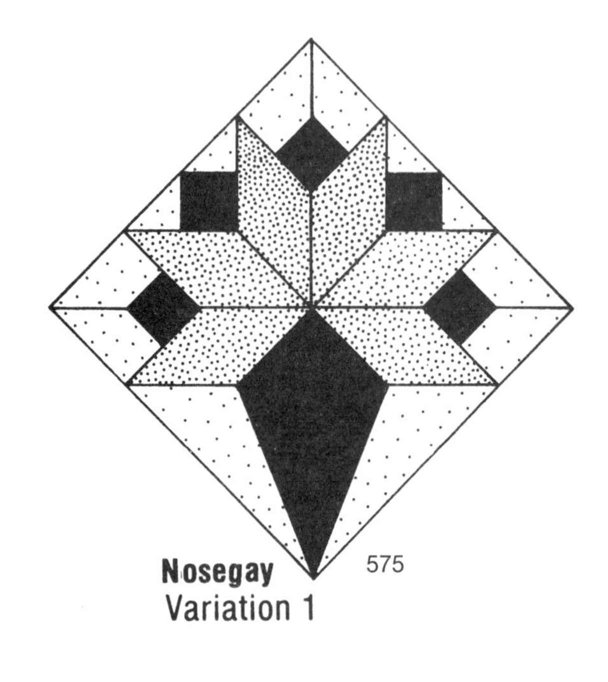

Nosegay
Variation 1

575

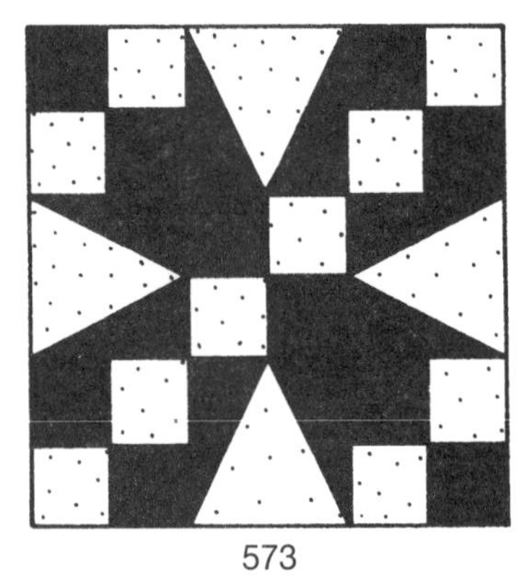

54-40 or Fight

573

St. Gregory's Cross

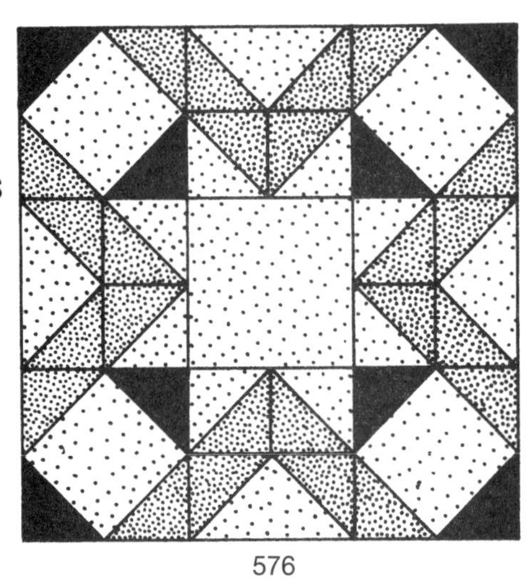

576

Squares

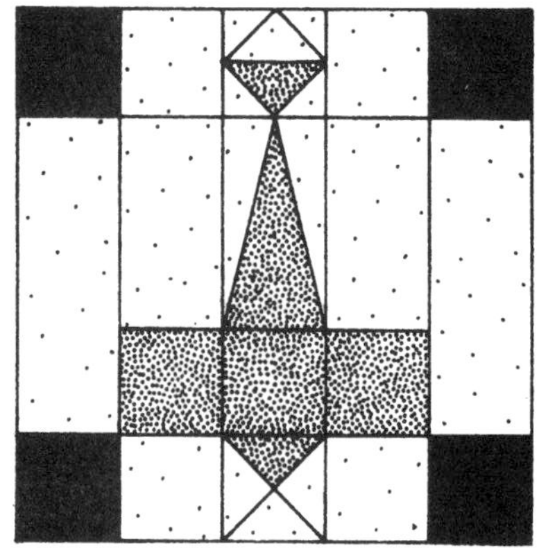
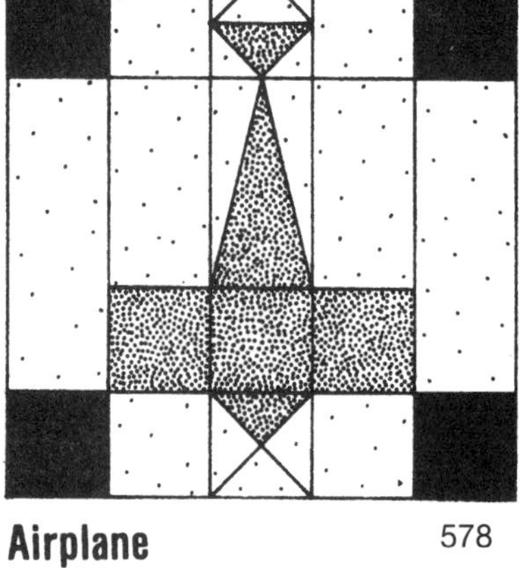

Airplane 578

Autumn Tints
Four-Patch, Var. 3

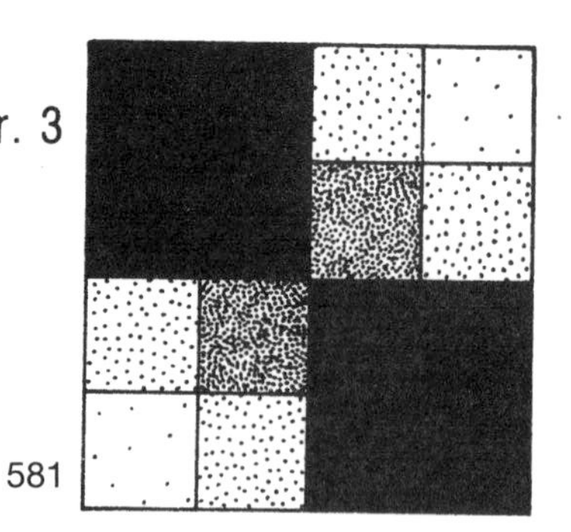

581

Baby Blocks Variation 1
Boxes, Var. 1
Cubework
Heavenly Stairs
Heavenly Steps
Pandora's Box
Tumbling Blocks

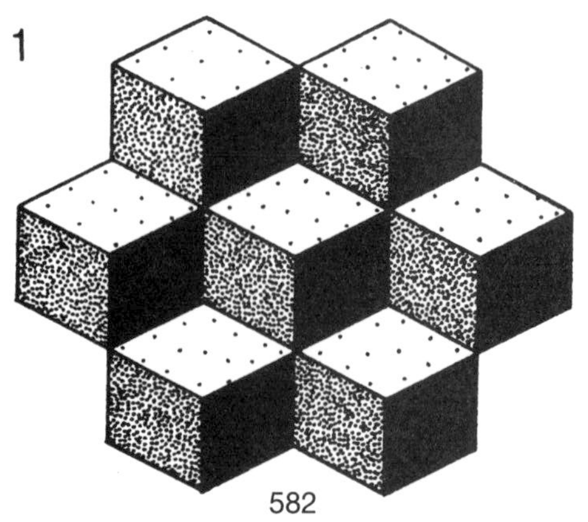

582

579

Album
Variation 3

Bachelor's Puzzle
Variation 1

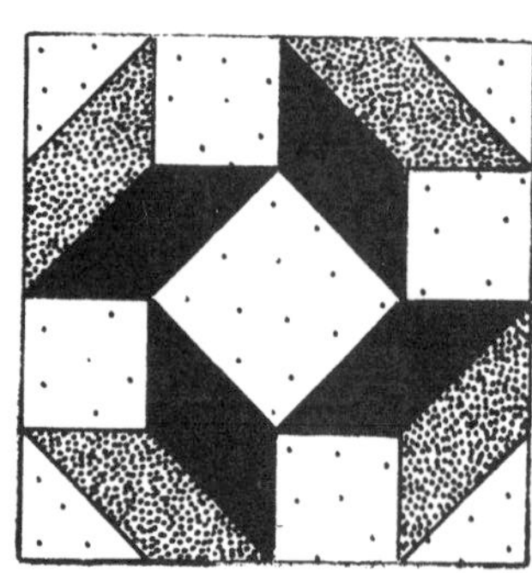

583

Album Patch

580

Bachelor's Puzzle Variation 2 584

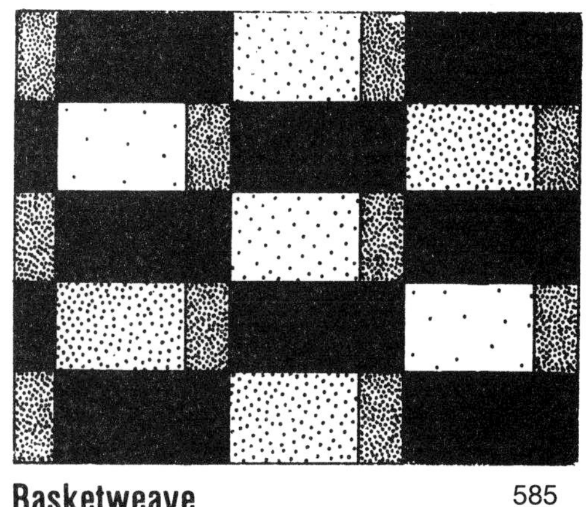

Basketweave 585

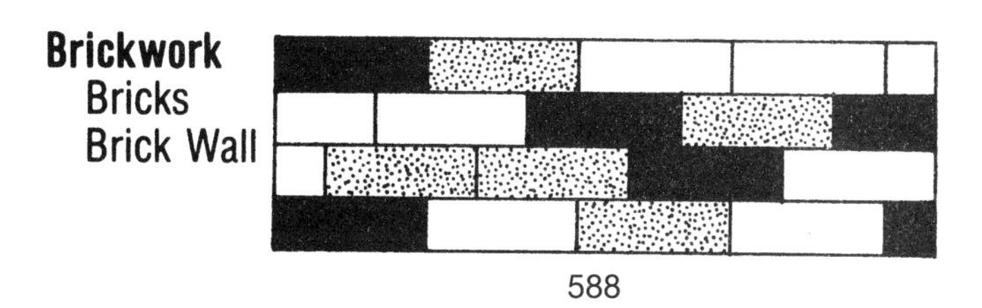

Brickwork
Bricks
Brick Wall

588

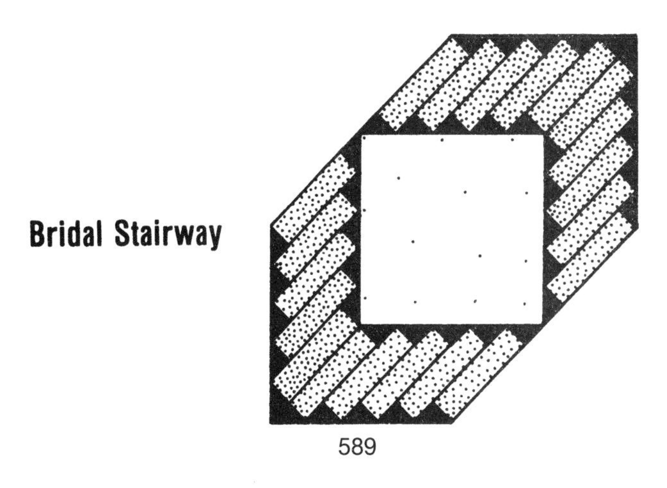

Bridal Stairway

589

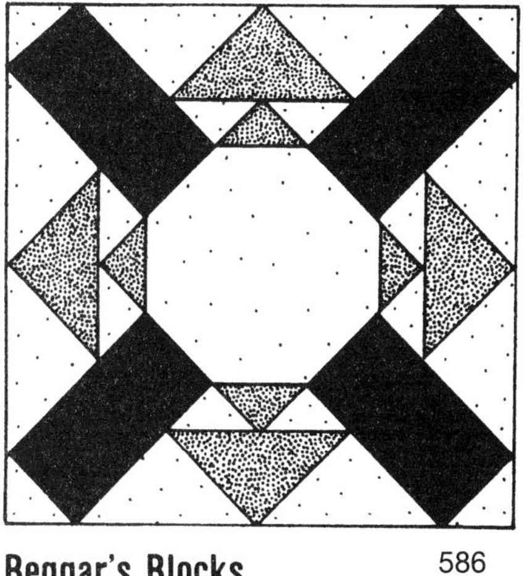

Beggar's Blocks 586
All Kinds

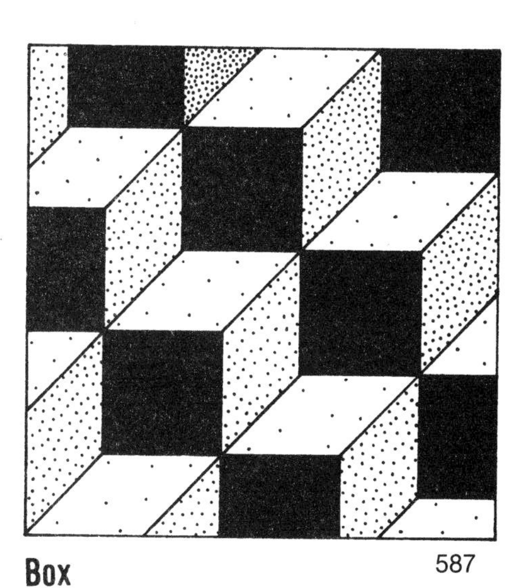

Box 587

Burgoyne Surrounded
Burgoyne's Quilt
Road to California, Var. 2
Wheel of Fortune, Var. 2

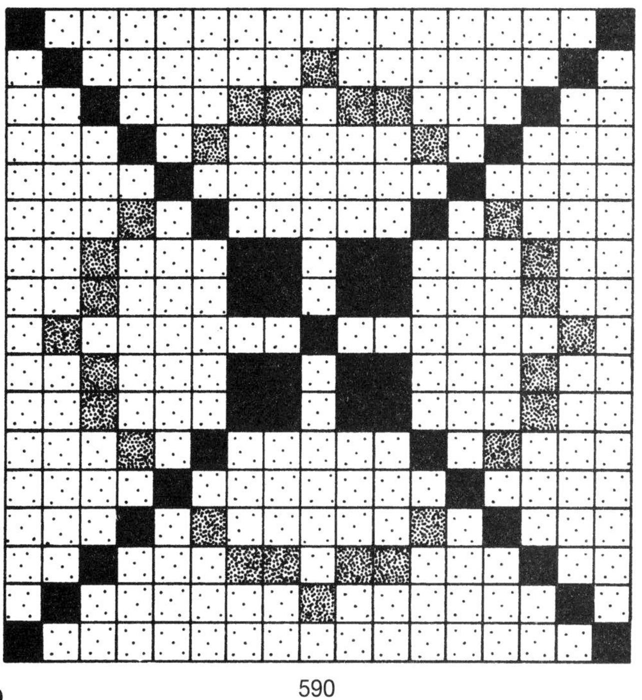

590

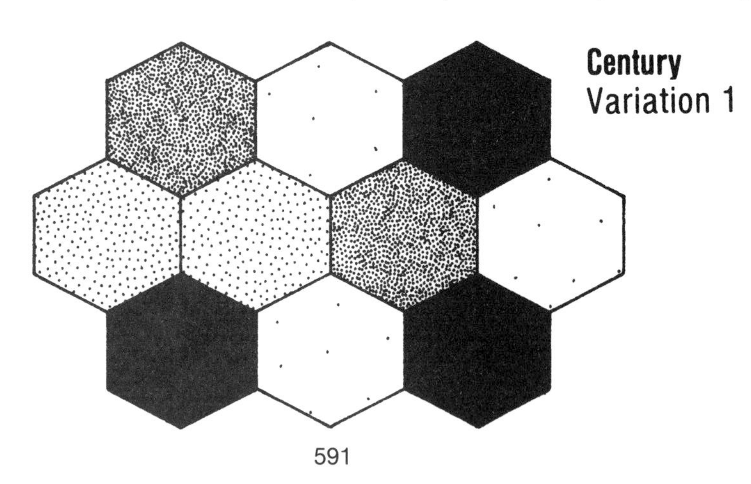

591

Century
Variation 1

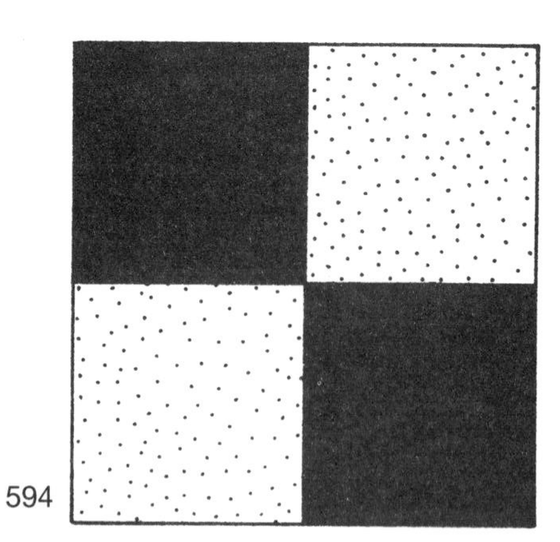

594

Checkerboard Variation 2

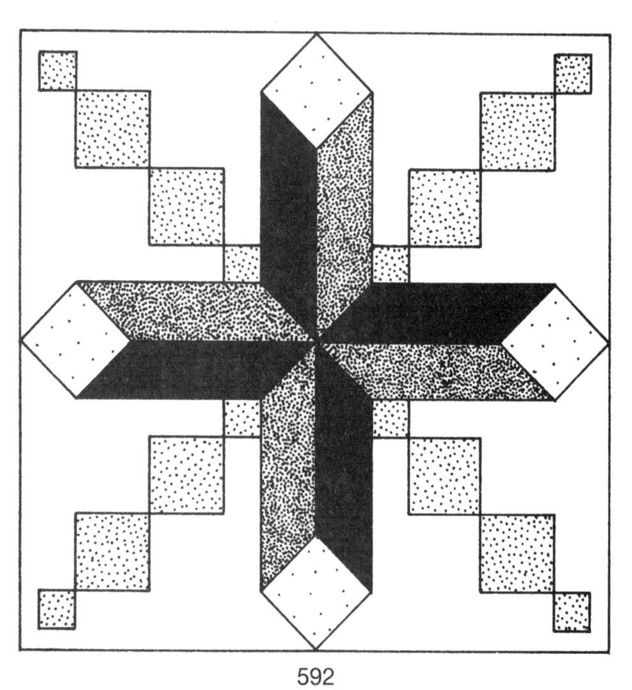

592

Century of Progress

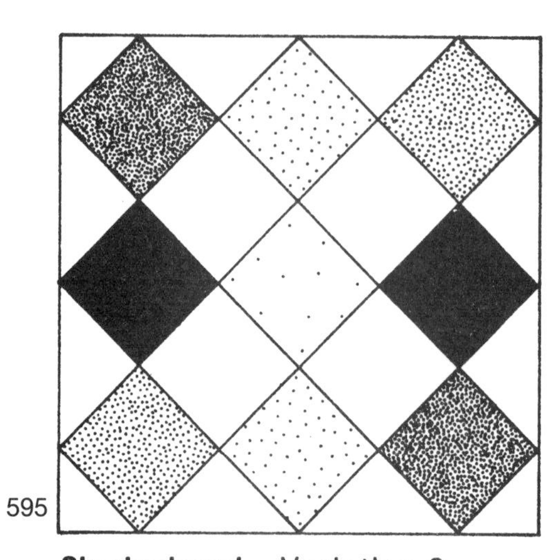

595

Checkerboard Variation 3

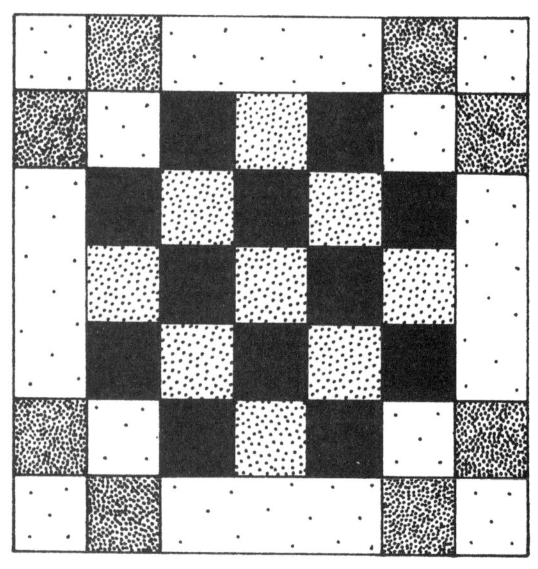

593

Chained Five-Patch

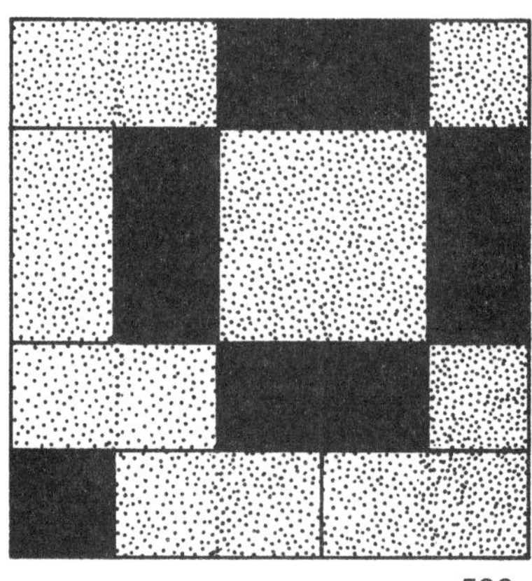

Children's Delight 596

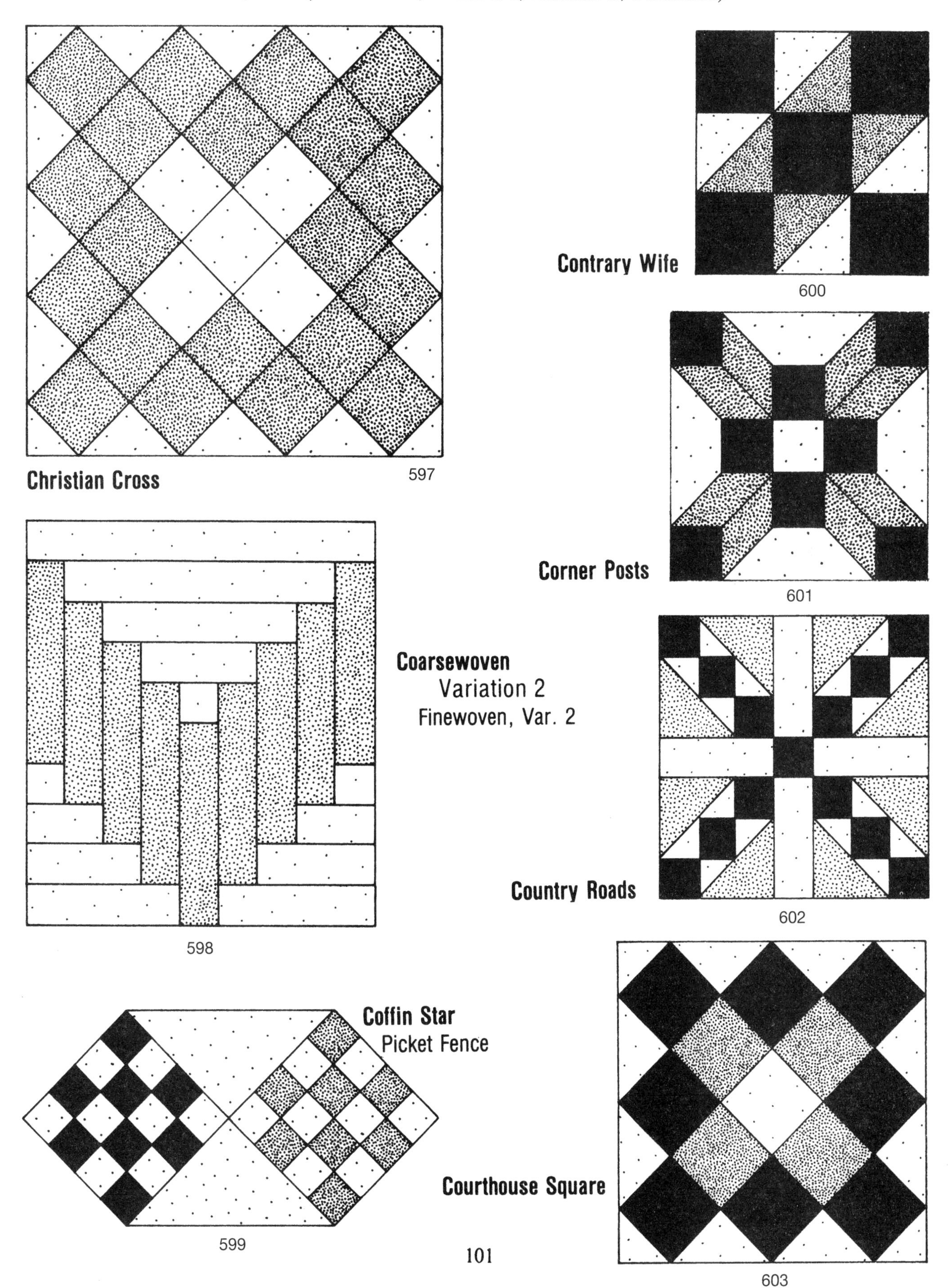
Christian Cross
597
Contrary Wife
600
Corner Posts
601
Coarsewoven
Variation 2
Finewoven, Var. 2
598
Country Roads
602
Coffin Star
Picket Fence
599
Courthouse Square
603

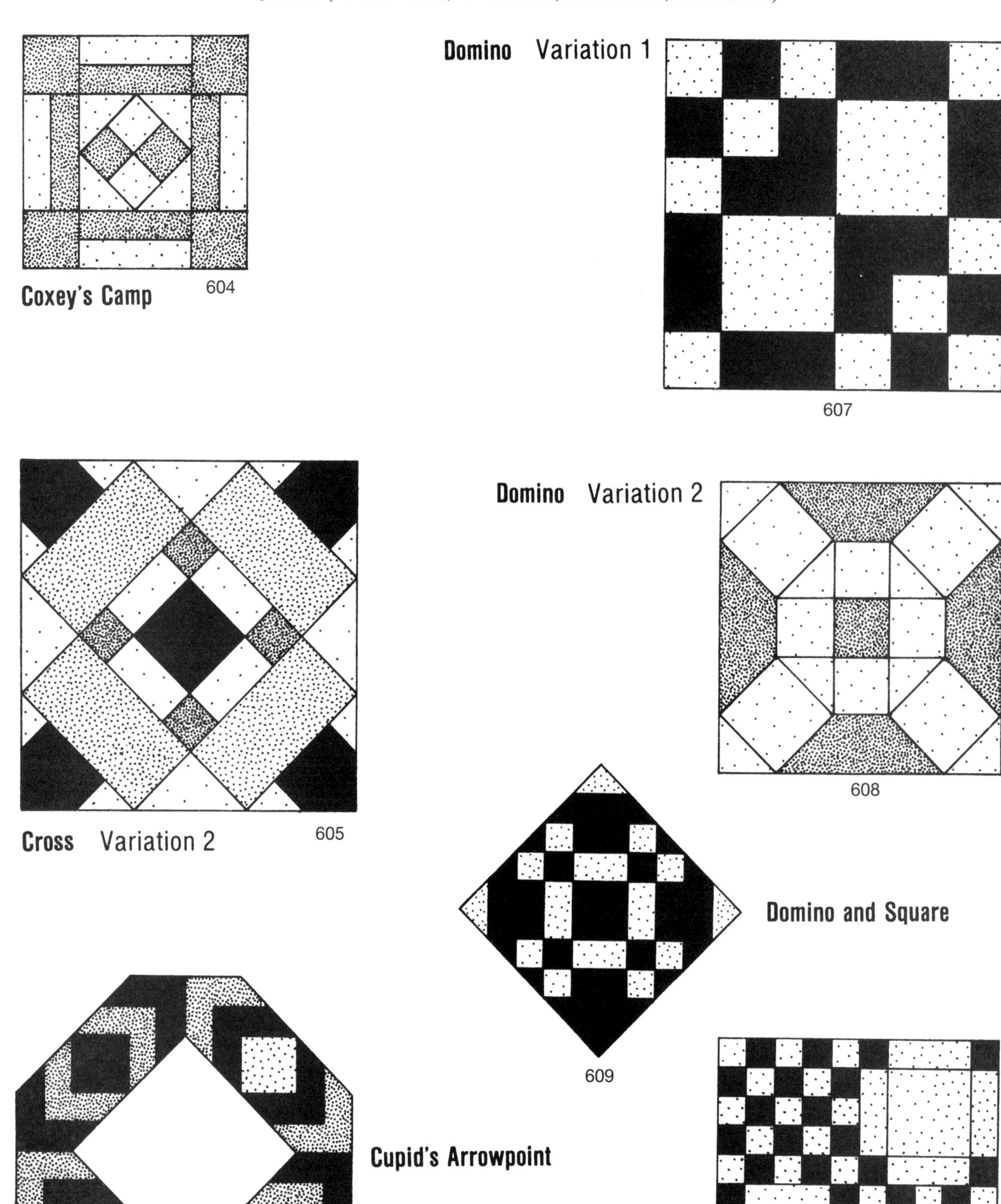

Coxey's Camp 604

Domino Variation 1

607

Domino Variation 2

608

Cross Variation 2 605

Domino and Square

609

Cupid's Arrowpoint

606

Double Irish Chain
Double Irish Cross

610

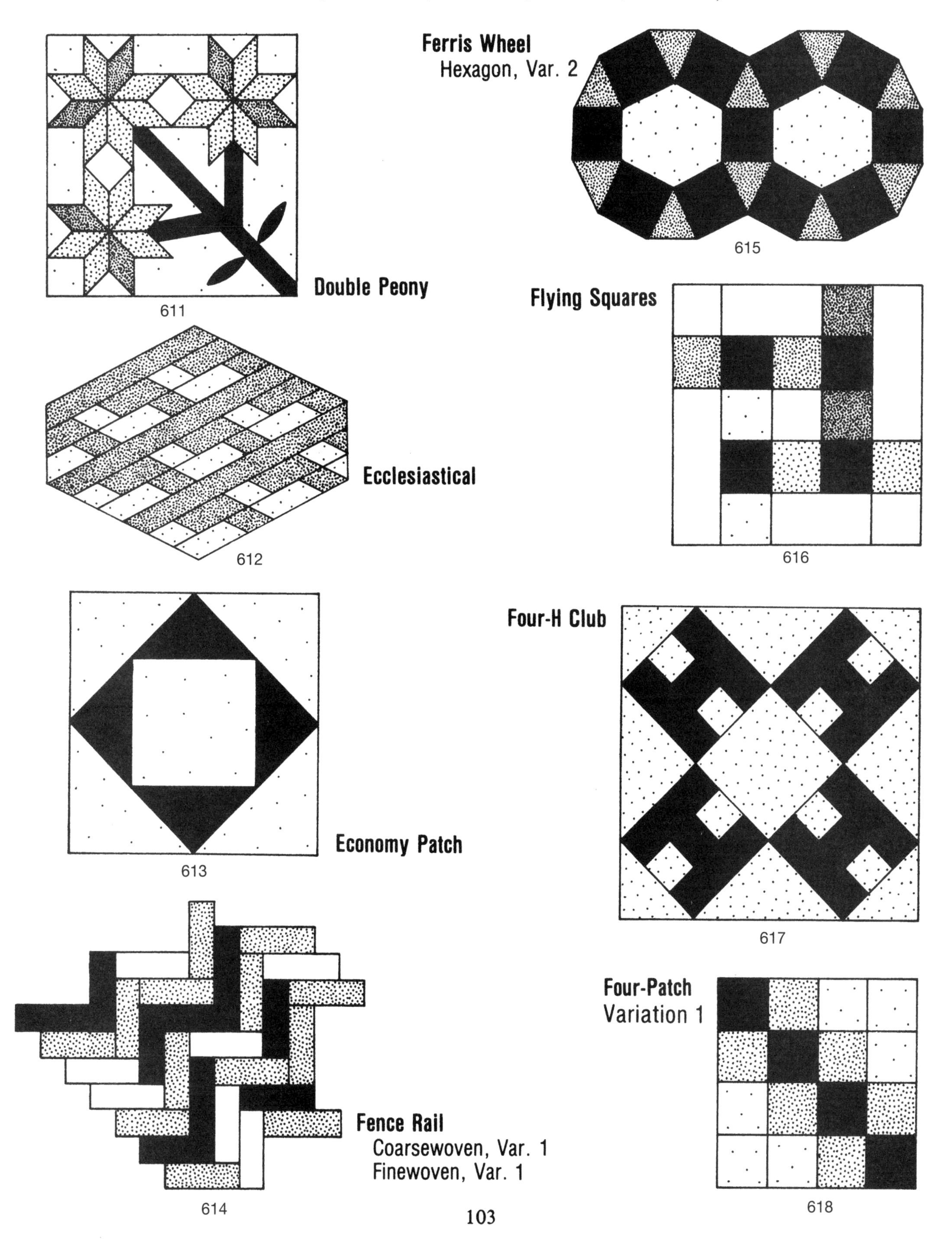

Double Peony

611

Ecclesiastical

612

Economy Patch

613

Fence Rail
Coarsewoven, Var. 1
Finewoven, Var. 1

614

Ferris Wheel
Hexagon, Var. 2

615

Flying Squares

616

Four-H Club

617

Four-Patch
Variation 1

618

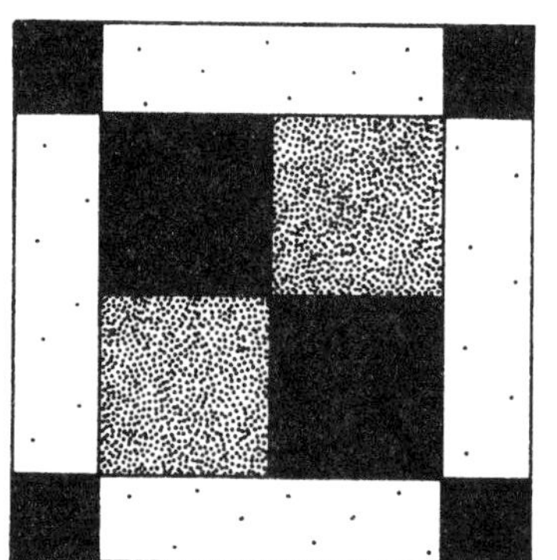
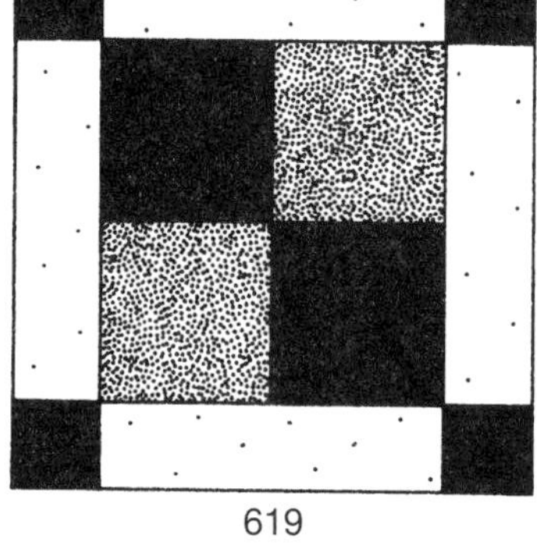

619

Four-Patch Variation 2

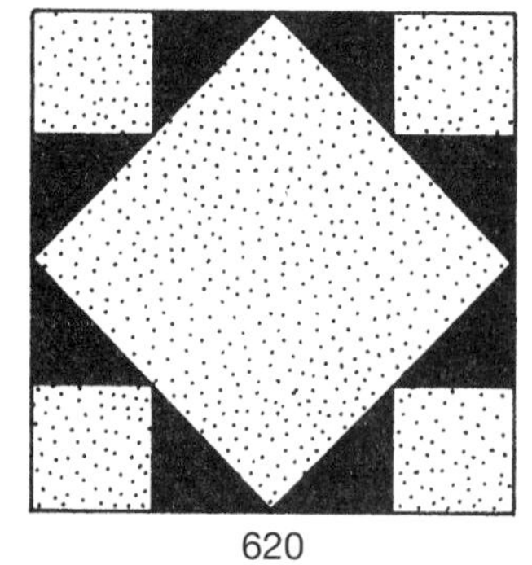

620

Four-Square

621

Friendship Square

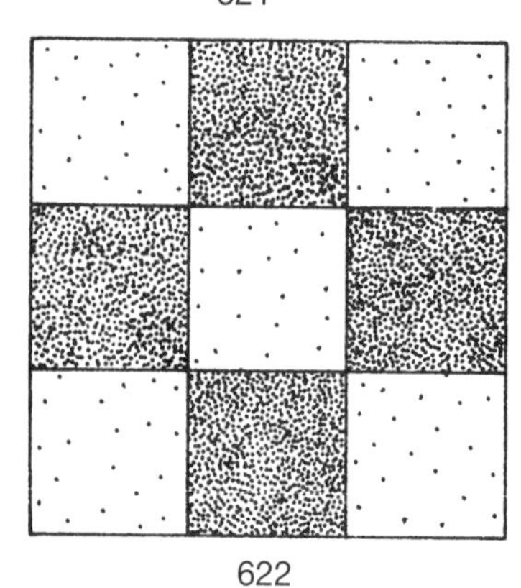

622

Fundamental Nine-Patch
Single Irish Chain

623

Garden Maze
Sun Dial
Tangled Garter
Tirzah's Treasure

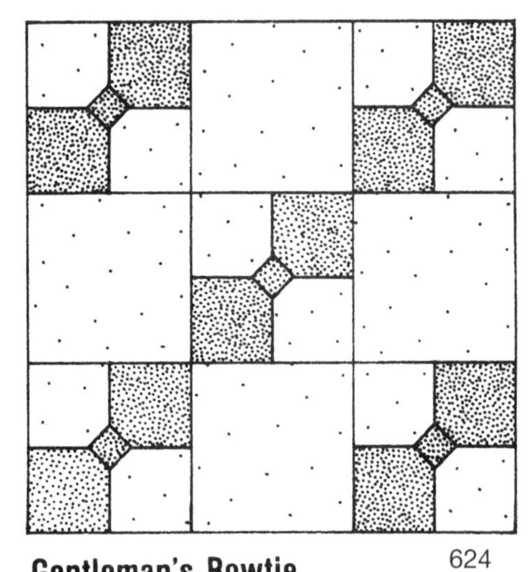

624

Gentleman's Bowtie
Bowtie
Joseph's Necktie

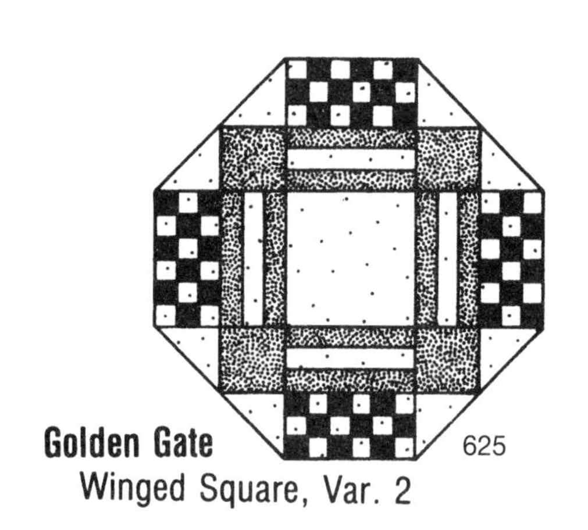

625

Golden Gate
Winged Square, Var. 2

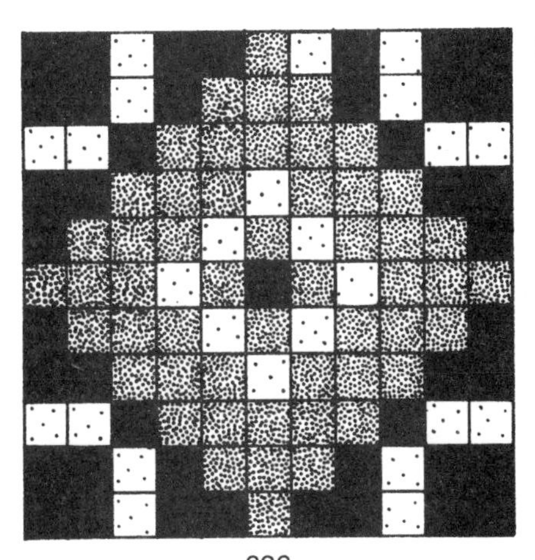

626

Golden Glow Variation 2

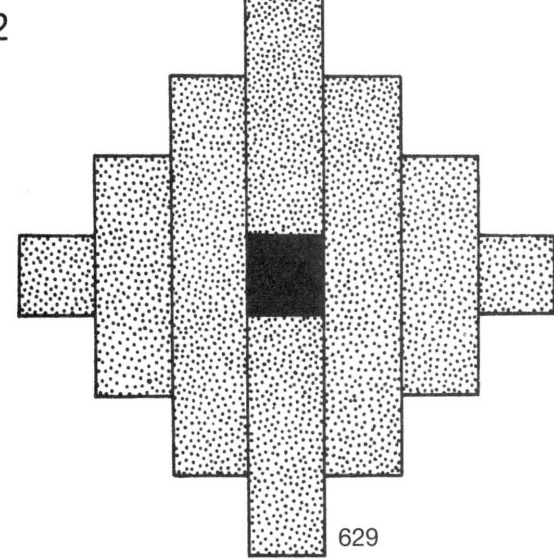

629

Granny's Flower Garden

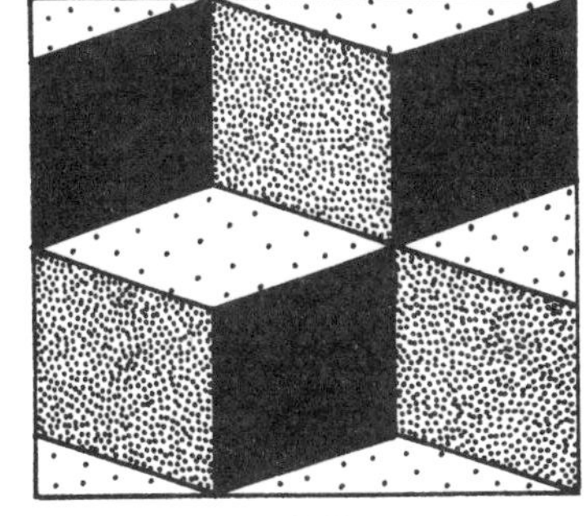

627

Grandma's Red and White

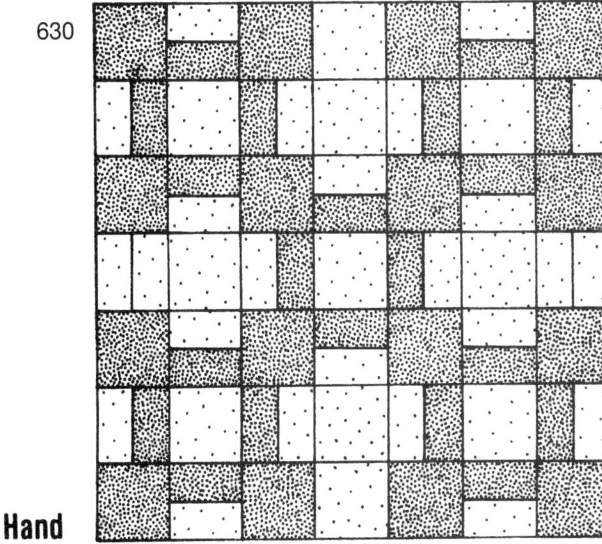

630

Grandmother's Flower Garden

Flower Garden
French Bouquet
Grandma's Garden
Honeycomb, Var. 1
Job's Troubles, Var. 1
Martha Washington's Flower Garden
Mosaic
Rainbow Tile
Rosette
Spider Web, Var. 1

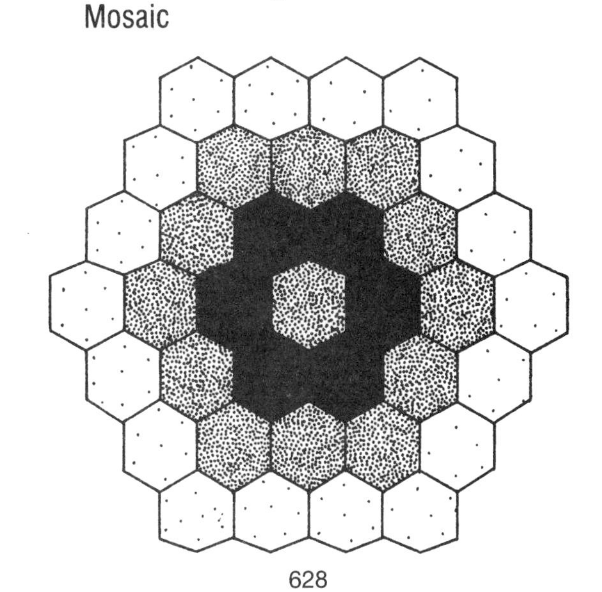

628

Hand

California Oak Leaf
Sassafras Leaf
True Lover's Knot, Var. 2

631

Hanging Diamond

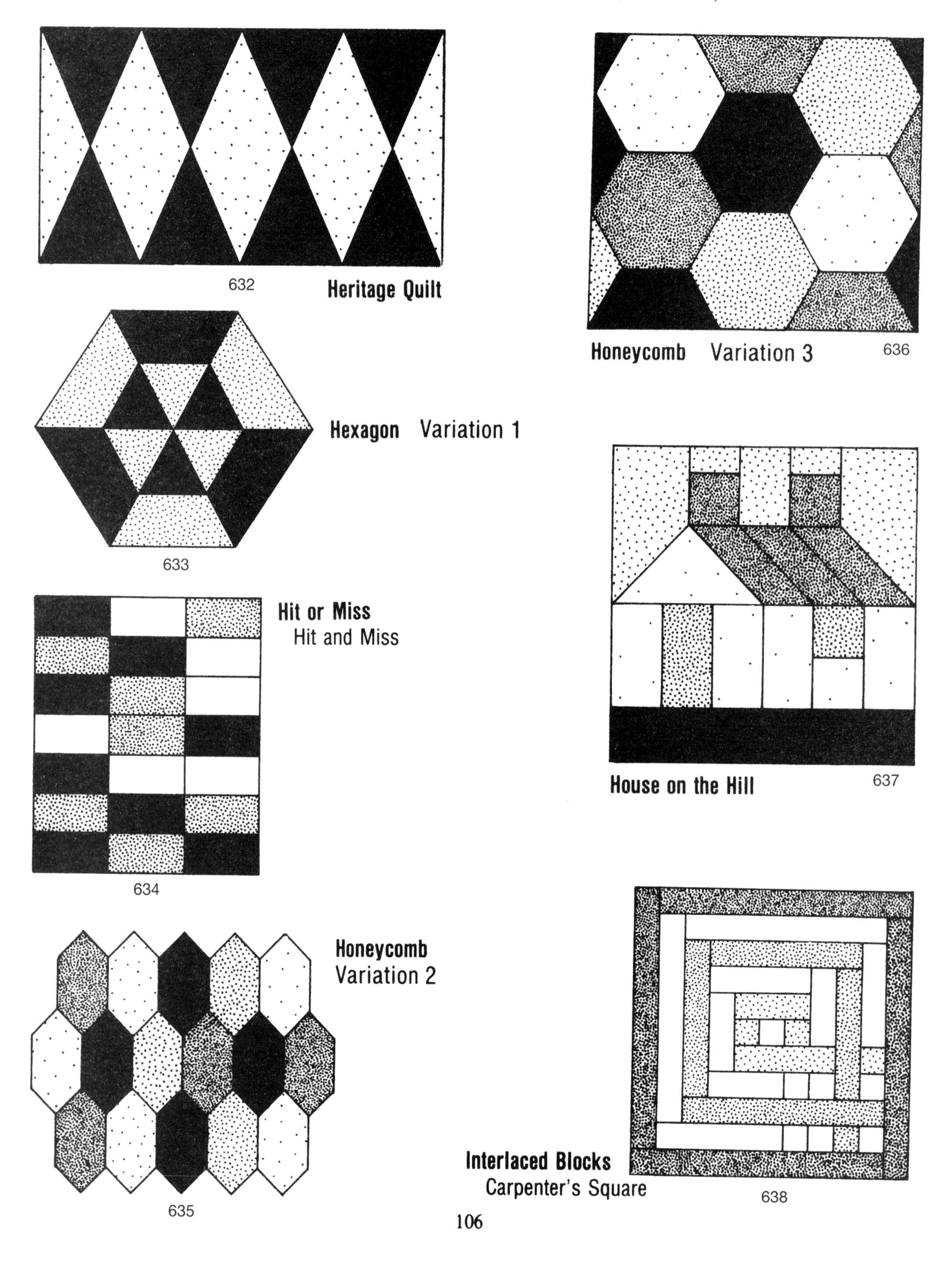

632 **Heritage Quilt**

Honeycomb Variation 3 636

Hexagon Variation 1

633

Hit or Miss
Hit and Miss

634

House on the Hill 637

Honeycomb
Variation 2

635

Interlaced Blocks
Carpenter's Square

638

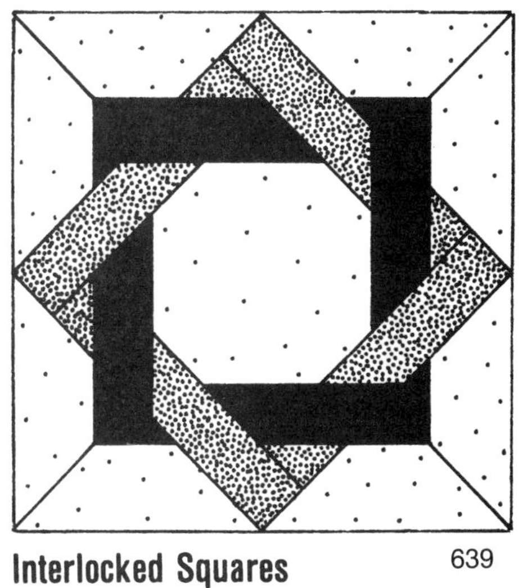

Interlocked Squares 639

640

Irish Chain Variation 2
Double Nine-Patch

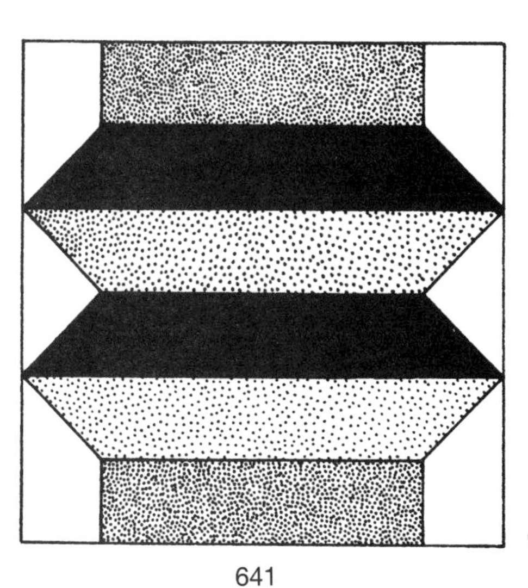

641 **Japanese Lantern**

Kansas Dugout

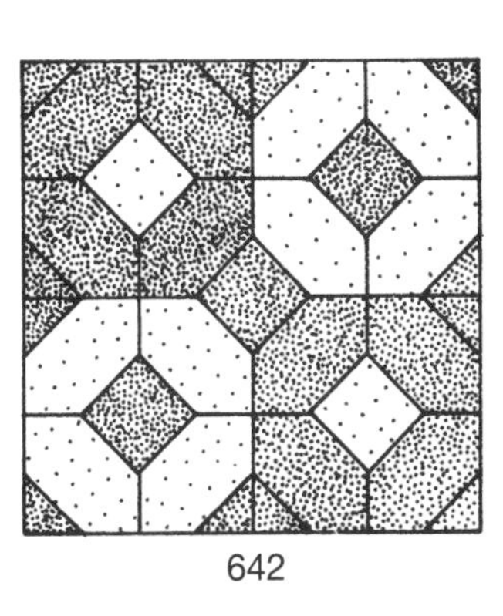

642

Kite's Tail

643

Leavenworth Nine-Patch

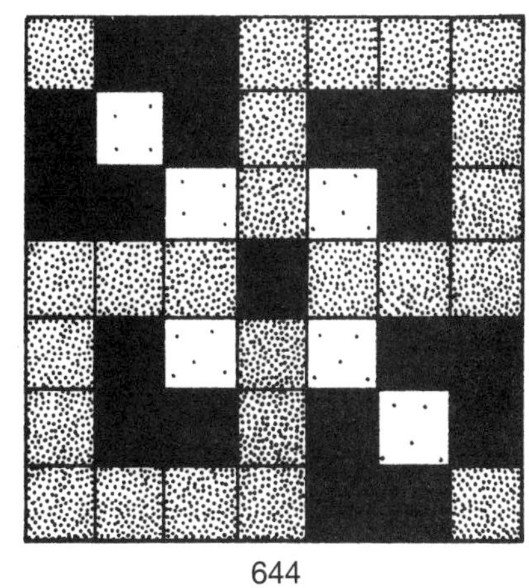

644

Letter H

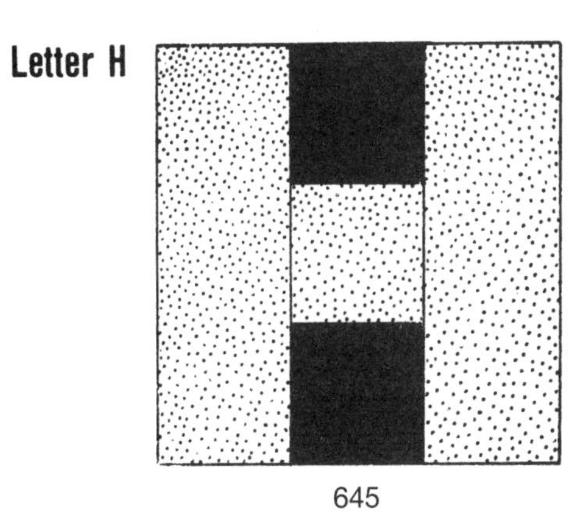

645

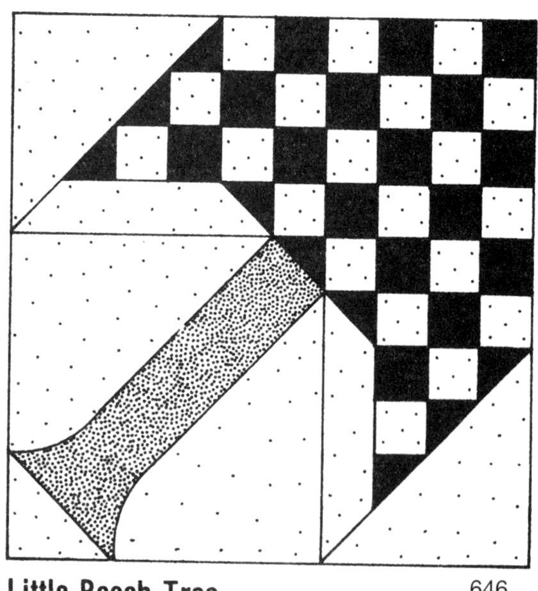

Little Beech Tree 646

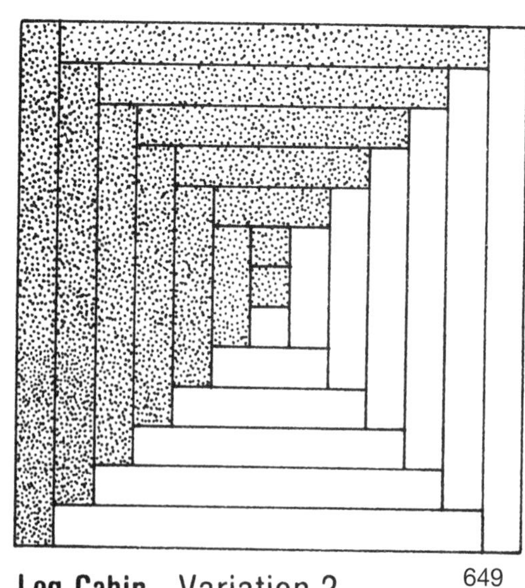

Log Cabin Variation 2 649
Courthouse Steps

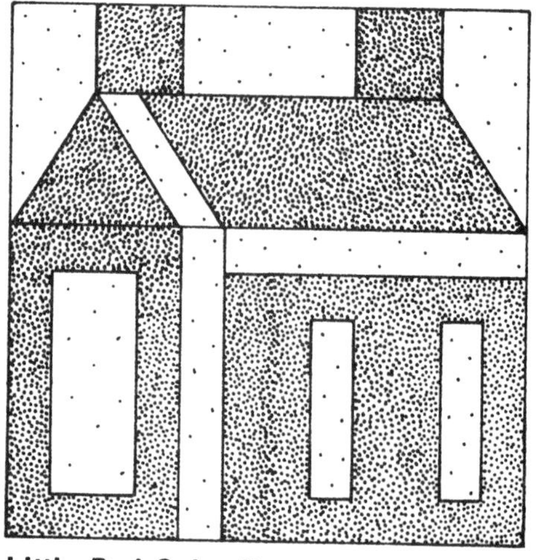

Little Red Schoolhouse 647

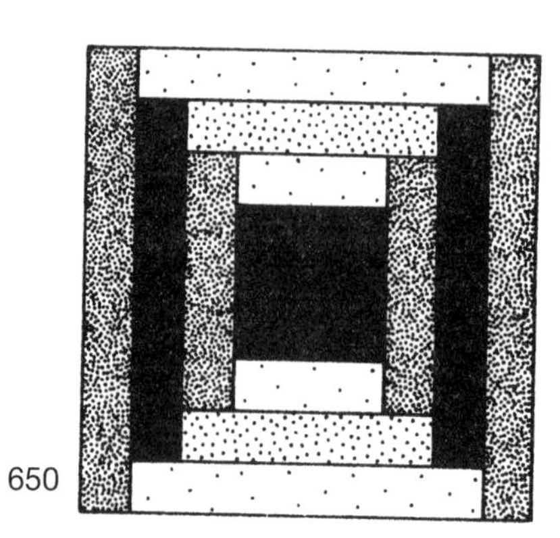

650 **Log Cabin** Variation 3

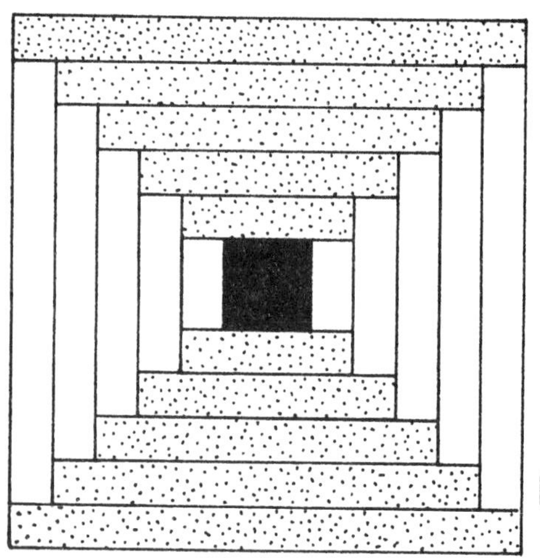

648

Log Cabin Variation 1
Old-Fashioned Log Cabin

Log Cabin
Variation 4

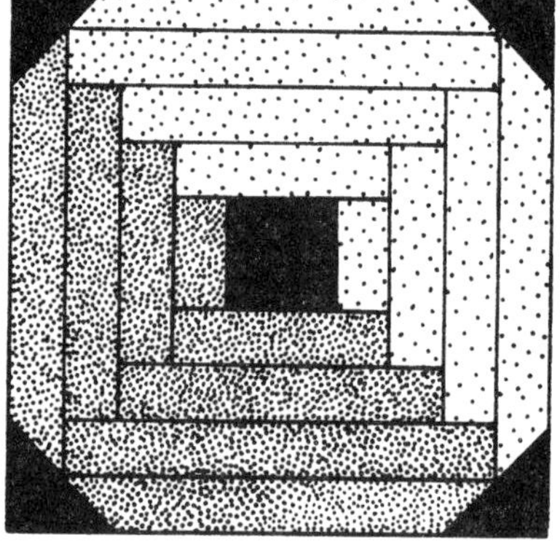

651

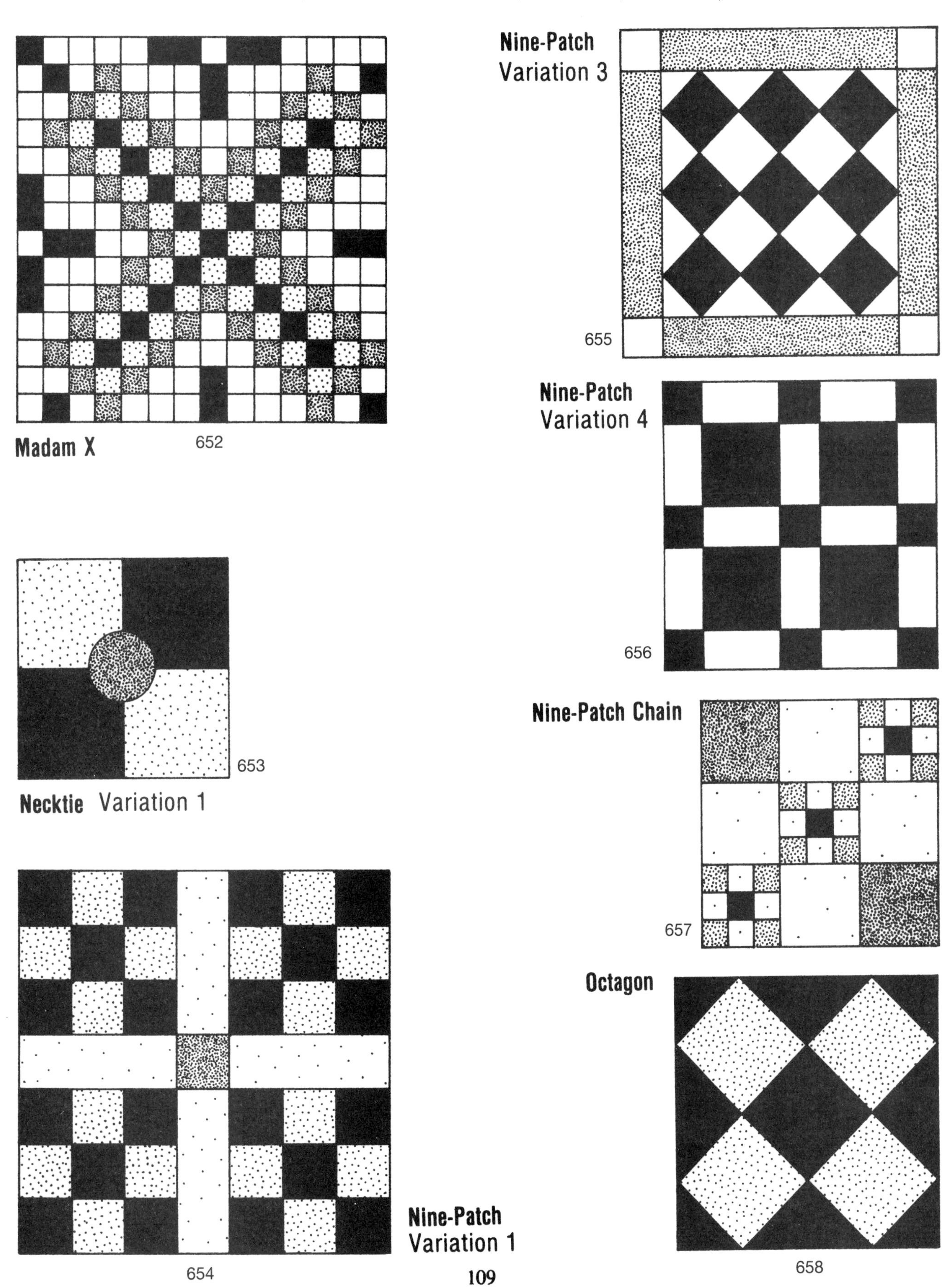
Madam X
652
Nine-Patch
Variation 3
655
Nine-Patch
Variation 4
656
653
Necktie Variation 1
Nine-Patch Chain
657
Octagon
654
Nine-Patch
Variation 1
658

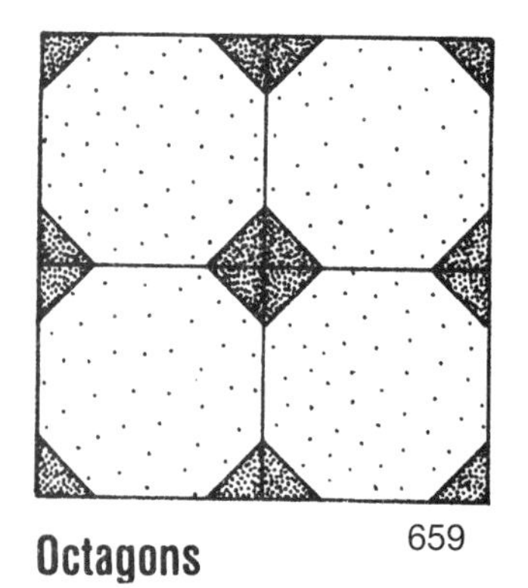

Octagons 659

Patience Corners

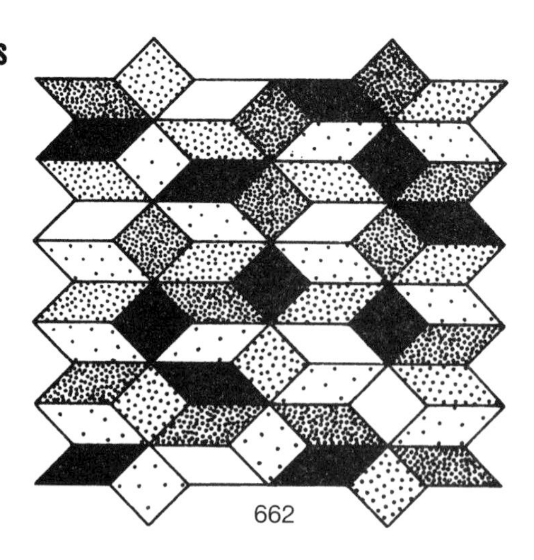

662

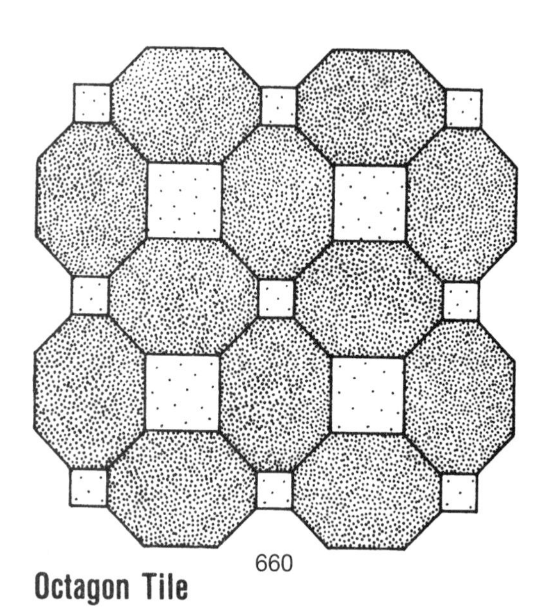

Octagon Tile 660

Peony

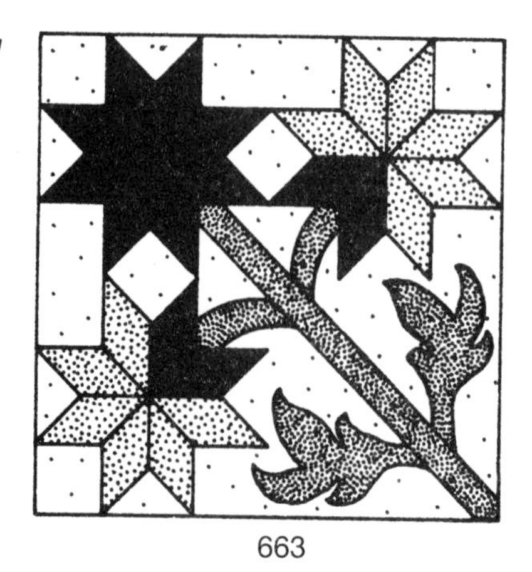

663

Patience Corner

661

Pineapple
Chestnut Burr
Church Steps
Maltese Cross, Var. 2

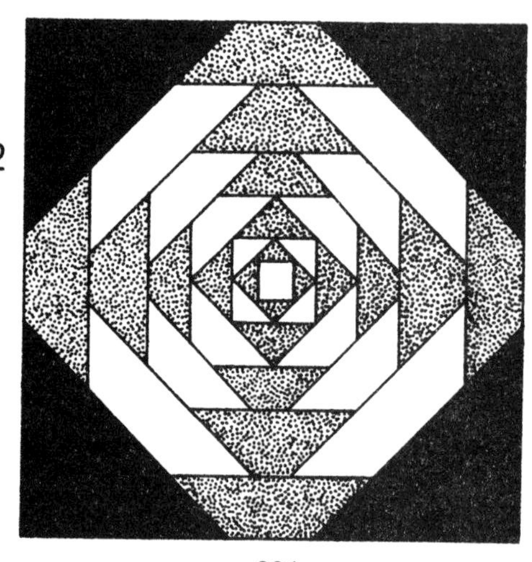

664

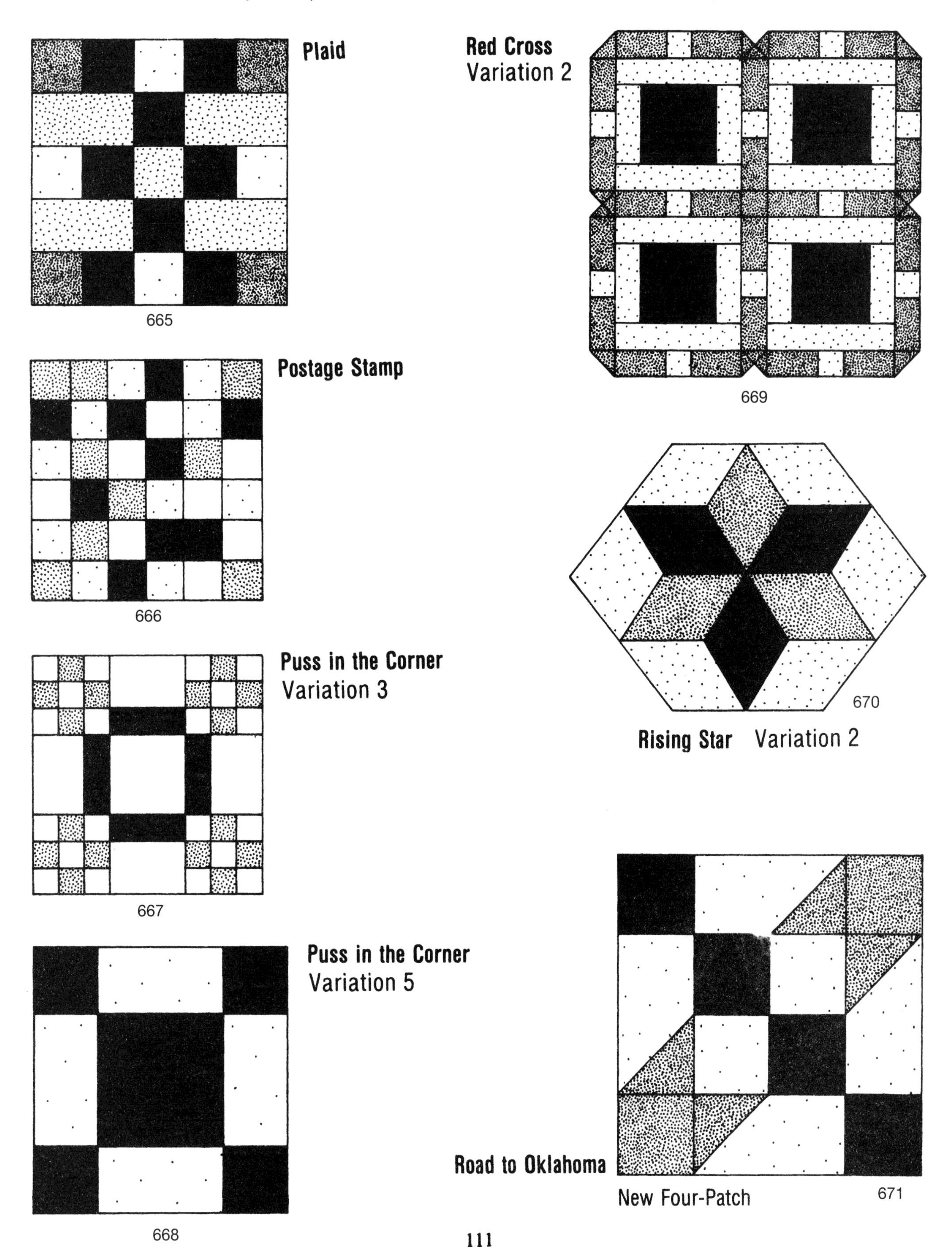
Plaid
665
Postage Stamp
666
Puss in the Corner
Variation 3
667
Puss in the Corner
Variation 5
668
Red Cross
Variation 2
669
670
Rising Star Variation 2
Road to Oklahoma
New Four-Patch
671

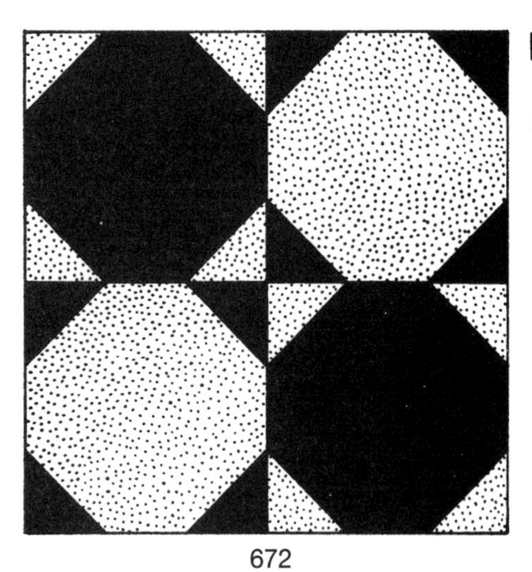

Robbing Peter to Pay Paul
Variation 5

672

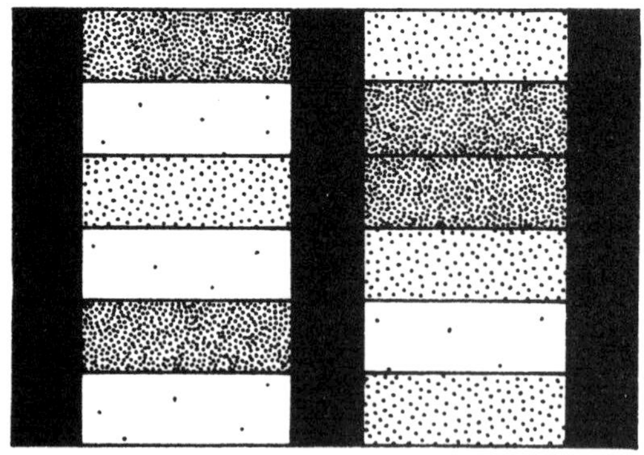

Roman Stripe Variation 1

676

Rocky Glen
Variation 3

673

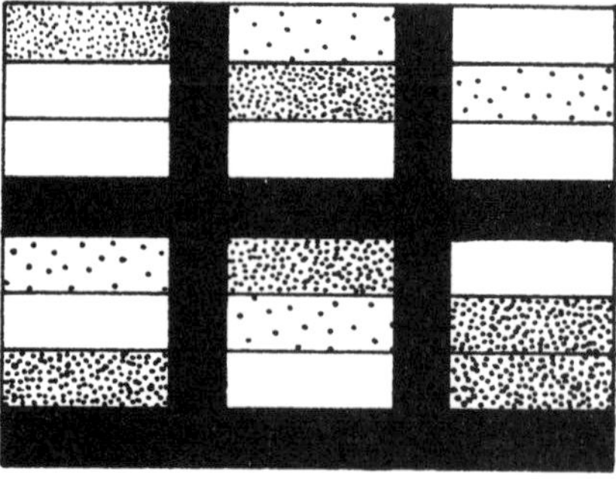

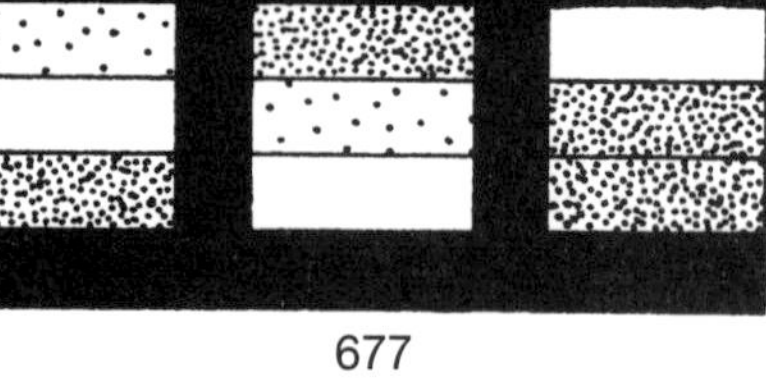

Roman Stripe Variation 2
Roman Square, Var. 1

677

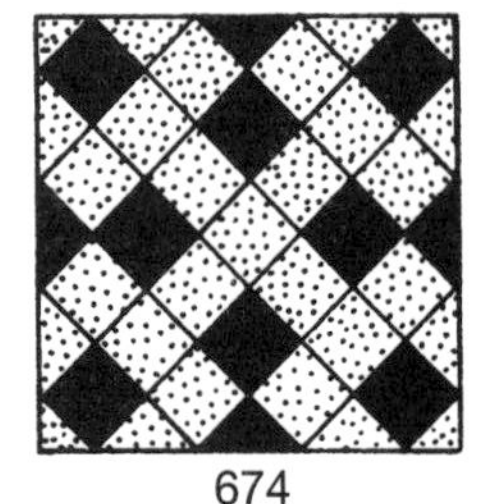

Roman Cross

674

Roman Wall

678

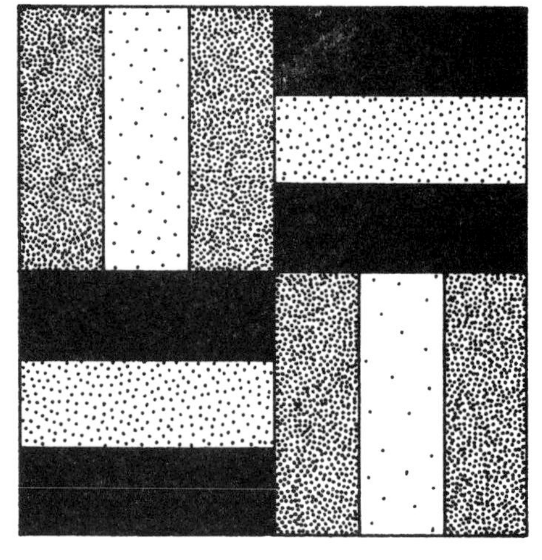

Roman Square
Variation 2
Roman Stripe Zigzag

675

Sawtooth
Variation 7

679

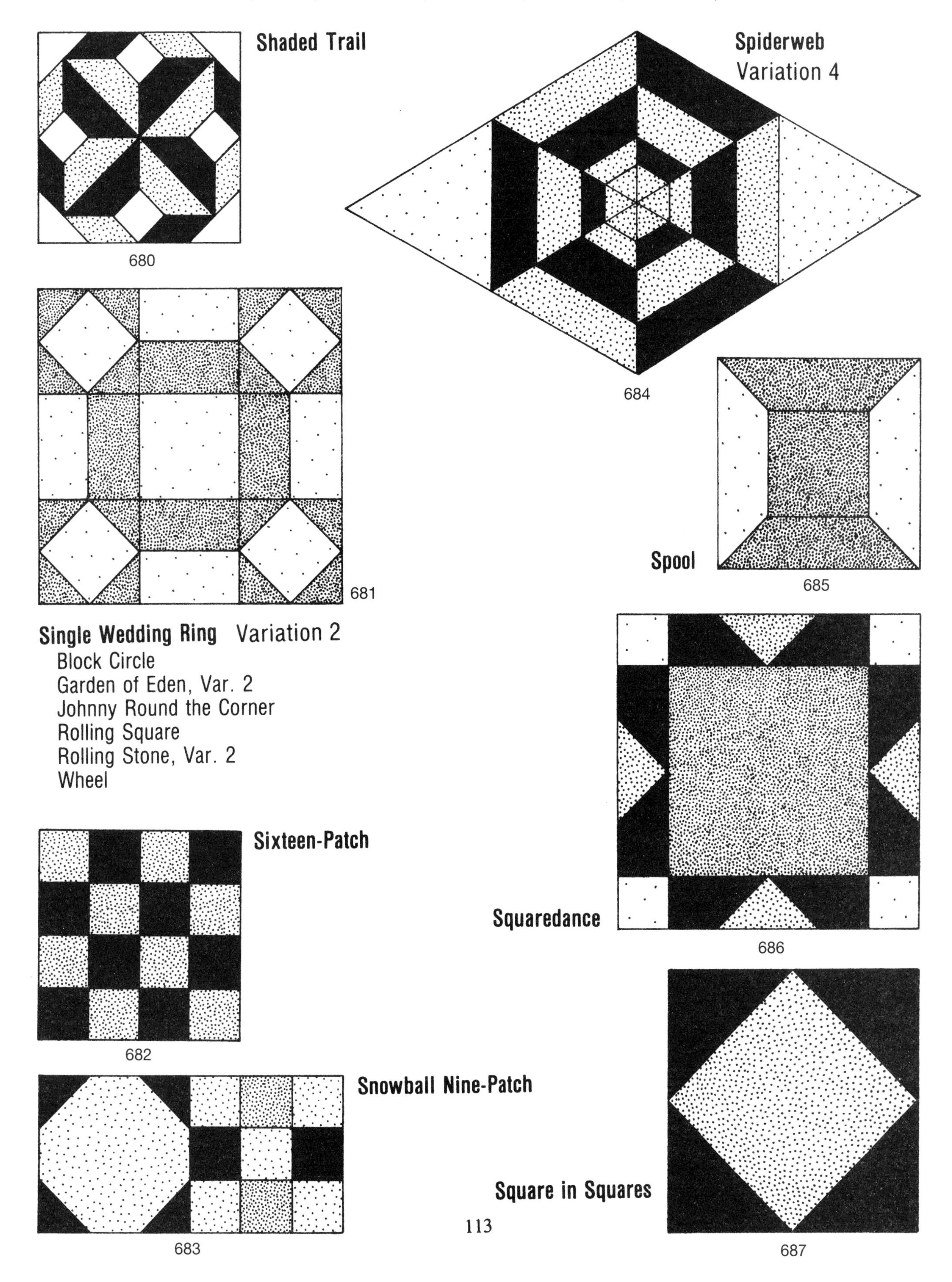

Shaded Trail

Spiderweb Variation 4

Single Wedding Ring Variation 2
Block Circle
Garden of Eden, Var. 2
Johnny Round the Corner
Rolling Square
Rolling Stone, Var. 2
Wheel

Spool

Squaredance

Sixteen-Patch

Snowball Nine-Patch

Square in Squares

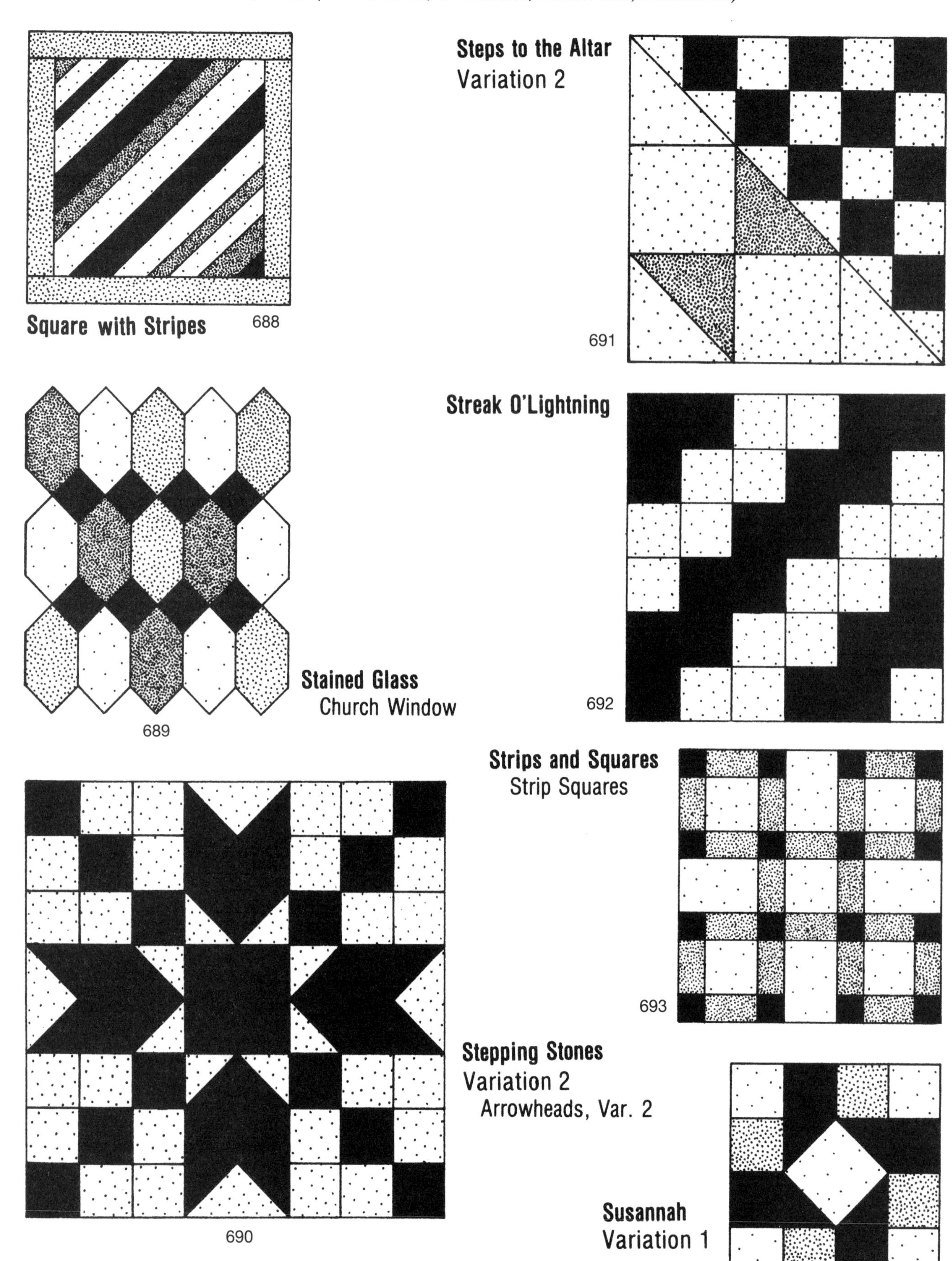

Square with Stripes 688

Stained Glass
Church Window
689

Stepping Stones
Variation 2
Arrowheads, Var. 2
690

Steps to the Altar
Variation 2
691

Streak O'Lightning
692

Strips and Squares
Strip Squares
693

Susannah
Variation 1
694

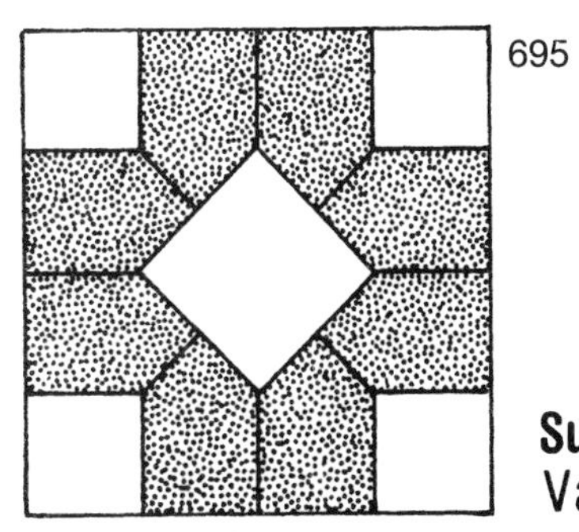
695

Susannah Variation 2

696

Susannah Variation 3

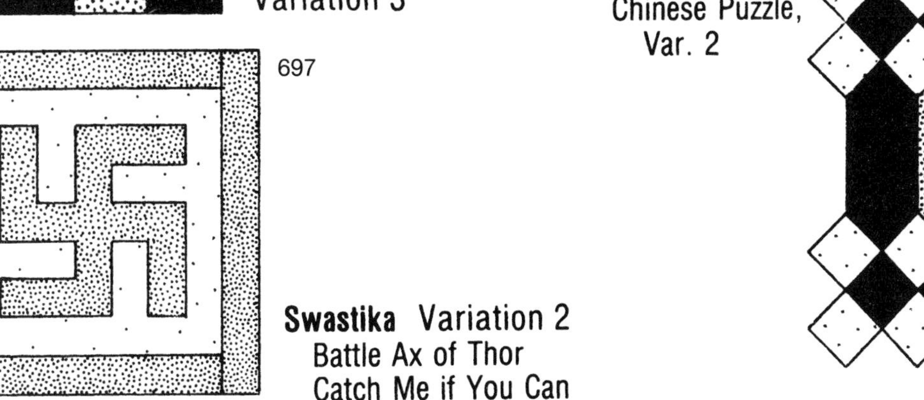
697

Swastika Variation 2
Battle Ax of Thor
Catch Me if You Can
Chinese 10,000 Perfections
Favorite of the Peruvians
Heart's Seal
Mound Builders
Pure Symbol of Right Doctrine
Wind Power of the Osages

Tam's Patch

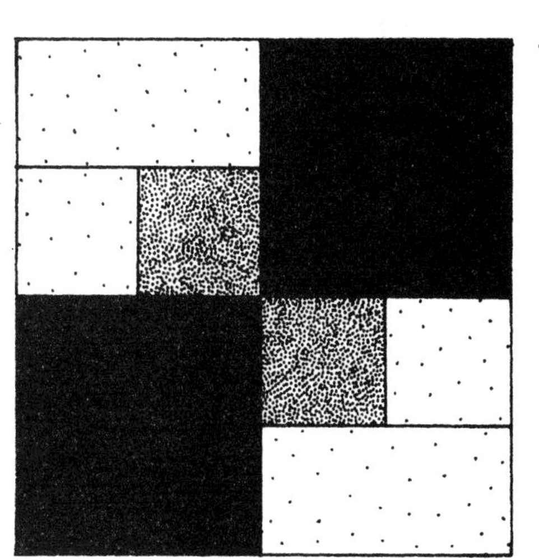
698

Tic Tac Toe Variation 1
Kitty Corner, Var. 1
Puss in the Corner,
Var. 4

699

Tile Patchwork
Chinese Puzzle,
Var. 2

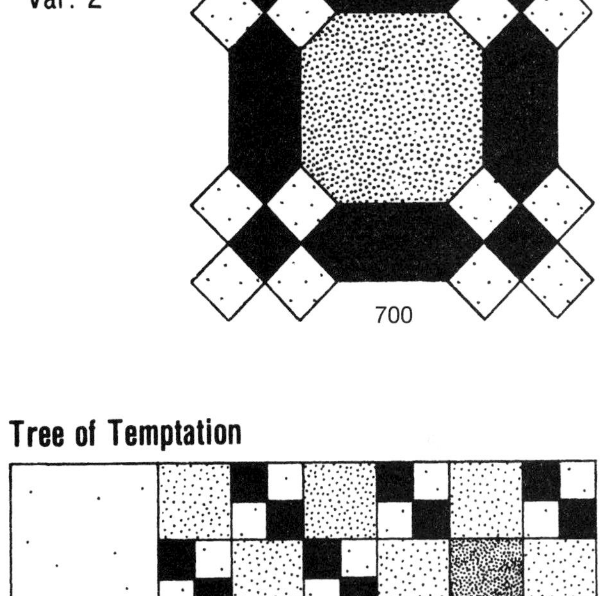
700

Tree of Temptation

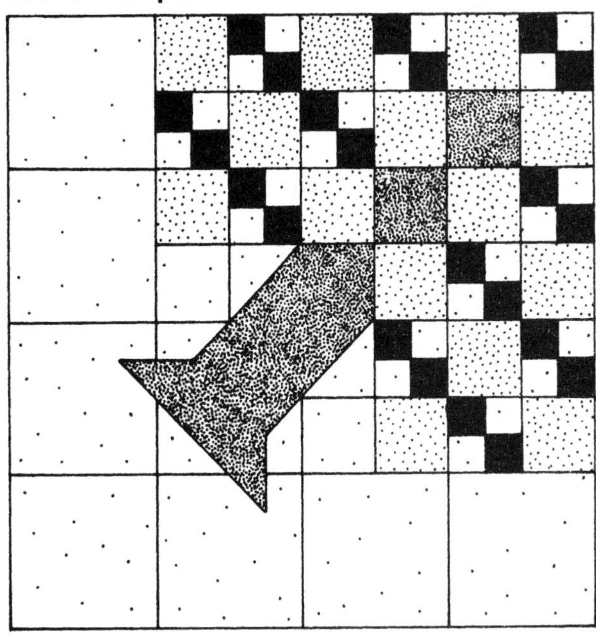
701

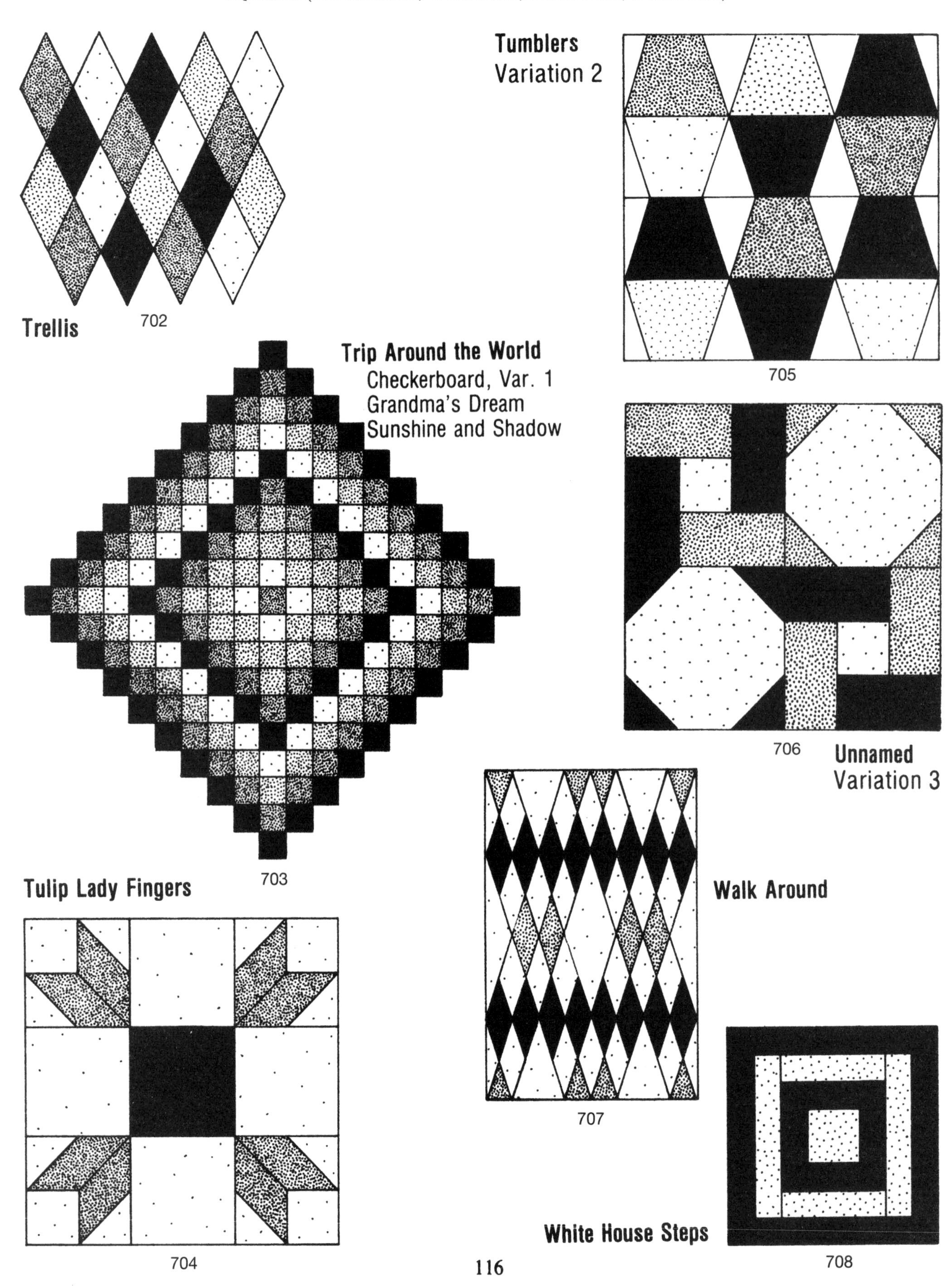
Trellis
702
Tumblers
Variation 2
705
Trip Around the World
Checkerboard, Var. 1
Grandma's Dream
Sunshine and Shadow
703
706
Unnamed
Variation 3
Tulip Lady Fingers
704
Walk Around
707
White House Steps
708

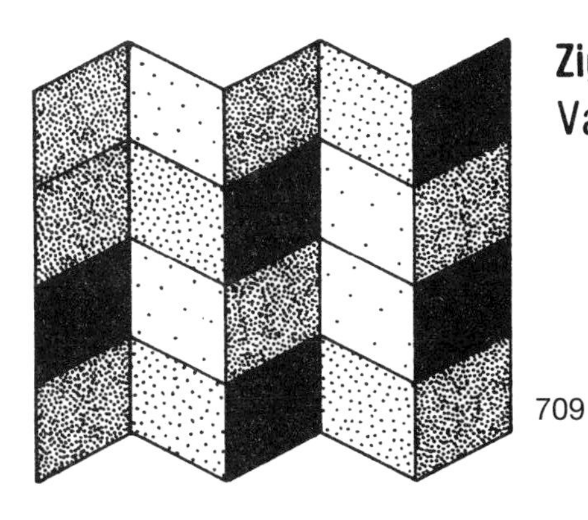

709

Zigzag
Variation 2
Snake Fence, Var. 2

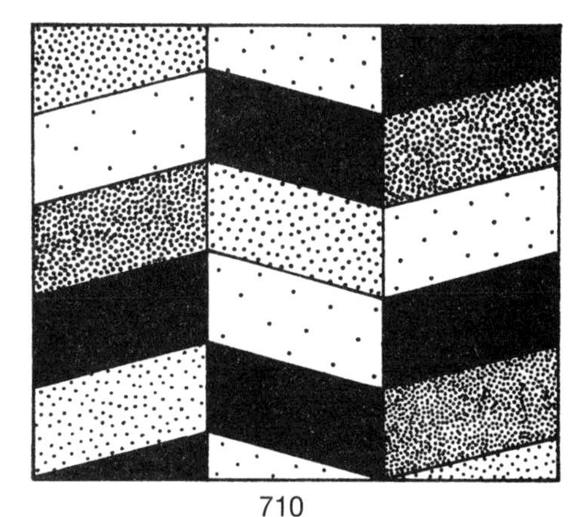

710

Zigzag
Variation 3

711

Zigzag Block

SUPPLEMENT

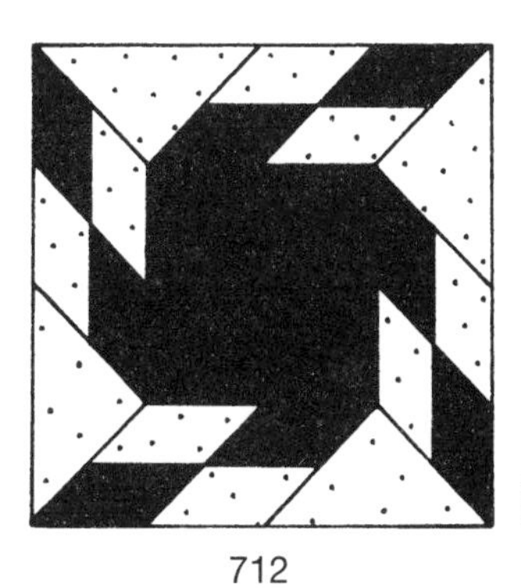

712

Flying Bats

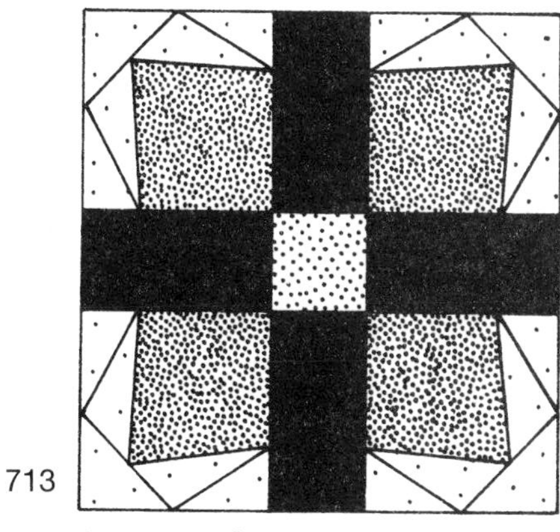

713

Star and Cross Variation 3

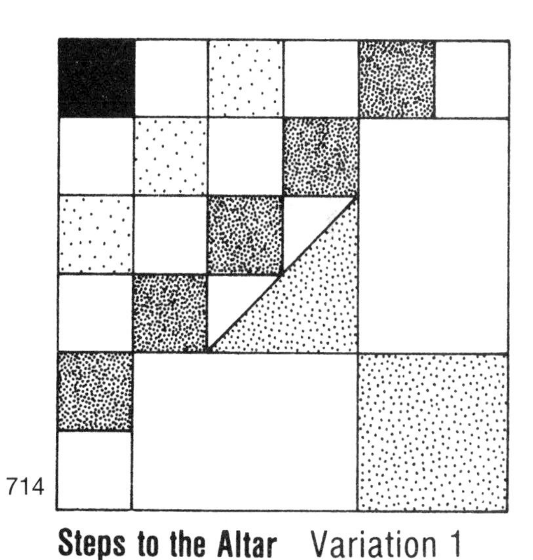

714

Steps to the Altar Variation 1

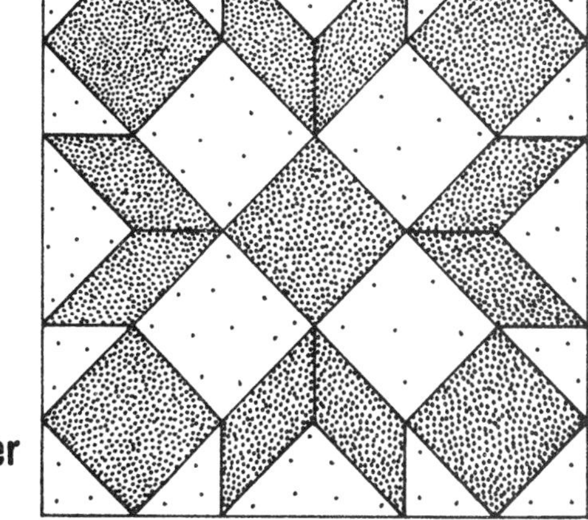

715

Swing in the Center
Variation 2

BIBLIOGRAPHY

Bicentennial Quilt Book, McCall's Needlework & Crafts, Editorial Director, Rosemary McMurtry, McCall Pattern Co., New York, 1975.

ERICSON, HELEN M., *Helen's Book of Basic Quiltmaking,* Groh Printing Co., Emporia, Kansas, 1973.

FINLEY, RUTH E., *Old Patchwork Quilts,* Charles T. Branford Co., Newton Centre, Mass., c. 1929, reprinted 1970.

The Foxfire Book, Editor, Eliot Wigginton, Anchor Books/Doubleday, Garden City, N.Y., 1972.

GRAFTON, CAROL BELANGER, *Traditional Patchwork Patterns,* Dover Publications, Inc., New York, 1974.

GREEN, SYLVIA, *Patchwork for Beginners,* Watson-Guptill Publications, New York, 1972.

GUTCHEON, BETH, *The Perfect Patchwork Primer,* Penguin Books Inc., Baltimore, 1973.

Heirloom Quilts, McCall's Needlework and Crafts, Editorial Director, Rosemary McMurtry, McCall Pattern Co., 1974.

HINSON, DOLORES, A., *A Quilter's Companion,* Arco Publishing, Inc., New York, 1973.

HOLSTEIN, JONATHAN, *American Pieced Quilts,* Viking Press, New York, 1972.

LARSEN, JUDITH LA BELLE & GULL, CAROL WAUGH, *The Patchwork Quilt Design & Coloring Book,* Butterick Publishing, New York, 1977.

LITHGOW, MARILYN, *Quiltmaking & Quiltmakers,* Funk & Wagnalls, New York, 1974.

MAHLER, CELINE BLANCHARD, *Once Upon a Quilt,* Van Nostrand Reinhold Co., New York, 1973.

The McCall's Book of Quilts, Editors of McCall's Needlework & Crafts Publications, Simon & Schuster/The McCall Pattern Company, New York, 1975.

MCKIM, RUBY SHORT, *One Hundred and One Patchwork Patterns,* Dover Publications, Inc., New York, 1962.

Mountain Artizans, An Exhibition of Patchwork and Quilting, Museum of Art, Rhode Island School of Design, Providence, 1970.

Mrs. Danner's Fifth Quilt Book, Editor, Helen M. Ericson, Groh Printing Co., Emporia, Kansas, 1972.

Mrs. Danner's Quilts, Books 1 and 2 combined, Editor, Helen M. Ericson, Groh Printing Co., Emporia, Kansas, 1971.

Mrs. Danner's Quilts, Books 3 and 4 combined, Editor, Helen M. Ericson, Groh Printing Co., Emporia, Kansas, 1973.

ORLOFSKY, PATSY & MYRON, *Quilts in America,* McGraw-Hill Book Co., New York, 1974.

PETO, FLORENCE, *Quilts & Coverlets,* Chanticleer Press, New York, 1949.

Quilter's Newsletter Magazine, Editor-Bonnie Leman, Leman Publications, Inc., Denver.

Quilt World, Editor-Barbara Hall Pedersen.

150 Years of American Quilts, The University of Kansas Museum of Art, Lawrence, Kansas, 1973.

INDEX

Index of Names